Library of
Davidson College

SCRIBNER REPRINT EDITIONS

A COMPANION

TO VICTORIAN

LITERATURE

THE YOUNG QUEEN VICTORIA
From a water-color sketch by A. E. Chalon in the National Portrait Gallery of Scotland

A COMPANION TO VICTORIAN LITERATURE

Thomas Marc Parrott
PRINCETON UNIVERSITY

Robert Bernard Martin
PRINCETON UNIVERSITY

AUGUSTUS M. KELLEY • PUBLISHERS
CLIFTON 1974

First Published 1955
(New York: Charles Scribner's Sons)
Copyright 1955 by Charles Scribner's Sons

RE-ISSUED *1974* BY
AUGUSTUS M. KELLEY · PUBLISHERS
Clifton New Jersey 07012
By Arrangement with CHARLES SCRIBNER'S SONS

Library of Congress Cataloging in Publication Data

```
Parrott, Thomas Marc, 1866-1960.
  A companion to Victorian literature.

  (Scribner reprint editions)
  Reprint of the ed. published by Scribner, New York.
  Includes bibliographies.
  1. English literature--19th century--History and
criticism. 2. Great Britain--History--Victoria,
1837-1901.  I. Martin, Robert Bernard, joint author.
II. Title.
[PR461.P3 1974]      820'.9'008           77-157691
ISBN 0-678-02772-2
```

All rights reserved. No part of this book may be reproduced in any form without the permission of Charles Scribner's Sons.

PRINTED IN THE UNITED STATES OF AMERICA
by SENTRY PRESS, NEW YORK, N. Y. 10013
Bound by A. HOROWITZ & SON, CLIFTON, N. J.

Contents

Preface   vii

Part I. *History of the Age: Political, Social, and Literary*

    I. THE PRELUDE   3
    II. THE VICTORIAN COMPROMISE   25
    III. THE GOLDEN AGE   46
    IV. THE TWILIGHT   74

Part II. *Shaping Forces of the Age*

    I. THE INDUSTRIAL REVOLUTION   111
    II. THE ADVANCING DEMOCRACY   122
    III. THE NEW SCIENCE   140

Part III. *Major Authors of the Age: Biography and Collateral Reading*

    ARNOLD   153
    CHARLOTTE AND EMILY BRONTË   159
    BROWNING   164
    CARLYLE   171
    DICKENS   178
    GEORGE ELIOT   186
    HARDY   192
    HUXLEY   198
    KINGSLEY   204

CONTENTS

MEREDITH	210
MILL	217
MORRIS	222
NEWMAN	228
ROSSETTI	235
RUSKIN	241
SWINBURNE	248
TENNYSON	254
THACKERAY	261
TROLLOPE	269

Part IV. *Chronological Table*   275

Index   299

Preface

Each period in history disdainfully regards the problems of the age immediately preceding it, throwing away its inherited solutions of man's eternal dilemmas with all the arrogance of a young man rejecting his father's advice, with all the contempt of a woman discarding last year's hat. It is only in maturity that the son finds with astonishment how much his father seems to have learned.

In the first quarter of our century, nothing could have been more completely moribund than regard for the wisdom of nineteenth-century England. The very word "Victorian" came to have a derogatory sound, with overtones of hypocrisy, prudishness, self-satisfaction, and a devastating lack of humor. If Lytton Strachey was more amusing than his contemporaries in poking fun at *Eminent Victorians,* he was at least representative of what 1918 thought of the preceding century.

But family traits persist, and the young man discovers that after all he is the true son of his father, that he has inherited all the family problems. What disturbed the Victorians troubles us, and the community of concern binds us to them as we are bound to no other great period of history in England. Elizabethan and Augustan literature may remain perpetually young for us, but we seldom read the great literary works of those periods for an insight into Elizabethan or Augustan society; most of the contemporary social problems which moved the writers of those ages to creation have little but antiquarian interest for modern readers, and they seem curiously remote when compared to the problems of the Victorians.

An age which has painfully survived two great wars and the accompanying doubt and frustration has found that it can no longer afford to neglect the experience of its parent age. With a greater sense of tolerance of their failures, with the perspective gained by the passage of time, with the surprise of the newly-matured son looking at his father, we are beginning to take serious stock of what the Victorians have to offer us. In both England and America there has been a wide revival of interest in the period and particularly in its literature. In recent years there has been a flood of books on the Victorians: history; criticism; above all, biography; and there is no present sign that the high-water mark has been reached. Even the "standard" editions of Victorian novels and poetry, which seem to take up two-thirds of the shelf-room in most home libraries, are being dusted and re-read. Part of this renewed interest undoubtedly comes from the attractive, if fallacious, view of the period as one of comparative safety, free of the tortures of intellectual and moral doubt. A more intelligent appraisal of the era would see the interests it held in common with our own, and particularly the humanistic struggle it made to preserve a place of dignity for the individual in a world expanding its political, scientific, and religious boundaries so rapidly that he could no longer know his own niche.

But for most people the real fascination of the Victorian period (the limits of which, for the purpose of this book, are 1832 and 1892, the dates of the first Reform Bill and the death of the poet laureate) is in the splendor of its literature. Not since the Elizabethan era have there been so many great and near-great poets living at the same time. The serious essay and the imaginative recreation of history held a whole generation of readers. Above all, the age is that in which prose fiction reached maturity in the widely-differing styles of Dickens, Thackeray, George Eliot, the Brontë sisters, Trollope, Meredith, Hardy, and a score of lesser novelists. Only in the drama is there a noticeable lack of great works; many of the greatest authors attempted writing for the stage, but never with any real success. If this was not the greatest of critical ages, it was perhaps because there was insufficient emotional detachment; the Victorians took to heart their religion, their politics, and even their aesthetics, so it was not surprising that they usually lacked the calm impartiality of the ideal critic.

The close connection between Victorian literature and its historical background is indicated by its very association with the name of the reigning queen. Her personal influence on literary matters was slight, but letters during her reign reflect the society for which she set the tone. In this period, as in no other, there was a constant awareness of the duty of the writer as interpreter, often as popularizer, of the intellectual issues of the times. The typical progression of thought was that of Ruskin, moving from a purely artistic interest to awareness of a world unfit for art, to an attempt to reform that world and make it a decent place for the joint habitation of man and art. Something of the movement of political thought may be seen in the contrast between Landor and William Morris. Landor, living on into the middle of the nineteenth century as an anachronistic relic of an earlier era, was an aristocratic "radical," filled equally with loathing for tyranny and dislike of the common people. At the end of the period Morris actually spoke and took part in the demonstrations for the socialist movement. The poles of thought in other fields are shown in the contrast between the spokesman of religious authority, Newman, who was basically disinterested in natural science, and Darwin's champion, Huxley, who was the voice of agnosticism. Between the extremes of these men there were many shades of opinion, but of all the major Victorian writers, only two seem indifferent to all matters political, religious or scientific: D. G. Rossetti, absorbed in the life of art, and Emily Brontë, interested only in a wind-swept moor and the dark places of the spirit. For the average reader any real understanding of the literature of Victoria's reign must therefore include some knowledge of the intellectual and historical climate in which it was written, and the purpose of this book is rather to provide background for the student of that literature than to evaluate its artistic merit. Obviously, knowledge of his background can only be the first step in understanding and judgment of any artist, but in the case of the Victorians it is an indispensable step.

The book is divided into three major parts, each of a level intended not for the specialist, but for the general reader or for the college student making a first serious study of the period. The first part treats the historical background of nineteenth-century England, from the pre-Victorian era after the Battle of Waterloo, 1815, through the beginning of the Victorian age with the passage of the Reform Bill,

1832, to its close with the death of Tennyson in 1892. Each chapter contains a short discussion of the literature of the period treated. The second part contains three chapters on new forces in Victorian life and thought: the Industrial Revolution, the Advancing Democracy, and the New Science. In the third section of the volume the series of short biographies of major authors, suggested reading lists, and lists of the most important original works, criticism, and biography, is intended primarily for the reader who is making his initial acquaintance with these writers, but a more advanced student will find that section useful as preparation for detailed investigation. The book is rounded off with a chronological table of historical, political, and literary events in England, with parallel dates for major happenings in Continental and American literature.

It remains only to say that this book is the result of genuine coperation between its authors; there has been so much mutual help and criticism at all stages of the writing that it is no longer possible to disentangle the work of the two, and both accept full responsibility for the entire volume.

T. M. P.
R. B. M.

Part I

HISTORY OF THE AGE

Political, Social, and Literary

Chapter I

The Prelude

1815–1832

The literature of the Victorian age reflects more fully and critically the political and social-economic aspects of English life than the literature of any previous period. The age is one of transition from a semi-medieval agricultural to an almost completely democratic and urban-industrial society. It is impossible to understand the life and literature of the Victorian age without some knowledge of the period from which it emerged. This companion to Victorian literature accordingly begins with a chapter on the preceding period, the Prelude, 1815-1832, including a survey of the condition of England in 1815, its institutions and active forces, followed by a brief historical sketch of the progress in this period of liberal thought and action.

No period in English history is quite so sharply divided from those which precede and follow it as that which is marked at the beginning by Waterloo, 1815, and at the end by the passage of the Reform Bill, 1832. Waterloo brought to a victorious close England's long war against revolutionary and Napoleonic France. While it lasted this war put a stop to the movement for constitutional and moderate reform begun under Pitt in the 1780's, and when the victory was won the government attempted to continue in the time of peace the strict control of public life and thought that had seemed necessary in wartime. The passage of the Reform Bill marks the end of this attempt.

The intervening period is one of governmental repression and popular reaction; it bears little likeness to the Victorian age of gradual political and social progress. So far as literature reflects this period it reveals the opposing forces which divided the nation; on the one hand the conservatives: Wordsworth, Southey, and Scott; on the other hand the rebels: Blake, Byron, and Shelley. A striking instance of this division is found in two poems on the death of George III: Southey's eulogy of the King, *A Vision of Judgment*, 1820, and Byron's parody of Southey's poem with his fierce denunciation of George, *The Vision of Judgment*, 1821.[1] Yet all these writers, conservatives and liberals, belong to the romantic age of English literature; it is only toward the close of the period that voices begin to be heard which carry on into the Victorian age: those of Carlyle, Macaulay, and the young Tennyson (pp. 23-4).

England in 1815 was a constitutional monarchy, but the monarch still retained prerogatives which gave him far more power than is now possessed by a monarch who is merely the symbol, often, it is true, the almost worshipped symbol, of the unity of the Commonwealth of Free Nations. He had the power to dissolve Parliament and so to force a general election, and the right to appoint and dismiss Prime

---

[1] It is characteristic of the period that the publisher of Byron's poem was fined £100 "for endangering the public peace."

THE PRELUDE 5

Ministers. The royal veto on legislation had not been exercised since 1692, but the King still had the power to block legislation by forbidding the introduction of measures to which he was opposed. As late as 1831, the Prime Minister had to obtain the King's consent to the introduction of the Reform Bill.

In spite of these powers the monarchy sank in this period to a lower level of popular favor than it had known since the reign of James II. A modern historian speaks of the "savage hatred" of the royal family in 1820. With this strong statement we may compare Shelley's sonnet, *England in 1819:*

> An old, mad, blind, despised, and dying King —
> Princes, the dregs of their dull race who flow
> Through public scorn, mud from a muddy spring —
> Rulers who neither see nor feel nor know,
> But leech-like to their fainting country cling.

It is, perhaps, doubtful whether in 1819 the dying King was really despised except by radicals and rebels. When he sank into incurable madness, 1811, he was generally mourned as "the good old King." But Shelley's "public scorn" of the Princes finds a parallel in the comment of so good a royalist as Wellington who called them "the d-dst millstone about the neck of any government."

George III had nine sons. There is a contemporary character sketch of the oldest, who succeeded him as George IV in 1820: "a more contemptible, cowardly, selfish, unfeeling dog does not exist than this King."[2] He came to power as Prince Regent, 1811, loaded

---

[2] Charles Greville, from whose *Journal* these words are quoted, was a born aristocrat, as a boy a page to George III, later for years clerk of the Privy Council. His *Journal,* published after his death as the *Greville Memoirs,* 1875, 1885, and 1887, reveals an intimate acquaintance with the life of the Court. A later Victorian estimate of George IV appears in Thackeray's lectures, *The Four Georges.*

with a debt of perhaps half a million pounds. It was paid by the Treasury, but repeated payments never kept him out of debt. His dissipated life and his desertion of his political friends soon forfeited what popularity his easy good humor had gained. He was hissed in the streets in 1814 and the windows of his coach were stoned and broken when he drove to open Parliament in 1817. The climax of his unpopularity was attained in 1820 when he tried to divorce his wife on the ground of alleged adultery. The death in 1817 of his one legitimate child, Princess Charlotte, opened the succession to the throne to a brother or a brother's child, and three bachelor brothers married in haste in hope of becoming the lucky father.

None of the royal family incurred quite the odium that attached to George, but against most of the Princes there was just cause for complaint. Frederick, Duke of York, his second brother, the soldier of the family, was appointed Commander in Chief in 1798 in spite of repeated failure in the field. In 1809 he was involved in a public scandal when it became known that his mistress, Mary Anne Clarke, had been selling commissions in the army signed by him.[3] In an investigation which followed, 196 members of the House of Commons voted against him and he was forced to resign. He was, however, promptly re-instated in 1811 when George became Regent. Like all his family York posed as a zealous Protestant and his speech in the House of Lords, 1819, is said to have postponed Catholic Emancipation (p. 19) for ten years.

William, Duke of Clarence, the sailor prince, kept the lovely actress, Miss Jordan, for twenty-five years,

[3] Some time later Mrs. Clarke, whom he had deserted, threatened to publish his letters and had to be bought off with a cash payment of £7,000 and a handsome pension.

and she rewarded his devotion with many children.[4] Reduced to poverty by their demands, he tried to marry one rich heiress after another, but his uncouth behavior scared them off; he was, in fact, suspected of showing incipient signs of his father's insanity. He became King in 1830 and his informal, not to say indecent, manners gave great offence in Court circles. Wellington, his first Prime Minister, found him "reasonable and tractable," which probably means that he would do as he was told. It was fortunate for England that so biddable a King was on the throne during the struggle for Reform.

Ernest Augustus, Duke of Cumberland, fifth son of George III, was, perhaps, the most heartily detested of all the Princes.[5] In spirit a German Junker rather than an English lord, he was bitterly opposed to any measure of reform. Had he become King of England instead of Hanover, where he followed William, his accession would almost certainly have caused an armed revolution.

Edward, Duke of Kent, the fourth son of George III, was the sole inheritor of his father's sober virtues. Sincerely pious, he was a member of various charitable organizations, and openly favored Catholic Emancipation. A year after Princess Charlotte's death he married a German Princess and died when their child, Victoria, later Queen of England, was a baby six months old.

Prominent in the public eye as royalty was, it was by no means the ruling force in England; the main function of the royal family seems to have

[4] Greville says that William was surrounded by "a numerous progeny of bastards."

[5] In 1810 an ugly rumor got about that he had murdered his valet whom he was known to have abused. He was probably innocent, but as late as 1832 he had to prosecute a pamphleteer who stated that the rumor was generally believed.

been to cling "leech-like" to the Treasury. Power rested in Parliament, then as now consisting of two chambers, the Lords and the Commons, but the composition of these bodies was then very different. The House of Lords no longer consisted mainly of members of the great Whig families who had ousted the last Stuart King and thereafter dominated the House of Hanover. From the beginning of Pitt's administration, 1783, the upper house had been deliberately packed with newly created peers, drawn mainly from the minor gentry, the mercantile, and the professional classes. These peers represented the newly rich, swollen with the wealth that in the eighteenth century poured into England from her foreign trade and her colonies.[6] The first desire, however, of a newly enriched Englishman was to acquire a landed estate, since only the possession of land then conferred the stamp of gentry on its owner. The Lords, then, old and new, were a compact body representing the "landed interest." Along with the lay peers sat the Bishops of the state Church who were appointed by the King and could be relied on to vote as a unit against all legislation repugnant to the monarch. Legislation, then as now, originated in the Commons; the function of the Lords was to amend, reject, or finally accept a bill sent up to them. Their consent was necessary to the King's signature which transformed a bill into a law, and since their consent to measures of reform was usually refused, the record of the Lords in this period is one of consistent opposition to changes demanded by the country.

Since the power of the purse which controlled executive action rested in the lower house, it was by far the more powerful of the two chambers.

[6] Pitt is said to have maintained that every man worth £10,000 a year ought by rights to be a peer.

Theoretically the House of Commons was a representative assembly freely elected to carry out the will of the people. Actually it represented only a small fraction of adult Englishmen. Members were returned from all the English counties and from a limited number of boroughs. Each county, large or small, returned two members elected by voters possessing land to the annual value of forty shillings. Voting was by word of mouth at the polls and the influence of great landlords upon their neighbors and tenants usually decided any contest. Some counties, indeed, were regarded as practically the private property of a great nobleman.[7]

Borough members outnumbered those from the counties by about four to one and were consequently the dominating power in the Commons. The boroughs varied in size from populous Bristol to the deserted village of Old Sarum, but great modern cities like Manchester and Birmingham, not yet recognized as boroughs, had no representatives. Within the boroughs the number of electors varied from Westminster with 17,000 voters to Gatton with only one. The universities of Oxford and Cambridge returned two members each. Some boroughs had household suffrage; elsewhere only "rate-payers" (*i.e.* payers of local taxes), freemen of the borough, or members of self-perpetuating corporations had the franchise.[8] In general the right of voting, says Trevelyan, was "as irregular as an extravagant and comic fancy could have made it." Many boroughs had so few voters that local elections were notoriously

[7] In Cumberland after a long and expensive rivalry between two noble families an amicable arrangement was made by which each of them sent up one member to Parliament.

[8] In Edinburgh a self-perpetuating board of thirty-three alone possessed the franchise. In 1831 they elected a Tory over Jeffrey, the editor of the *Edinburgh Review*, in spite of many petitions in favor of Jeffrey.

decided by patronage or by outright bribery. These were the so-called "pocket boroughs," in the pocket, as it were, of their owners. In 1827 Croker, a practical politician, reckoned that over one third of the seats in the Commons were controlled by landed patrons. Yet this unrepresentative body more than once expressed the general will of the nation. It did so when it supported the ministry during the long war with France, and it was this unreformed House that finally passed the first Reform bill, if only by one vote (p. 21).

Any description of the governing powers of England at this time must take the Church into account, for the state Church was an active branch of the government. Bishops voted in the House of Lords, and throughout the country clergymen sat on boards of magistrates to direct local administration, execute local justice, and levy local taxes, the "church rates" for the upkeep of the church, upon dissenters as well as upon communicants. Closely identified with the land-holding gentry from whom their ranks were mainly recruited, clergymen of the state Church might be relied on to stand firm against all attempts to alter the *status quo*. Yet this state Church was far from being in reality the Church of the nation. Probably one half of professing English Christians belonged at this time to other denominations; most of them were Methodists, a body expelled from the state Church in the reign of George III for excessive "enthusiasm." Dissent was strong in the towns, as the Church was in the country, and Methodists, allied with smaller sects like the Quakers, took the lead in many humanitarian and political movements.

The general condition of England in 1815 was far from happy; the reaction which followed the war left all classes divided and disturbed. The landowners were startled by the sudden fall in the price of wheat which forced them to reduce the rents they had steadily raised during the war.[9] The only remedy they saw was to secure from Parliament a protective measure, the Corn Law of 1815, which forbade the importation of wheat until the market price reached 80 shillings a quarter, an excessive figure in the money value of that time.[10] This, of course, raised the price of bread and was bitterly opposed by businessmen and workers, but in a Parliament dominated by the landed gentry it took a generation of protest and agitation to get the law repealed. The privation which the high cost of bread imposed on the peasant led, naturally, to his poaching on the land where the gentry preserved game: pheasants, hares, and rabbits.[11] The poor man wanted a bit of meat; the squire was determined that it should not be taken from his land, and set up man-traps and spring-guns to keep off trespassers. In 1816 Parliament passed the harshest of the game laws which condemned a peasant to transportation for seven years if caught at night with a net on him, this being regarded as *prima facie* proof of his guilt. The gulf between the landowners

---

[9] Byron in his *Age of Bronze,* 1823, taunted the landed interest with having promoted the long war especially for this purpose:

> Year after year they voted cent. per cent.,
> Blood, sweat, and tear-wrung millions — Why? for rent!
> ....
> The peace has made one general malcontent
> Of these high-market patriots; war was rent!

[10] The student should remember that in England "corn" means wheat, barley, rye, and oats collectively, or more specifically wheat, never our American "maize." A "quarter" is eight bushels.

[11] Cf. Carlyle's repeated thrusts at "double-barrelled game-preservers," especially in his epitaph on Count Zähdarm (*Sartor,* II, iv), and Tennyson's sneer at

> these old pheasant lords,
> These partridge-breeders. — *Aylmer's Field.*

and the working class in town and country steadily widened and deepened; it was not until near the close of the period that a rising generation of the gentry, threatened with armed revolution, joined the middle and lower classes in a common effort for reform.

Business in England had on the whole flourished during the war, but it had been risky to an alarming degree. Sudden changes in the strict traffic laws made it something like a gamble. The slump that followed the war closed many factories and threw thousands of men out of work. Obsessed by the fear of a proletarian revolution, business supported the war Combination Laws which prohibited trade unions, not repealed till 1824. The introduction of new machines into factories lessened the demand for labor, and since organized strikes were illegal, labor's protest often took the form of sabotage in smashing the machines. The prosecutions for rioting and sedition which followed such action increased the bitter feeling between labor and employers, but in general business was readier than the landed gentry for measures of social and political reform.

The state of the urban worker at this time was indeed deplorable. The mushroom growth of manufacturing towns during the war had drawn into them thousands of farm and village workers. These newcomers were housed in wretched slums, and the life of men, women, and children in factories and mines was indescribably miserable. Social legislation and state control were almost unknown and measures of reform were opposed by both employers and theoretical economists. It is not surprising that discontent was bitterest and that propaganda for radical reform and even for armed revolution found the readiest listeners in the new towns.

The condition of the agricultural laborer was,

perhaps, even more hopeless than that of the urban worker. Stripped of his old rights of pasturage and free fuel by the enclosure of the common lands, he gradually lost also his home industries, spinning and weaving, to the machines in the new factories and sank into desperate poverty. An attempt to aid him had been made in 1795 — the "Speedhamland Act" — but instead of receiving higher wages, he was given the dole, an allowance from the local rates dependent on the price of bread, to be increased or diminished as that rose or fell. This allowance not only stripped the peasant of every motive for prudence and economy but imposed a heavy burden on the local taxpayer.[12] Unable to unite for mutual protection like the town workers, the peasant class in the greater part of England was completely pauperized.[13] Only the most daring spirits found escape from their lot in poaching, in revengeful burning of the big farmers' ricks, and even in highway robbery.[14] Such acts brought down upon them the hand of the cruel penal laws. As late as 1830 a riotous assembly of starving field-hands clamoring for a living wage was dispersed by the military; three of their leaders were hanged and over four hundred others were shipped as convicts to Australia. Even the life of the mill-hand and the miner seemed better, and there was a steady drift of farm workers into the town. The general condition of England was evidently in desperate need of reform, but

[12] In 1813 this "poor rate" cost England five times the amount levied for all other local expenses.

[13] A contemporary observer, quoted by Trevelyan, *British History*, p. 249, remarked: "An English agricultural labourer and an English pauper, these words are synonymous. He pilfers when occasion offers, and teaches his children to lie and steal. . . . He is depraved through and through, too far gone to possess even the strength of despair."

[14] Tennyson's *Rizpah* is a tale of this time.

neither political party was able and willing to undertake the task. The Tories, in power for most of this period, did indeed toward its close put through certain minor reforms, but they resolutely opposed the one great necessary change, a reformed electoral system. The Whigs, generally out of office, were divided among themselves and anxious to avoid any taint of revolutionary activity. Fortunately there were other forces able to exert an influence for good without engaging in party strife. The strongest, numerically at least, of these forces was composed of the so-called Evangelicals.[15] This was not a sect, but a body of Christians, fired with the enthusiasm that Wesley had generated, yet still adhering to the state Church. Composed in the main of middle class citizens and members of the minor gentry, they were at once devoutly religious and eminently practical. They promoted missionary work at home and abroad, founded schools for poor children, and organized societies for the promotion of various reforms. Their efforts were particularly directed against slavery. In spite of the law, dating back to 1776, that no slave could be held on English soil, the slave trade flourished till it was outlawed in 1807, and another quarter of a century passed before slavery was abolished in the British colonies (p. 26). This reform was accomplished by persistent agitation directed by societies, largely composed of Evangelicals, organized for this specific purpose, and such societies were later to become one of the main agencies in arousing public opinion to demand parliamentary reform.

A less numerous, but very efficient, group of reformers sprang directly from the teaching of Jeremy Bentham, 1748-1832. Essentially a man of the

---

[15] A good account of Evangelicalism appears in Lord David Cecil's life of Cowper, *The Stricken Deer*.

eighteenth century with its characteristic stress upon reason rather than emotion, Bentham set himself from the beginning of his career to think out rational reforms in all phases of society. He was no revolutionary; in fact he ridiculed the doctrine of "natural rights." This temper recommended him to conservative politicians who were willing to accept specific proposals promoting the "greatest good of the greatest number"—Bentham's slogan—so long as they did not endanger the security of the state. Beginning with proposals for bringing order into the chaos of English law, Bentham ended as an outspoken champion of parliamentary reform, and lived just long enough to see the passage of the Reform Bill. To this result his disciples had, each in his own way, largely contributed, for Bentham had exerted a profound influence on many men of many minds: jurists, economists, philosophers, and practical politicians. They did not form a political party, but they were united in their efforts to effect something useful by legal means. The name "Utilitarian" was later applied to this group by one of Bentham's followers, John Stuart Mill (p. 217), and "Utilitarianism" became one of the dominant trends of Victorian thought. The Utilitarians lacked the zealous enthusiasm of the Evangelicals; they were realists, free-thinkers, and positivists. Yet their goal, the good of the state, was, in fact, identical with that of the Evangelicals, the relief of humanity, and the two often united in urging minor measures of reform before their final triumph in the passage of the epoch-making bill.

Historically this period of prelude falls into two unequal parts, the point of separation being marked by the death of Castlereagh, 1822, the chief of postwar ministers. The first is one of strict governmental repression; the second of an intermittent progress toward social, if not political, reform. The Tories were in power till near the end of the period, but there was marked difference between the high and dry Tories of the war days: Castlereagh, Sidmouth, and Eldon, and the new men, Canning, Peel, and others who came into power after them.[16] Only Wellington holds over in office and Wellington was a good soldier who knew how and when to retreat.

The year of Waterloo, 1815, was one of economic distress, but the only measure passed to relieve it was the Corn Law (p. 11). The following year saw the repeal of the wartime income tax; this gave relief to the propertied class but embarrassed governmental finances. The bad harvest of 1816 caused great distress as the price of bread rose, but the rioting that followed was sternly repressed. There was more rioting in 1817; in reprisal the right of *Habeas Corpus* "was suspended and a series of prosecutions of the press" drove Cobbett, the most daring propagandist of the day, into exile in America, whence he was later to bring back the body of the old revolutionary, Tom Paine.

In 1819 the first feeble Factory Act was passed, forbidding children under nine years to work in cotton mills. Victoria, daughter of the Duke of Kent, was born in May of that year. In August there occurred the most startling exhibition of the government's determination to suppress the popular demand for reform. Some 60,000 unarmed men and women marched into St. Peter's Fields, Manchester, for the lawful purpose of presenting a petition for parliamentary reform. The local magistrates ordered the arrest of the chief speaker, and when the crowd resisted called upon a troop of hussars to charge them. There was, indeed, less loss of life than might

---

[16] These statesmen appear in Shelley's *The Masque of Anarchy*, 1819, masked as Murder, Hypocrisy, and Fraud.

have been expected; about a dozen men and women were killed and some hundreds injured, but a wave of wrath at this brutal violation of popular rights swept over England. Shelley in Italy caught the echo of the outcry and wrote his flaming *Masque of Anarchy*, calling on the men of England to rise and shake their chains to earth, but Leigh Hunt, editor of the liberal *Examiner*, did not dare to print the poem. The Prince Regent congratulated the magistrates — one of them a clergyman — upon their action, but "Peterloo," as the affair came to be called in derisive contrast to the glorious victory of Waterloo, was long remembered and resented by the workers of England.

Since there was some doubt as to the legality of the magistrates' action in this case, the government decided to make the law quite clear. They passed the notorious *Six Acts* forbidding large public meetings, authorizing all magistrates to confiscate seditious literature, and imposing a crushing stamp-tax on periodical publications. This marks the high tide of Tory repression; the public reaction was such that Wellington himself feared universal revolution.

On the death of George III, 1820, the Regent became King as George IV. His wife, from whom he had long been separated and who had been living a somewhat irregular life on the Continent, announced her intention of returning to claim her position as Queen. George countered by forcing his reluctant ministers to institute proceedings for divorce on the ground of her alleged adultery. The English sense of fair play was shocked by this action; George's liaisons were notorious, and it was secretly known and generally believed that he was the husband of Mrs. Fitzherbert at the time when he married the unfortunate princess who became his queen. Accordingly when the Queen returned she received a triumphant welcome. Macaulay, then an undergraduate at Cambridge, greeted her as "The Daughter of the People" in a copy of verses whose enthusiasm surpasses their poetic merit. After a long trial, during which much dirty linen was washed in public with no definite result, the government decided to drop the case and buy the lady off with a pension of £50,000 a year.[17] The excitement died down and did not flare up again even when she tried to force her way into the coronation service, 1821, and had the door of Westminster Abbey slammed in her face. The whole affair contributed to the public disgust with the government and for the first time in his life Wellington was hissed in the streets of London.

In 1822 Castlereagh, perhaps the most hated man in England, went mad and killed himself.[18] He was succeeded as the chief power in the government by Canning, one of Pitt's young disciples. Canning promptly broke the ties that linked England to the reactionary powers on the Continent and joined the United States in promulgating the so-called Monroe Doctrine, the first joint action of the English-speaking nations in a world policy, a promise of better things to come. At home Canning put through several social reforms; the penal laws were modified along the line of Bentham's proposals; the death penalty for some two hundred felonies was abolished. There was also a slow but steady progress toward freer trade and commercial reciprocity. In

[17] Shelley's comic-satiric drama, *Oedipus Tyranus or Swellfoot the Tyrant,* expresses the contempt of a good republican for the government's proceedings. Only seven copies were sold in London before it was stopped by the Society for the Prevention of Vice.

[18] Byron's bitter attack on him in the *Dedication* to *Don Juan,* 1818, and his indecent epitaphs on hearing of his death express the hatred of liberal thinkers. Later judgments recognize Castlereagh's ability as a statesman in the Napoleonic War and in his negotiations with the United States.

1824 the law prohibiting trade unions was repealed and the *Westminster Review* (p. 219) was founded to preach the gospel according to Bentham. In 1827 University College was opened in London to offer higher education to dissenters still debarred from Oxford and Cambridge.[19]

The repeal, 1828, of the obsolete *Test and Corporation Acts* paved the way to the more important measure of Catholic Emancipation.[20] For some two centuries English Catholics had suffered under heavy disabilities; they were debarred from the learned professions and denied admission into Parliament. Popular feeling, expressed in the "No Popery" cry, joined with the prejudices of successive kings to prevent their emancipation. Strange as it may seem it was the staunch Conservative Wellington, head of the government after Canning's death, 1827, who espoused the Catholic cause. He seems to have done so for military rather than for social reasons. Recent illegal elections in Ireland of Catholics as members of Parliament had convinced him that unless emancipation was granted, there would be an outbreak of civil war in that country, where even in peace an army larger than that in India was required to keep order. Accordingly in 1829 Peel, Wellington's leader in the Commons, pushed through an emancipating bill by the slender majority of four votes. Since it was certain that the Lords would reject it, Wellington and Peel begged the King to use his influence with the upper House. He refused to do so and accepted their resignation with tears, only to call them back and submit. With the King's authority

---

[19] Its later union with the Church of England King's College created the great University of London of today.

[20] These Acts, dating back to the Restoration, prohibited dissenters from holding any national or municipal office. They were, as a matter of fact, habitually violated.

behind him Wellington had little trouble with the Lords. While their action was pending Macaulay asked a friendly peer how the Duke would manage it. "Easy enough," was the reply, "He'll say 'My Lords, attention! Right about face! March!'," and so it proved. The high and dry Tories never forgave Wellington, and the dons of Oxford visited their wrath on Peel by rejecting him as their representative at the next election. While still in office, however, Peel put through a reform with which his name is still associated; he founded the Metropolitan Police Force, the so-called "Peelers," better known today as the "Bobbies" in memory of Sir Robert. This fine body, which replaced the medieval night-watchmen, was limited to London, but similar forces were soon organized in all large English cities. Their calm control of mobs put an end to the need of such military intervention as had caused the massacre of Peterloo.

George IV died in June, 1830, and the Duke of Clarence became King as William IV. While the general election that regularly followed the accession of a new King was proceeding, the news reached England of a second French Revolution, "the glorious three days of July," that drove Charles X, the last of the Bourbons, from the throne. An armed revolt in Paris ended after fierce street fighting in the fraternization of the military and the rioters and in the confirmation of the liberal Prince, Louis Philippe, as King of the French. The fall of the reactionary Bourbons was hailed with joy in England, for in this revolt there had been none of the terroristic excess which had formerly shocked English liberals into opposition. On the contrary it now seemed as if France had led the way toward the goal so long deferred in England, the formation of a popular Parliament. The general approval of the liberal victory in France increased the return in the reform. It did not, however, come to blows. In December, 1831, a third slightly modified bill was sent up to the Lords. This time they did not reject it but claimed the right to amend it at their leisure. Thereupon Grey resigned and the King called on Wellington to take the reins. The old soldier accepted, but soon found that even his own party would not stand by him at the risk of civil war.

During a ten-day intermission while the Duke tried in vain to form a ministry, the country showed a firm determination to secure the passage of "the bill, the whole bill, and nothing but the bill." People refused to pay taxes, and strong petitions urged the Commons to refuse to vote supplies. The King, less obstinate than his father or brother, recalled Grey and gave him a written pledge to create enough peers to swamp the Lords. The mere threat was sufficient; when the bill came once more before them it was passed by a good majority. In France an armed revolution overthrew the monarchy in three days; in England it took months of popular agitation and parliamentary debate to destroy the old regime. In France, however, the new popular monarchy lasted only eighteen years; in England a constitutional monarch still sits on the throne.

Yet it must not be thought that the Reform Bill gave England a truly democratic government. It was, in fact, a characteristic Victorian compromise between the clamor of the radicals for manhood suffrage and the refusal of the stern and unbending Tories to accept any change. So far from being a democratic measure the Bill actually took votes away from hundreds of workers in such boroughs as Westminster (p. 9) and in general barred most of the working class from the franchise. When the second Reform Bill was under discussion, 1864, Gladstone asserted that only about two per cent of urban current English election of members pledged to parliamentary reform.

At the first meeting of the new Parliament Wellington was challenged as to the intention of the government. He replied that Parliament in its present form possessed the entire confidence of the country and that if he had to frame a new system of representation, he would do his best to imitate so excellent a model. This uncompromising declaration doomed the Tory government, which soon resigned. Earl Grey, the old Whig leader, then became Prime Minister. In March, 1831, the first Reform Bill was introduced, so sweeping in its measures as to provoke the derisive laughter of the Tories. After an angry debate, in which Macaulay, returned from a "pocket borough," made one of his brilliant speeches, the second reading was carried by the majority of one, a majority made possible by the recent admission into Parliament of Irish Catholic members. A letter of Macaulay's, March 3, 1831, gives a vivid picture of the excitement that reigned while the votes were being counted and of the exultation at the Liberal victory. As Parliament dispersed at four in the morning the Liberal members were cheered in the lobby; even the cabby who drove Macaulay home thanked God for their triumph.

The fight was not yet over. In April the government was beaten in committee and Grey persuaded the King to order a new election. In this the Liberals gained a decisive victory, and a second Reform Bill passed the Commons by a majority of 136. The Lords, however, rejected it by 41 votes, a majority composed of the new peers (p. 8) and the bishop who voted in a body against it. Rioting at once broke out in the country; in Bristol a furious mob burned the palace of the Tory Bishop; in the North working men were arming and drilling to fight fo workers had the right to vote. It is impossible to dwell here upon the details of this historic measure.[21] Suffice it to say that the Reform Bill broke the long monopoly of political power by the landowning gentry and transferred a great part of it to the middle class inhabitants of the new great towns. With the passage of this Bill in 1832 the Victorian age in its political aspect begins. Three later reforms in 1867, 1884, and 1918, were needed to make England the democracy it is today. Yet these measures were the necessary, if unforeseen, consequences of the first, and they came in time to be recognized as such. Over none of them was such a battle waged as was fought over the first. We shall see in the next chapter what use the coalition of liberal landowners and well-to-do citizens made of their newly acquired power.

The period covered in this chapter belongs in the history of English literature to the romantic movement. As it draws to a close in the eighteen twenties the lights are one by one dimmed or extinguished, and its close is marked by the death of Scott in 1832. It is still early for the full revelation of Victorian literature, but faint signs of its emergence are beginning to appear. Carlyle, the first-born of the great Victorians, 1795, attracted some attention by his contributions to the growing interest in German literature and thought in his *Life of Schiller*, 1823-4, and his translation of Goethe's *Wilhelm Meister*, 1824-7. The young Macaulay's brilliant essay on Milton in the *Edinburgh Review*, 1825, was the first of a long series of literary and historical studies that won for him a wide popularity. Disraeli today is remembered rather as a Victorian statesman than as a writer of fiction, but he had made his mark as a

---

[21] They may be found neatly summarized in Trevelyan's *British History in the Nineteenth Century*, pp. 239 ff.

novelist before he attained political eminence. His *Vivian Grey,* published anonymously in 1826-7, was the first of a number of his novels that dealt, among other things, with contemporary social and political ideas. The last of these, *Endymion,* appeared in 1880, shortly before his death. Tennyson alone of Victorian poets began in this period to show signs of his future greatness. His poetic genius developed early; while still a schoolboy he and his brother Charles collaborated in *Poems by Two Brothers,* 1827. At Cambridge he won a prize for poetry with *Timbuctoo,* 1829, and published a little volume of verse, *Poems Chiefly Lyrical,* 1830. A later volume, *Poems,* 1833, consisted mainly of verses composed during his residence at Cambridge. These two volumes were unfavorably reviewed and attracted little attention, but they served to introduce a future Laureate to all true lovers of poetry. Robert Browning's *Pauline,* 1833, was, no doubt, composed in this period, but this poem was completely ignored and showed, in fact, little promise of Browning's later achievement.

Chapter II

The Victorian Compromise

1832–1848

About two hundred thousand new voters, *ca.* 50% of those still qualified to exercise the franchise, took part in the election of members to the House of Commons of the first reformed Parliament. The composition of the House, however, did not differ greatly from that of former Parliaments. The landed interest was still represented by some five hundred members, of whom about half were sons of noble families. On the other hand a little group of radical Benthamites was elected and lost no time in making its influence felt. The temper of the House was favorable to reform; the majority felt that they had been elected to put into action the will of the people. Even the Tories under the leadership of Peel accepted the new electoral law as a "final and irrevocable settlement" and began to call themselves "Conservatives,"[1] ready to conciliate "the sober-minded and well-disposed" part of the nation.

[1] "Conservative" in its political sense first appears in 1830. The term was adopted by Peel and soon superseded "Tory." Greville says: "Peel does not intend that there shall be a Tory; there must be a Conservative party."

One of the first acts of the new Parliament was to abolish negro slavery in the colonies (p. 14). During the long struggle toward this goal the abolitionists were often taunted with their indifference to the sufferings of "white slaves" in English mines and factories, and it was, therefore, fitting that the government should take prompt steps to remedy intolerable conditions at home. The first effective Factory Act was passed in 1833, fixing the working hours for children, and, what was more important, appointing inspectors to enforce the law. This halfway measure was supplemented in 1842 by the Ten Hours Bill limiting the hours of work for women as well as for children, and definitely establishing the right of the state to control working conditions.[2]

Parliament proceeded in 1834 to grapple with the widespread pauperization caused by outdoor relief (p. 13). The Poor Law substituted for this a system of "work-houses" in which applicants for relief were obliged to live under strict control. The hardship imposed by the new law, especially on women and children, provoked a bitter resentment which finds striking expression in the first chapters of *Oliver Twist*.[3] The board presiding over the workhouse where young Oliver is immured had established, says Dickens, "the rule that all poor people should have the alternative of being starved by a gradual process within the house, or by a quick one out of it." An example of the "quick process" appears in a later chapter, XXIII, where Bumble, the Beadle, tells how a starving applicant for relief was given a pound of potatoes and half a pint of oat-

---

[2] It was in connection with the passage of this Bill that Miss Barrett wrote *The Cry of the Children*. It appeared in *Blackwood's*, 1843.

[3] Especially resented was the enforced separation of husband and wife in the work-house.

meal. As the uncooked food was of no use to him he went away and died in the streets, "an obstinate pauper," but the great principle of outdoor relief, "to give the paupers exactly what they don't want," was firmly maintained. The Poor Law was a characteristic Benthamite measure passed with more regard for order and consistency than for human feelings. Yet it was a staunch Benthamite, Chadwick, head of the commission to enforce the law, who led the movement in 1848 to pass the first Public Health Act, striking at one of the chief causes of pauperism, insanitary living conditions.

Lord Grey, the Prime Minister, resigned in 1834, but the Whig government was carried on under Lord Melbourne. In 1835, another important measure, this time political rather than social, was passed, the Municipal Corporations Act. This law abolished the old, inefficient, and often corrupt, administration of the boroughs by close and sometimes self-perpetuating corporations. For these the new law substituted municipal councils elected by the ratepayers. This was a necessary consequence of parliamentary reform, and it is a proof of the general acceptance of that measure that Peel promoted the bill in Commons and Wellington quieted the rebellious Lords. This truly democratic measure broke down the rule of a petty local aristocracy and threw open municipal offices to dissenters, liberals, and radicals, who by custom, if not by law, had long been excluded.

William IV died on June 20, 1837, and was succeeded by his niece Victoria (p. 7). From 1821, when the last of his two children died, Victoria had been regarded as his eventual successor and had been carefully trained in complete seclusion for her future duties. The accession to the throne of a young and lovely girl was to cause a complete change in the nation's attitude toward the monarchy (pp. 4-8). At the time of the Reform Bill the Russian Ambassador wrote the Czar that if Victoria ever came to the throne she would be swept off it by "a rising tide of republican sentiment." Republican sentiment, indeed, ran high among the working classes in William's day, and even such a typical liberal as Macaulay looked forward to a possible overthrow of the monarchy. In a letter of June 17, 1834, he wrote: "For the public I shall, if this Parliament is dissolved, entertain scarcely any hopes. I see nothing before us but a frantic conflict between extreme opinions; a short period of oppression, then a convulsive reaction, and then a tremendous crash of the Funds, the Church, the Peerage, and the Throne." The tide of republican sentiment, however, began to ebb early in the young Queen's reign; there was no demand for a republic in the People's Charter (p. 31), which presented the extreme views of English radicals. Victoria's popularity was increased by her love-match with her cousin Albert, by her happy family life as the mother of a brood of children — nine of them in seventeen years — and by her long widowhood after Albert's death in 1861. It was not till toward the close of the century that such irreverent comment as Kipling's *The Widow of Windsor* or Max Beerbohm's caricatures became possible.

Melbourne was Prime Minister when Victoria came to the throne, and except for a brief interval he continued to serve her for the next four years. His kindly consideration and gentle manners completely won the young Queen's heart and it is hardly too much to say that he made a constitutional monarch out of a young woman who at times exhibited the

THE VICTORIAN COMPROMISE

self-will characteristic of her Hanoverian ancestors.[4] Melbourne was a hold-over from the gay society of the Regency, an old Whig with little taste for reform, and it is not surprising that under him the fortunes of the Whig party steadily declined.[5] A general election in 1841, fought on a half-hearted Whig proposal to reduce the duty on corn (p. 11), threw them out of office, and the Conservatives under Peel came back to power.

Sir Robert Peel, the son of a rich factory owner, inherited his father's business ability and at once proceeded to give England what might be called a business administration. It was sorely needed, for the economic condition of the country was deplorable.[6] Carlyle's *Past and Present* (p. 174), 1843, paints a lurid picture of the "condition of England," with about a million and a half paupers on relief and over two hundred thousand sitting idle in "workhouses" where no work was done.

Undernourishment, familiar in this century in a Europe devastated by war, was prevalent to the point of starvation in an England at peace. Dickens tells us in *Oliver Twist* of the suffering of the urban poor and Elliott in his *Cornlaw Rhymes*, 1828, sets their misery to the tune of *Robin Adair:*

> Father clamm'd thrice a week — [starved]
> God's will be done!
> Long for work did he seek,
> Work he found none.

[4] It is said that he was the only person who ever fell asleep in the Queen's presence and she would not let him be waked.

[5] As William Lamb he is best known as the husband of Lady Caroline, the maddest and unhappiest of Byron's loves.

[6] It was about this time that Friedrick Engels, the friend and associate of Karl Marx, was living in Manchester. His experience of life in an English factory town went into his book, *The Condition of the English Working Class*, which became one of the foundation stones of proletarian political economy.

> Tears on his hollow cheek
> Told what no tongue could speak:
> Why did his master break? [fail]
> God's will be done.

The prime cause of this condition was a business depression due in large measure to the obsolete restrictions on trade, to duties imposed both on imported raw materials and on exported finished products. Rapidly becoming a manufacturing and trading country, England was peculiarly ill-adapted to such restrictions, and Peel was clear-sighted enough to abolish them, taking step after step in the direction of free trade. To compensate for the loss of revenue from such duties he reimposed the old income tax and thus for the first time in years balanced the national budget. One tariff barrier, however, he long hesitated to attack, the Corn Law, which protected the interests of the landowning class. For the repeal of this law the Anti-Corn Law League had been agitating since 1839 by methods taken over from the struggle for parliamentary reform, by mass-meetings, public addresses, and widespread distribution of printed propaganda.[7] A great body of the nation demanded "total and immediate repeal," but the landowners opposed any considerable change, and it was they who had elected Peel and supported his reforms. His natural reluctance to break with his party was overcome in the autumn of 1845 by a bad harvest in England combined with the almost total failure of the potato crop. This failure bore hard on the English poor, but in Ireland, where half the wretched peasantry, "the worst housed, the worst fed, and the worst clothed of any in Europe" maintained a bare subsistence on potatoes alone, it was an absolute calamity, the notorious Irish famine.

[7] John Bright, one of England's greatest orators, played a principal part in this agitation.

Over a million people are reported to have died of hunger and of the pestilence which followed famine. Cheap bread, Peel became convinced, was an immediate necessity, and to secure it he pushed through with the aid of the Whigs and the reluctant support of a minority of his own party the repeal of the Corn Law, 1846.[8] The landowners were furious at what they called their leader's betrayal of his party, and on the very night when the repeal bill passed the House of Lords, Peel was howled out of office in the Commons by a coalition of angry Tories, led by the brilliant young Disraeli, and Whigs eager for the spoils.

Parallel with the struggle for free trade there ran another movement, political rather than economic. It aimed at a wider extension of the franchise and with it a more direct control of legislation by democratic forces. This movement took the form of a demand for the enactment of a People's Charter, a nineteenth century parallel to the medieval Magna Carta, and accordingly came to be known as Chartism. The origin of this demand lay in the disappointment of the working classes with the results of the Reform Bill. They had looked to that measure as the first step on the road to democracy; they saw that on the contrary it had actually disfranchised many of them, and that neither political party had any intention of moving further. In the words of an old Chartist, written long after the collapse of the movement: "The political history of the fourth and fifth decades [1830-1850] is the history of the

---

[8] Carlyle, no lover of parliaments, wrote to Peel in that year praising his action: "By and by . . . all England will say what already many a one begins to feel, that whatever were the spoken underactivities in Parliament — and they were many on all hands, lamentable to gods and men — here has a great veracity been done in Parliament, . . . a strenuous, courageous and manful thing."

anger of working men with the classes and political parties which made promises of enfranchisement and broke them."⁹ In 1838 the Workingmen's Association drew up the People's Charter with its famous six points: annual parliaments, universal suffrage, the secret ballot, equal electoral districts, no property qualification for members of Parliament, and, as a natural consequence, the payment of members.¹⁰ We may note that all of these demands except the first have been attained in the democratic governments of England and the United States, and the American biennial election of Congressmen differs but slightly from the Chartist plea. At that time, however, these demands were regarded as revolutionary, and a Chartist was looked on with the same fear and abhorrence as a Communist is today. Carlyle, indeed, who called himself "no Tory but one of the deepest . . . of radicals," was sympathetic enough with the movement to offer its followers some advice in his pamphlet, *Chartism*, 1839, but they would not hear him.¹¹ The general alarm was naturally heightened by the fiery language of many Chartist leaders, wordy demagogues like Feargus O'Connor, rather than genuine representatives of labor. An armed revolt of Welsh miners actually occurred in 1839, but it was easily suppressed and its leaders were condemned to death.¹² A series of prosecutions by the Whig government swept hundreds of prominent Chartists into prison, and for a time the driving force of the movement weakened.

In 1842, however, a fresh attempt was made to promote the people's cause, this time by constitu-

⁹ Thomas Cooper, *Thoughts at Fourscore*, 1885.
¹⁰ Universal meant manhood suffrage; woman suffrage was suggested but never urged.
¹¹ Carlyle's *Chartism* was struck off a list of books for a working man's library by the committee in charge.
¹² The sentence was commuted to transportation for life.

tional means. A petition demanding the adoption of the Charter, ostensibly signed by three million persons, was presented to Parliament. In the debate that followed, Macaulay, a sincere liberal, declared universal suffrage "fatal to all the purposes for which government exists and utterly incompatible with the very existence of civilization." Only a few radicals in the Commons supported the petition; an overwhelming majority refused a hearing to the petitioners. Six years later, 1848, events on the Continent, especially the overthrow of the Orleanist monarchy in France and the establishment of the French Republic, rekindled the hopes of the Chartists. "France has a Republic; England must have the Charter," declared their organ, *The Northern Star*. Karl Marx came to England to invite the Chartists to join a congress of working men determined to secure world-wide liberty. Another petition was drawn up, this time to be carried to Parliament by a great procession to be assembled in a London suburb. In case the petition was rejected, the Chartists resolved to appeal directly to the Queen, asking her to dissolve Parliament and appoint ministers who would enact the Charter into law. London was swept by a panic, but the government took prompt measures against anything like a Parisian revolution. The Queen was sent out of harm's way; Wellington stationed soldiers at key points in the city, and 170,000 special constables were sworn in to support Peel's police force.[13] The procession was forbidden, and the petition, signed by millions of names, was taken to Parliament in three cabs. On examination it appeared that many of the signatures were in one and the same hand; others like those of Victoria Rex, Wellington, and Mr. Punch, were foolish frauds. The petition was scornfully rejected, and

[13] Among them was Louis Napoleon, then an exile in England.

the assembly of Chartists, far less numerous than had been planned, quietly dispersed. Such was the ignominious end of Chartism.

The cause of this failure is obvious. Not only were the Chartists badly organized and incapably led, but Chartism was never a truly national movement. Dominated by class-consciousness, it rejected alliance with the strong middle class then winning its long fight for free trade. On the other hand it was regarded with distrust by the trade unions in which skilled laborers were steadily enrolling. It was essentially a proletarian movement for revolutionary change, and no such movement is ever likely to succeed unless the nation as a whole is in such distress as to welcome almost any change. But by 1848 the "condition of England" had so improved under Peel's guidance that the proletariat's demand for a democratic charter fell on deaf ears. The nation as a whole was content with the Victorian compromise of the Reform Bill and was willing to wait nearly twenty years before taking the next step in advance. But Chartism was not altogether a failure. It failed, indeed, to obtain its revolutionary demands, but it educated the working class politically and taught them to combine in claiming a share in the government of the nation. It was another stage in the long democratic process which culminated a century later in the victory of the Labor party and the formation of a Labor government.

During the time that Chartism rose and fell, other movements, social and economic rather than political, were developing which finally produced happier results for the working class. One of these, the co-operative, can be traced back to the life work of one man, Robert Owen, 1771-1858. A young Welshman of little education but immense energy, Owen became manager of a cotton mill when only nineteen years of age. Later, 1800, as manager and part owner of mills at New Lanark in Scotland, he inaugurated a series of social reforms that were to exert a profound influence. Convinced that character was determined by environment, he set himself to improve the conditions under which his workers lived. For the children in his mills, many of them very young, he organized infant schools, the first in Great Britain. He opened a store where workers could get standard goods at fair prices; he greatly improved their housing and sanitation and exercised a strict control over the sale of liquor. So successful were his efforts that New Lanark came to be regarded as a model industrial community; it was visited and praised by reformers from the Continent as well as from England.

Over this experiment Owen presided in paternalistic fashion, but his ideas developed along socialistic and co-operative lines.[14] He was an early advocate of state regulation of factory conditions, but he came to believe that the improvement of working class life depended upon the will and ability of the workers to unite and co-operate. His vision of the future was one of small socialized communities, guided by the motto, "all for one and one for all."[15] Unfortunately Owen's avowed hostility to all forms of religion alienated the very classes, especially the Evangelicals, from whom he should have drawn support. His Grand National Association of All Nations, 1835, which proclaimed that labor was the sole source of wealth and that competition must give place to socialized production, was a hopeless failure. Original, eloquent, and visionary, Owen was in many ways too far in advance of his time.

[14] The word "socialism" first becomes current in connection with Owen's work.

[15] In 1826 Owen founded such a community at New Harmony, Indiana, but it soon failed because of the motley crew of theorists and idlers that it attracted.

The one permanent result of Owen's varied labors was the co-operative movement. This took practical shape when Owenite workers opened in 1844 the store of the Rochdale Pioneers in the heart of industrial England. From this small, honestly and efficiently managed store, which distributed all profits among its members, there sprang a movement which pushed on to the production as well as the distribution of goods, and before the close of the century spread over England and crossed the sea to America. It was essentially democratic since the election of managers and the general control of business depended upon the vote of the members, and each member, man or woman, had one vote. The co-operative movement has been called one of the causes of the "social transformation of Great Britain."

The trade union movement of this period falls into two distinct periods. Outlawed by the Combination Act, 1800, which branded any combination in restraint of trade as conspiracy, trade unions regained a legal status in 1824 and obtained the right of collective bargaining, the keystone of trade unionism. The revived trade unions succumbed for a time to the eloquence of Owen and indulged in wild dreams of a Grand National Trades Union which would wrest all power from masters and owners. This provoked reaction, and a class war broke out in which even the Liberal government of the thirties took sides with the employers. The transportation for seven years of a group of Dorset farm hands, 1834, for even attempting to form a union was an act worthy of the harshest Tory government.[16]

[16] It is a proof of the growth and strength of public opinion in England that the outcry against this sentence forced the government to pardon and recall the men within two years.

There was a marked revival of trade unionism in the next decade; several strong unions were founded in the early forties. These unions tried to avoid strikes; they set themselves definite and limited objectives: the defense of their members against injustice and the education of labor by schools and trade journals. The whole movement profited in this decade by the rapid concentration of factories in the growing towns, a natural result of the sudden expansion of railways in England.

It has been said that modern urban industrial England dates from the victory of the railway over the highroad. The steam engine, originally employed to pump water out of coal mines, was used on roads as early as 1825 to transport passengers between the northern towns of Stockton and Darlington. The pace of the "daily coach" on this line was so slow that the train was preceded by a mounted man to warn pedestrians off the track. More important was the opening of a line in 1830 between the great cities of Manchester and Liverpool.[17] Construction proceeded slowly at first as the railway had to compete with the well-organized coaching system, but by 1840 over 1,200 miles of railways had been built. In fact the first years of this decade saw what has been called the "railway mania" of wild speculation in railway shares. This was brought about partly by the energetic activity of Hudson, the "railway King," who rose from a small shop-keeper to be the controller of over a thousand miles of railroad. The boom was followed by a crash, and Hudson died bankrupt.[18] Systematic reorganization followed

[17] This line ran through the little "rotten borough" of Newton, and an early passenger commented on the absurdity of Newton's having two members in Parliament while Manchester had none.
[18] One of Carlyle's *Latter-Day Pamphlets* (p. 72) mocks at a proposal to erect a statue to Hudson as a modern hero.

his fall, and by 1850 the victory of rail over road was complete. The triumph of the rail can be traced in the novels of Dickens; in *Pickwick*, 1836, there is no mention of a railway; travel is entirely by coach and postchaise; but in *Dombey and Son*, 1848, the antiquated coach system of France is compared unfavorably with the efficient English railways.[19]

Some of the immediate results of this development of the railway may be noted. It furnished employment for thousands of unskilled workers in the construction of the lines, greatly lessened the army of the unemployed, and served to avert the armed revolt of labor which had seemed imminent in the thirties. It also helped to prevent the recurrent semi-famine periods in England by furnishing quick transport to the cheap food that poured in after the repeal of the Corn Law. Perhaps its most important result was the attraction of country factories dependent on water power into towns where they could use steam generated by the coal which the railways carried. And these towns served as magnets to draw the unemployed or underpaid agricultural laborer into their factories, and sooner or later into some trade union.

Parallel with these political and social-economic currents ran a religious movement, less wide-spread than they, but destined to exert a profound influence on later Victorian life and literature. This was the so-called "Oxford Movement," rightly so-called since it was in the University of Oxford that it started, flourished, fought, and finally failed. It is hard for any one today familiar with American colleges, or even with twentieth century Oxford, to realize the

---

[19] Carker, the villain of this novel, is run over by a train, as Huskisson, a prominent politician, had been at the opening of the Manchester-Liverpool line.

character of that University at the beginning of the Victorian era. The Oxford colleges of that day have been called by a sympathetic historian of the movement as "ecclesiastical as the chapter of a cathedral." The heads of the various colleges were priests of the state Church; the tutors and fellows were celibates in holy orders; undergraduates were obliged upon admission to affirm their acceptance of the Thirty-Nine Articles, embodying the doctrine of the Church, and, in consequence, all dissenters were excluded.[20] Clerical Oxford was at ease in Zion so long as the Tory government lasted, but with the beginning of reform the University awoke to a sense of impending change, and its temper was shown by its rejection of Peel for his support of Catholic Emancipation (p. 19). With the advent of a Whig ministry supported by the reformed Parliament, the danger became apparent. The Church party in politics, notably the bishops, had steadily opposed all movement towards reform, and now the victorious reformers turned upon them. The Whig Prime Minister bade the bishops "put their house in order" and the radical wing of his party demanded the disestablishment of the Church. Lord Grey had no notion of such a sweeping move, but one of the early acts of his government was to lay hands on the English Church in Ireland and to suppress ten bishoprics supported by taxes on the Roman Catholic peasantry. This assertion of state control broke the old alliance between Church and state; it was denounced by Keble in a University sermon in 1833 as an act of "national apostasy."

Keble, a brilliant scholar who had left Oxford to become a country clergyman, was looked on in the University as something like a saint; his little

---

[20] An attempt in 1835 to abolish this regulation was defeated by a vote of five to one.

volume of verse, *The Christian Year*, 1827, was already a sacred book treasured by devout souls along with the Bible and the Book of Common Prayer. His famous sermon, often called the origin of the Oxford Movement, summoned the Church to take arms against "the robbers of the shrines, come to reform where ne'er they came to pray," and his call was answered by a little group of Oxford scholars and clergymen who took over the established practice of propaganda by the printed word and began writing and circulating a series of *Tracts for the Times*.[21]

The leader of this group was John Henry Newman (p. 228), the University Preacher, who at this time exerted an extraordinary influence upon the youth of Oxford, especially by his Sunday afternoon sermons in St. Mary's, the University Church. These sermons profoundly affected life in the University and in the Church; indifference gave way to zeal and self-seeking to self-sacrifice; *credo in Newmanum* was the brief creed of many a simple soul ready to follow wherever he might lead. Newman was perhaps less successful with the highly controversial *Tracts* than with his sermons, but he threw himself with all his energy into this form of propaganda. He wrote most of them himself and in the first number proclaimed the doctrine which was to be the ruin of the movement at Oxford. This was the dogma of the "Apostolic Succession," according to which the priesthood ordained by Christ in his apostles had been successively transmitted by the laying-on of hands through the Dark and Middle Ages and the Reformation to the Anglican clergy of the nineteenth century. This divinely founded

---

[21] Hence the name "Tractarian" often applied to the movement. It was also called "Puseyite" after the great scholar, Pusey, associated with its early stages.

and mystically transmitted priesthood formed a Church, Newman held, apart from and above the state. State interference with the Church was, therefore, little less than sacrilege. This dogma, however, denounced at the time by the liberal Arnold of Rugby as a "profane heraldic theory," was the keystone of Rome's claim to sole and supreme authority. Rome could boast an uninterrupted succession of priests; the Anglican claim since the Reformation was historically doubtful. Newman's more ardent followers in their contempt of the Reformation and their hatred of political liberalism were perceptibly drawing near to Rome; some of them, in fact, went over publicly. Finally Newman's *Tract XC*, 1841, precipitated the crisis. This closely reasoned analysis of the Thirty-Nine Articles was designed to show that they contained nothing contrary to the essential faith of Rome, even though they denounced her errors. Naturally, though apparently to Newman's surprise, the publication of this tract roused a fierce storm. If Newman's conclusion was correct, a Roman Catholic, or at least a "Romanizer," could sign the articles, and thereafter hold any post whatever in Oxford or in the Church. The conservative orthodox clergy felt that their defenses had been attacked from within their walls. The heads of colleges solemnly denounced the *Tract* and posted their denunciation in the schools and colleges of the University to protect, Newman said scornfully, undergraduate youth from the contagion of his heresy. At the request of the Bishop of Oxford, Newman's ecclesiastical superior, the publication of the *Tracts* was stopped, Newman severed his connection with the University and after some delay joined the Roman Catholic Church, 1845.

Newman's secession ended the movement at Oxford; the liberals had won the battle, and they went on later to transform the whole ancient clerical constitution of the University (p. 39). Yet the spirit Newman had breathed into the Church was not quenched. A modern historian declares, perhaps too smartly, that the movement found the English clergy "mere gentlemen; it left them theologians and priests." Kingsley, no friend of the movement, confesses that it had greatly improved the quality of the country clergymen and had awakened hundreds, perhaps thousands of cultivated men and women.[22] This awakening revealed itself in a new reverence for the priestly office, in an insistence on the catholicity of the Church's doctrine, and on the mystical significance of the Eucharist. A novel phase of the movement shortly appeared in the devoted missionary work of Anglican churchmen in the squalid urban slums of the day.[23]

Matthew Arnold once asserted that Newman had adopted "an impossible solution" for contemporary doubts and difficulties. It did not seem impossible to poets less critical and more emotional than Arnold: to Coventry Patmore, Alice Meynell, Gerard Manley Hopkins, Lionel Johnson, and others, who found in the Church of Rome a refuge from the arid materialism of the age. The influence of the movement was seen even in the work of men like Keble and Pusey who remained steadfast in the national Church, in the once popular novels of Charlotte Yonge and in those of Arnold's niece, Mrs. Humphry Ward, and with special force and beauty in Shorthouse's *John Inglesant,* 1880, rightly called "the one great religious novel of the English language."

The first period of the Victorian age covering the years from the Reform Bill, 1832, to the collapse

---

[22] In his *Preface* to the fourth edition of *Yeast,* 1859.
[23] Like the Rev. Eustace Hanna in Kipling's *Badalia Herrodsfoot.*

of Chartism, 1848, drew to an end in England in profound peace. Since Waterloo, 1815, there had been no war to disturb the condition of the country, and the nation took advantage of the peace to compose, temporarily at least, its political and economic difficulties. England was now rapidly advancing to the dominant position as a manufacturing, trading, and colonizing power which she was to hold for the greater part of the nineteenth century. Only in Ireland was there still distress and unrest, but Ireland had been so weakened by famine and pestilence and by the emigration of so much of her vigorous youth that a serious revolt had become impossible. A foolish demonstration led by Smith O'Brien in 1848 was easily put down by a body of "Peelers."

It is in this time of peace that the literature characteristic of the Victorian age begins to appear. Carlyle, the oldest of the great Victorians, accomplishes in fact all his best work from *Sartor* to *Oliver Cromwell*, 1845, within its limits; Ruskin, destined in many ways to continue Carlyle's mission, speaks out for the first time in *Modern Painters* (Volume I, 1843). After the long silence that followed the chill reception of his early work, Tennyson establishes himself as the most popular poet of the time with his *Poems* of 1842. Browning achieves a certain measure of success with *Paracelsus*, 1835; fails badly with *Sordello*, 1840, and slowly regains a hearing from an audience, fit though few, with the series of *Bells and Pomegranates*, 1841-6. Miss Barrett, a far more popular author, gains applause with two volumes of *Poems*, 1844, but the work by which she is best known today, *Sonnets from the Portuguese*, 1849, was written after her marriage. In fiction, perhaps the chief glory of Victorian literature, Dickens is the first to hit the mark with *The Pickwick Papers*, 1836; he follows it up with his first real novel, *Oliver*

Twist, 1838, and with a swift series of successes to *Dombey and Son,* 1847-8, at the end of the period. His great rival, Thackeray, after squandering his talent on ephemeral contributions to periodicals, comes through with his first considerable novel, the little read, but wholly admirable, *Barry Lyndon,* 1844; *Vanity Fair,* usually esteemed his masterpiece, rounds off the period in 1847-8. Disraeli's now forgotten, but historically important, political novels, *Coningsby* and *Sybil,* date from 1844 to 1845. The Brontë sisters, Charlotte and Emily, startle the sober Victorian world with *Jane Eyre,* 1847, and *Wuthering Heights,* 1848.

The year 1848, which saw England at peace, was one of revolution on the Continent. The Parisian revolt of February which overthrew the Orleanist monarchy and established the shortlived Second Republic kindled a fire that spread far beyond France. Northern Italy rose to drive out the Austrians; Venice and Rome declared themselves republics, and Sicily revolted against the Bourbon King of Naples. Hungary shook off the Austrian yoke, and the King of Prussia was forced by street fighting in Berlin to grant his people a constitution. The fire, however, was soon extinguished; Russian armies trampled it out in Hungary; Austria reconquered her Italian provinces; a French army overthrew the Roman Republic and the Sicilian revolt was crushed with such cruelty that French and English admirals, on station off the island, intervened to stop the massacre. Order reigned again in Berlin, and the conservative Prince of Prussia, who had fled into exile, returned to become later the first German Emperor. England took no active part in these Continental wars, but she offered at least an asylum to political refugees of all shades from King Louis Philippe and the Prussian Prince to republicans like Kossuth and

Mazzini. English workingmen mobbed Marshal Haynau, known as "the hangman of Austria," and England joined with France in supporting Turkey's refusal to surrender refugees to Russia. It was to Italy, above all, in her struggle for liberty, that English sympathy went out, finding generous expression later in the poems of the Brownings and in Meredith's novel *Vittoria,* 1867.

The average Briton, on the other hand, was only too apt to look upon these revolutions with a somewhat smug satisfaction that things were better in England, a temper dramatically expressed by the words put into the mouth of a Tory member's undergraduate son in the conclusion of Tennyson's *The Princess:*

> Yonder, whiff! there comes a sudden heat,
> The gravest citizen seems to lose his head,
> The King is scared, the soldier will not fight,
> The little boys begin to shoot and stab,
> A Kingdom topples over with a shriek
> Like an old woman and down rolls the world.
>
> . . . .
>
> Revolts, republics, revolutions, most
> No graver than a schoolboys' barring out.[24]

It was with something of this conviction, soon to be shattered, that all's well in the English world, that the nation moved forward into what is known as the Golden Age of Victorianism.

[24] It is perhaps worth noting that these lines first appeared in the third edition of *The Princess,* 1850, that is after the collapse of the Continental revolution of 1848.

Chapter III

The Golden Age

1848-1868

There is no sharp break between the first and second periods of the Victorian age like that between the first and its prelude. After the collapse of Chartism the nation continued quietly on its way untroubled by any fear of revolution. A Whig government was broken only at brief intervals by the Conservatives, themselves near enough to the Whigs to offer them repeatedly places in the cabinet. Until nearly the close of the period there was no strong demand for radical change. Politically the nation was content with things as they were, more interested in the expansion of commerce and in the observation of events abroad than in reform at home. This state of mind is exemplified by the leadership of Lord Palmerston during most of this period. Born in 1784, Palmerston held minor offices during the Napoleonic wars, joined the first Reform government, and became in turn Foreign Secretary, Home Secretary, and Prime Minister, and died in harness, 1865, at the age of eighty-one. He called himself an old Whig, but at heart he was a typical conservative John Bull. Always a popular character, he relied on the support of the nation to maintain him in office against the dislike of the court, the opposition of radical politicians, and the hostility of reactionary foreign governments. A warm friend, at times an active helper of revolutionary movements on the Continent, he, like the nation, was satisfied with what had been attained at home, and to the end of his life opposed a further advance of democracy in England.

Yet it would be wrong to believe that no reforms were made in England during this period. The Factory Act of 1850 confirmed state control over industry, shortened the hours of labor, and established the principle of half-time on Saturday. Little by little the state began also to play a part in the long neglected education of youth. It did not yet dare to insist on compulsory schooling, but in 1850 it created a Ministry of Education, granted increasingly liberal subsidies to voluntary schools, and in 1850 by regulating state grants, in accordance with the successful operation of the schools, "payment by results," did much to promote primary and secondary education. Reform in the universities, however, was postponed until the next period. The founding of the Working Men's College, 1854, in which such liberals as Kingsley and Thomas Hughes played a leading part, was an attempt to do by private means what the State left undone, to offer adult workers the opportunity of a liberal education. Gladstone, slowly moving from his early Tory and his High Church position, toward the liberal leadership of his later years, served repeatedly as Chancellor of the Exchequer, and his carefully planned budgets led the nation further along the road of free trade and prosperity. His proposed repeal of the paper duty, "the tax on knowledge," which hindered the publication of cheap books and newspapers, was rejected by the Lords in 1860, but in the next year he not only succeeded in repealing the tax, but forced the Lords to admit that taxation was exclusively the function of the Commons as the elected representatives of the nation.

Another financial reform destined to produce important results was the Limited Liability Act of 1853-6. Before this time the failure of a firm or company with which a man was connected left him responsible for all the debts of the concern. It was this which broke the heart and shortened the life of Walter Scott when the failure of the printing and publishing houses, in which he was a silent partner, saddled him with a crushing load of debt. After 1856 if a company was legally described as "limited," an investor was liable for only that amount which he had put into the business. This Act served as an invitation to the man with money lying idle in the bank to invest it where he had a prospect of gain and only a limited risk of loss. Few limited companies, indeed, were formed immediately after the passage of the Act, but before long their advantages were recognized, and money poured into them from the accumulating capital of a prosperous nation. One of the first results of this reform was the transformation of the old family firm into the modern type of stock company, and the successful development of these companies brought about a wider distribution of wealth and the rise of a social class unknown in earlier times, the so-called "rentiers" living happily and well on the income derived from their investments.[1] England was already on the way to the modern capitalistic state.

The success of a stock company depended mainly on efficient management, and the necessity for such management caused the steady replacement of in-

[1] Galsworthy's Forsytes are typical representatives of this class.

competent inheritors of a family business by trained and salaried managers. This change, indeed, was not altogether for the good. The manager's chief, if not his sole, aim was to secure the dividends demanded by the stock holders, and the stock holders were further removed from and so less interested in the working conditions of the laborers than the original founders of the business, though few founders managed their concerns with the kindly paternalism of Owen (p. 34).[2] The manager's difficulties were increased also by the growing number of workers under his control as one small business after another was absorbed by the stock company, and as a result the management of these early companies was apt to be deaf to the claims of labor.[3]

Trade unions during this period began to reorganize along what has been called "the new model." Small local unions combined to form national associations, and trades working in related lines joined in one central union. Thus the Amalgamated Society of Engineers, 1857, composed of various unions of mechanics, numbered at one time eleven thousand members. The leadership of these large unions gradually passed from the hands of professional agitators into those of elected and salaried officials, almost always workers who had risen from the ranks by industry and ability. Such leaders were able to meet the managers of the new stock companies on even terms, and were willing, as early agitators had not been, to enlist legal aid in the disputes between labor and management. Trade councils composed of such officials sprang up in

[2] Early hostile relations between founder and employee are vividly described in Charlotte Brontë's *Shirley*.

[3] The progressive growth of stock companies tended to the formation of the trusts and monopolies of later years, organizations more easily "nationalized" by socialist governments than their original small and scattered units could have been.

most industrial centers, working generally for conciliation rather than for war. In spite of occasional strikes in the fifties this period as a whole was one of peace between the organized forces of labor and management. Only toward its close when the design of industry to crush trade unionism became apparent, did the unions abandon their old policy of abstaining from politics (p. 37) and take part in the agitation for a second Reform Bill to give the workers the franchise denied by the first. Labor finally came to recognize that only by the possession of the franchise would it be able to secure the desired legislative reforms.

In the year of Gladstone's repeal of the "tax on knowledge" (p. 47) another reform, the Bankruptcy Act, 1861, limited, though it did not abolish, an abuse familiar to all readers of English drama and fiction, imprisonment for debt. By the old law a debtor could be clapped into jail by one of his creditors and held there till he had satisfied the claims of all of them. A merchant, indeed, could plead bankruptcy and come to some arrangement with his creditors, but an insolvent individual was at their mercy unless he fled the country.[4] The new law limited the period of imprisonment to one year and made possible a voluntary arrangement between debtor and creditor. Further amendments to the Act in 1869 and 1883 wiped out the last traces of the harsh old law.

Mention should be made in passing of the Great Exhibition of 1851, the first of many World Fairs. It was planned by Prince Albert primarily, perhaps, to show the world the flourishing condition of British

[4] Dickens' father spent some two years in a debtor's prison; imprisonment for debt is a common occurrence in Victorian, as in earlier, literature, and there are countless allusions to debtors living, like Beau Brummel, in exile in France.

business and to promote international trade. It was housed in the Crystal Palace of iron and glass erected in Hyde Park. Formally opened by the Queen it was visited by millions from England and the Continent.[5] By one of Fate's ironies this exhibition of the peaceful prosperity of England was staged at the opening of a decade that saw the nation involved in wars such as it had not known since the time of Napoleon.

Important in its bearing on Victorian life was the great expansion in this period of what was once called the British Empire, a term discarded nowadays. In India, partly by conquest, partly by peaceful annexation, one great province after another came under the control of the East India Company, still the intermediary between the various states of India and the British government. In 1852 the greater part of Burma was conquered and annexed. Meanwhile the English-speaking colonies were moving along the road of responsible self-government toward their present status of independent members of the Commonwealth of Free Nations. The Canadian provinces, the first to obtain responsible government, 1840, were united in 1867 in a federation as the Dominion of Canada, and were joined four years later by the vast territory of British Columbia. England had feared that self-government in the colonies would be but the first step in their complete separation from the mother country, but as early as 1855 Canada proved her loyalty by raising a regiment to support England in the Crimean War (p. 53).

Australia, regarded at first as a mere dumping ground for criminals sentenced to transportation, slowly acquired responsible self-government. The

[5] The newly founded travel bureau of Thos. Cook is said to have conducted over 150,000 tourists there.

development of sheep-farming and the discovery of gold, 1857, led to a rapid growth of population composed almost entirely of immigrants from the British Isles. In 1855 a new constitution for the various provinces was adopted, but it was not until 1900 that they were formally united in the Australian Commonwealth.

The twin islands of New Zealand had been annexed in 1840. Long troubles, culminating in war, 1860, with the Maoris, the finest race of the Pacific aborigines, came to an end in 1867, when the Maoris were given representation in the Colonial assembly. This body had obtained control over local affairs as early as 1856, for by that time the islands were rapidly filling with British settlers sent out by emigration societies. A sturdy and industrious population developed along democratic lines as in Australia, and like the Australians they were loyal to the mother country, joining with them in the famous Anzac expeditionary force of World War I.

The development of South Africa was very different from that of the other British colonies. The first white settlers at the Cape of Good Hope were Dutch, but England seized the colony, 1795, during her war with revolutionary France and retained it after 1815 as a way-station on the long voyage to India. For many years there was only a trickle of British emigration to South Africa and the Home Government had to deal with the backward and stubborn Dutch, the so-called Boers, as well as with the warlike tribes, Zulus and Kaffirs, on the north. In 1835-7 growing dissatisfaction on the part of the Boers led to the Great Trek in which a large body of them pushed northwards to escape British rule and to found the independent republics of the Orange Free State and the Transvaal. The history of South Africa during the latter part of the

THE GOLDEN AGE 53

nineteenth century is one of rather inglorious wars with the Boers and the native tribes. The discovery of gold and diamonds, 1867, led to an inrush of British settlers and finally to war, but the story of the long Boer War, the pacification of the country, and the Union of South Africa, 1910, belongs to the post-Victorian period.

England was more deeply stirred and her reactions more clearly reflected in literature by the wars in which the nation was engaged during this period than by the expansion of the colonies overseas. Some of these wars were petty affairs like the Persian War of 1856, or the expedition of 1868, which, without the loss of an English life, overthrew Theodore, the tyrant of Abyssinia. The long war with China, 1856-60, begun on a frivolous pretext and ending with the sack of the Imperial palace at Pekin, shocked the conscience of English liberals, but made little impression on the nation.[6] It was otherwise, however, with the two great wars of the 1850's, the Crimean and the Sepoy Mutiny.

England plunged into the Crimean war, 1854-6, with as little reason as any nation ever had for embarking in a major conflict. The ostensible cause of the war, the prevention of Russian aggression on Turkey, could have been removed before a shot was fired, but there were men and parties in Western Europe that were bent on war. Chief among these was Louis Napoleon, now Emperor of France by his *coup-d'état* of 1851. Napoleon had a personal grudge against the Czar Nicholas and wished to demonstrate the military power of his Empire by a successful war in which he was eager to enlist England as his ally. In this he was efficiently aided by Palmerston, who detested the Czar as the incarnate

[6] The Chinese seizure of the ship Arrow, which was flying, allegedly unlawfully, the British flag, was the occasion of this war.

enemy of liberalism. After long and futile diplomatic conferences on the Russian claim to protect Christian subjects of the Sultan, Turkey declared war on Russia and won some small success on her northern border; Russia replied by destroying the Turkish fleet in the Black Sea. This action, the so-called "Massacre of Sinope," provoked a cry of rage in England, and the demand for war rose to fever heat. Aberdeen, the peace-loving Prime Minister, the liberal John Bright, and even Prince Albert, were denounced as pacifists and Russophiles. The long peace since Waterloo had apparently generated such a temper in England that she was ready, indeed eager, for war, if it could be shown that it was a "good war" against a barbaric tyrant.[7] Accordingly in February 1854, England joined France in declaring war on Russia. They invited the other European nations to join them, but only the little Kingdom of Piedmont responded to the call and sent a small force to join the allies, a step that had important results for Italy thereafter.

The allies limited their aim to the capture of Sebastopol, the great Crimean fortress and naval station, the natural base for a Russian attack on Turkey. The campaign was bungled from the beginning; the only military glory for England was won by the stubborn stand of her infantry at the Alma and at Inkerman and by two daring cavalry charges at Balaclava. That of the Light Brigade has been immortalized by Tennyson; a more sober comment was that of a French observer: "magnificent, but it was not war."[8]

[7] This temper is reflected in the last section of Tennyson's *Maud,* 1855, and later in Meredith's *Beauchamp's Career,* 1875 (Chaps. III and IV).

[8] The more successful charge of the "Heavies," also hymned by Tennyson, has been generally forgotten.

A hurricane wrecked the British transport in the harbor whence the army was supplied, and during the bitter winter of 1854-5 the suffering of the troops was terrible. Ill fed, ill clothed, and scourged by sickness, English soldiers died like flies in the trenches and the miserably equipped hospitals. The shocking mismanagement of supplies was exposed in letters to *The Times* by the first, and perhaps the greatest, of war correspondents, William Russell. Unhampered by censorship he gave the English public such an appalling picture of the condition of the army that the Prime Minister was forced to resign his position to the energetic Palmerston. Florence Nightingale, the best trained and most efficient of English nurses, was sent to the Crimea, where she cut through red tape, broke down official obstruction, and reduced the death rate in the base hospital to a minimum. She ruined her health by her untiring exertion, but after her return to England she started a system of training nurses for civil as well as for military service. The Red Cross movement, starting in 1864, goes back, in fact, to her work in the Crimea.

After the death of the Czar, March, 1855, the war might have been ended, but Napoleon and Palmerston were determined at least to take Sebastopol. The Russians finally evacuated the fortress, the allies reduced it to a heap of ruins, and peace was signed at Paris in March, 1856.

England gained nothing by this costly war; the Christians in Turkey were left to the tender mercies of the Sultan with results that caused much trouble later (p. 89), and Russia was forbidden to keep naval vessels on the Black Sea, a limitation of power which in 1870 (p. 86) she treated as a scrap of paper. Perhaps the one permanent result in England of the war was a lasting suspicion and dread of

Russia. The Victoria Cross, England's supreme decoration "for valor," was first awarded by the Queen shortly after the Crimea.

The Treaty of Paris had hardly been signed when England was startled by the news of serious trouble in India. The Sepoy Mutiny must not be confused with the nationalist movement that in the twentieth century broke the tie that bound India to Great Britain. It was not a revolt of the people, merely a mutiny of Sepoys, the native troops in the service of the East India Company. There was a widespread rumor at this time that the Company was planning the forcible conversion of India to Christianity, and this fear was intensified by the issue to the Sepoys of cartridges smeared with beef and hog fat, the mere touch of which would degrade Hindoos and Moslems. Company after company of Sepoys refused to handle them and although individual mutineers were punished, no proper steps were taken to correct the evil. Absorbed in the Crimean War, England ignored the danger brewing in India, a danger increased by the fact that in the Company's army Sepoys greatly outnumbered British troops and that the artillery was almost entirely in their hands. Finally, in May, 1857, the first serious outbreak occurred at Meerut, where the Sepoys mutinied, freed comrades jailed for refusing to handle the cartridges, and sacked the English quarters, murdering women and children.[9] The mutineers then seized Delhi, the former capital of the Mogul empire and set up a senile descendant of the Mogul dynasty as the figurehead of a national rising. To prevent Delhi from becoming the capital of a rebellious native state it was imperative that it should be promptly re-taken, but the difficulties of the siege were enormous and it was not until Septem-

---

[9] Flora Steele's *On the Face of the Waters*, 1896, gives a vivid picture of this first phase of the mutiny.

ber that the Company's troops took the town by storm.

Meanwhile the war spread over central India. The garrison of Cawnpore, an English station, surrendered on a promise of safe conduct given by Nana Sahib, a native prince who had joined the Sepoys, but the men were shot down at once; the women and children were later hacked to pieces by hired murderers and their bodies were thrown into a well. The garrison of Lucknow took refuge in the Residency, where they endured a four months' siege, saving hundreds of women and children from the horrors of Cawnpore.[10] Havelok with his Highland regiment fought his way through to them, but was himself besieged there, and it was not until November that Sir Colin Campbell with fresh troops from England was able to withdraw the survivors. The storming of Delhi and the relief of Lucknow were the critical points in the war; after them there was no chance of a Sepoy success. By July, 1858, the mutiny was crushed; Nana Sahib vanished from the scene and the last of the Moguls was exiled from India.

In spite of the cry for vengeance on the murderers of women and children, the reaction of the British government was surprisingly lenient.[11] Individual Sepoys convicted of taking part in the massacres were hanged or blown from the mouths of cannon, but no sweeping punitive measures were taken. The Governor-General, indeed, was nicknamed "Clemency Canning" because he forbade indiscriminate revenge and the burning of native villages. It was plain, however, that the old administration of India

[10] Tennyson's *The Defence of Lucknow* celebrates this famous siege.

[11] So mild a man as Macaulay said: "I could look on without winking while Nana Sahib underwent all the tortures of Ravaillac. And these feelings are not mine alone."

divided between the Company and the Home Government must end, and Palmerston brought in a Bill for the Better Government of India. The Company, of course, opposed it, and their ablest servant, John Stuart Mill, drew up a strong petition in their defense. The Bill was still under discussion in Parliament when Palmerston was beaten by a vote on another issue. He resigned and the Conservatives, led by Lord Derby and Disraeli, came into power.

It is characteristic of the absence of real differences between English political parties at this time that the Bill which Palmerston had introduced was put through by Disraeli, an early example of "bipartisan policy." The Bill transferred all power in India from the Company to the Home Government. The Governor-General was replaced by a Viceroy, and on November 1, 1858, a royal proclamation declared that henceforth all acts of the India government would be done in the name of the Queen. In 1877 Victoria on the suggestion of Disraeli assumed the title of Empress of India, and the British "Raj" which lasted till 1947 was definitely established.

This India of the British "Raj" is portrayed in Kipling's tales and poems, a wonderful, at times a terrifying land, ruled by aliens for the benefit of natives, where peace was preserved by British soldiers and justice was administered by British civil servants. The remaining British fear was not of a native revolt but of an attack by the great power on the North, "the Bear that walks like a man." Kipling's India, of course, is gone forever.

A war, or rather a series of wars, which was followed with intense interest in England, was the "Risorgimento," the long fight for the liberation and unification of Italy. The first movement in this direction, 1848, had been crushed by Austria (p. 44), but after the Crimea, it was again renewed, and Victor Emmanuel, the soldier King of Piedmont, sought the help of Louis Napoleon. Napoleon had long sympathized with the cause of Italian liberty; he owed Piedmont a debt for her aid in the Crimea (p. 54), and he seems to have feared for his life at the hands of Italian conspirators unless he acted. Accordingly, when Austria attacked Piedmont, 1859, a French army entered Italy and won two great victories at Magenta and Solferino, June, 1859. Then suddenly Napoleon stopped fighting and in a personal conference with the Austrian Emperor at Villa Franca, July, 1859, arranged a peace which left Austria and Austrian satellites still in possession of large parts of Italy.[12] Moreover, as a price of this peace he exacted the cession to France of the Italian provinces of Nice and Savoy. Napoleon's apparent betrayal of his ally shocked liberal sentiment in England. The three leaders of the then Liberal government were all in favor of the Italian cause: Gladstone, who had himself seen the Bourbon tyranny at Naples, had denounced it as "the negation of God erected into a system of government"; Russell upheld the Whig tradition that a people had the right to choose their rulers; and Palmerston consistently favored the liberal movement in Europe. Feeling against Napoleon ran so high that for a time it seemed as if war might break out between England and France.[13] Napoleon, however, had no wish to break with England; a commercial treaty negotiated at this time relieved the tension, and the creation of the "Volunteers" in England dispelled the panicky fear of a French invasion.

[12] Two poems by Mrs. Browning, *Napoleon in Italy* and *First News from Villa Franca,* show the early enthusiasm and the later despair of sympathizers with the Italian cause.
[13] This is the date of Tennyson's *Riflemen Form,* with its sneer at Napoleon, "our faithful ally."

Meanwhile the Italians, deserted by Napoleon, took things into their own hands. The satellite states expelled their Austrian rulers and joined the Kingdom of Piedmont. The revolutionary leader, Garibaldi, conquered Sicily and Naples for King Victor, while England forbade Austrian or French interference. Victor annexed the Papal states, all but Rome itself, where the Pope was supported by French soldiers, and in October, 1860, he was hailed as King of Italy. Venice still remained in Austrian hands, but in 1866, when Austria was defeated by Prussia, it was restored to Italy, and after the fall of Napoleon at Sedan, Victor entered Rome and made it the capital of a free and united Italy. The "Risorgimento" had finally triumphed to the delight of all liberal Englishmen.

The Civil War in North America, 1861-5, had, naturally, a more immediate effect on English life and thought than the struggle for Italian liberty. After the secession from the Union of a group of slave-holding Southern states and the election of Jefferson Davis as President of the Confederacy, actual hostilities began with the Southern firing on Fort Sumter, April, 1861, and the Northern blockade of Southern ports. England promptly recognized the Confederacy as a belligerent, a step deeply resented in the North, although it did not imply the recognition of the seceding states as a nation. For political and military reasons Lincoln, never himself an abolitionist, proclaimed that his object was the forcible reclamation of these states, and this statement tended to confuse the case in England. The fundamental issue of slavery was overlooked, even by Englishmen who had abolished it in the British Empire. From the beginning of the Civil War English sympathy in general was with the South; Mill records "the rush of nearly the whole upper and middle classes, even those who passed for Liberals, into a furious pro-Southern partisanship." The romantic, emotional impulse which had led Englishmen to sympathize with subject peoples, Poles, Magyars, and Italians, revolting against oppression, now tended to picture the South as a people fighting for independence against a stronger military power. There was, moreover, a less creditable motive for English partisanship. The ruling classes, satisfied with the limited reform of 1832, had long regarded the growing power of American democracy with some fear and much dislike. Lincoln, an uncouth Westerner, the chosen leader of this democracy, became in English eyes the incarnation of this hated power. Although the most humane of men, he was stigmatized in English papers as a ruffian; *Punch* even caricatured him as a devil. The leaders of the English government, Palmerston, Russell, and Gladstone, were at heart inimical to the cause of the Union.[14] With Lee's invasion of Maryland, 1862, and his anticipated capture of Washington, they apparently agreed that the time had come for intervention. Along with France and Russia, England was to inform the North that the conscience of the world could no longer tolerate this fratricidal war. The project, however, was never put into effect; the other members of the ministry strongly opposed it, and Czarist Russia flatly refused to join in such an action. After Lee's retreat, following his check at Antietam, nothing more was heard of intervention.

Even earlier, however, an incident had occurred which brought England to the verge of war with the

[14] Russell told Parliament that the "subjugation of the South would be a calamity" and Gladstone, in a carefully prepared public address, asserted that "Jefferson Davis has made an army, was making a navy, and, what is more important than either, was making a nation."

North. Jefferson Davis decided to send two commissioners, Mason and Slidell, to Europe to urge the recognition of Southern independence. They embarked at Havana on the *Trent,* a British ship, and started for England; but the *Trent* was stopped by a U.S. man-of-war, November 8, 1861, whose captain seized them and carried them to prison in the North. This exercise of the old British "right of search and seizure" on the high sea, over which the War of 1812 had been fought, was hailed in the North with shouts of applause, in England with howls of rage.[15] Feeling ran high on both sides of the ocean, and, as it was generally believed in England that the commissioners would not be given up, preparations were made for the apparently inevitable war. English troops were rushed to Canada and the West India fleet was doubled. An official dispatch was composed demanding the prompt release of the prisoners with an apology for the act of "aggression," but, fortunately for both countries, it was shown to the Queen. Prince Albert privately suggested an amendment to the effect that Great Britain was willing to believe that the American captain had acted without the authority of his government, and this amendment, incorporated in the dispatch, saved the day.[16] Lincoln, who had no desire to involve his country in a war with England, directed Seward,

[15] Thackeray, though a good friend of America, expresses English feeling at that time in his *Roundabout Paper, On Half a Loaf,* where he speaks of "the roar of hate, defiance, folly, falsehood, which comes to us across the Atlantic." He says nothing, however, of the "explosion of feeling," noted by Mill, in England, where a contemporary observer stated that "if the country were polled 999 men out of a thousand would declare for immediate war." For American feeling at that time see *The Biglow Papers,* 1862.

[16] This dispatch was followed by another directing the British Minister to return unless the ultimatum were accepted within a week. Lincoln's reply came just in time.

then Secretary of State, to reply that the offending captain had in fact acted without orders and that the commissioners would be "cheerfully liberated." The storm blew over, but while it lasted there was no chance, Mill said, "of a hearing for anything favorable to the American cause."

In 1862 the British government was guilty of a graver offense against international law than this unauthorized act of the American captain. It was an accepted doctrine that a neutral should not furnish arms to either belligerent in a war, but English ship-builders more than once complied with the South's request for armed vessels to prey on Northern commerce. The most notorious of these ships, the *Alabama*, was almost completed when Adams, the American Minister to Great Britain, denounced her, presenting sworn evidence to Russell, the Foreign Secretary. Russell hesitated; legal papers were shifted from office to office, local authorities refused to act, and by the time he ordered her seizure, the *Alabama* had already sailed. With a Southern captain and a mainly British crew she ranged the seas for nearly two years, inflicting great damage on American commerce until she was sunk by the U.S.S. *Kearsarge*, 1864. Russell steadily refused reparation or redress, although he later confessed that he had been guilty of "criminal negligence." It was not until 1872 that a court of arbitration (p. 86) awarded damages to America.

Russell acted more promptly in the following year. The Lairds, builders of the *Alabama*, were now constructing two iron-clad rams for the express purpose of breaking the Northern blockade. The success of the *Merrimac* in Hampton Roads, 1862, had demonstrated the helplessness of the Northern wooden naval vessels against such antagonists; their appearance on the scene might even turn the tide of war.

Ostensibly they were being built for a French firm, and Russell at first felt that he had no right to detain them. After repeated futile appeals Adams finally sent him a note, September 5, 1863, saying that if the rams were not detained, "it would be superfluous for me to point out to your Lordship that this is war."[17] Within three days Adams was informed that the rams were stopped; they were, in fact, finally bought for the British navy.

Even though the government was unsympathetic and society positively hostile, the cause of the Union was not without friends in England. Politicians like Cobden and John Bright spoke for the North; Cairnes and Mill wrote in the same vein, and the great Duke of Argyll exerted his influence in court circles.[18] Among men of letters Monckton Milnes and Browning were conspicuous friends of the North. Yet the most devoted friends, under extreme difficulties, were the voteless workers in the cotton mills of Lancashire. This industry was then the most important in England; the annual value of English cotton goods was greater than the entire revenue of the kingdom. From early in 1861, however, the blockade stopped the flow of cotton from the South; mills were closed and thousands of workers were discharged. In 1862 the industry came almost to a standstill; by the end of the year half a million workers were on relief; but labor never begged the government to break the blockade. On the contrary the working men of Northern England regarded themselves as passive combatants in a war

[17] Henry Adams, the Minister's son, believed that this threat of war decided the case, but it later appeared that Russell had given secret orders to stop the rams before he received the note. The victories of Gettysburg and Vicksburg had probably wiped out Russell's *idée fixe* that the North was certain to lose the war.

[18] A splendid example of Bright's oratory is quoted in *The Education of Henry Adams*, Chap. XII.

THE GOLDEN AGE 65

of free against slave labor. At the close of the worst year the workers of Manchester sent an address of sympathy to Lincoln, which he acknowledged as an instance of "sublime Christian heroism." The worst passed over with relief pouring in from Canada, Australia, and even the Northern states, and with fresh supplies of cotton from India and Egypt; but labor did not forget and the "cotton famine" of 1862 contributed no little to the agitation for political reform a few years later.

With the end of the Civil War and the assassination of Lincoln there came a complete revulsion of feeling in England; even *Punch* paid a tribute to the martyred President in an elegiac poem and a famous cartoon.[19]

In 1865-6 a controversy developed which revealed the deep rift between liberal and conservative thought in England. In October, 1865, a Negro riot in the self-governing colony of Jamaica broke out, culminating in arson and the murder of some twenty whites; Eyre, governor of the colony, called out the military, and the local rising was promptly suppressed. Then there followed a series of punitive measures: some four hundred Negroes were executed; six hundred, including some women, were flogged; and a thousand Negro cabins burned. Gordon, a Negro member of the Colonial assembly, was charged with seditious language, and although he had not taken part in the riot, he was arrested and conveyed to the district where martial law was in force. There he was tried before a board of three young officers, condemned to death, and immediately hanged. When the news reached England a Royal Commission was

[19] An interesting reflection of the English attitude toward the North during the war appears in *The Education of Henry Adams*. It is biased by the author's anti-British sentiments and needs to be corrected by the later account in *The Adams Family*, 1930.

dispatched to investigate. Their report commended Eyre for his quick action, but suggested his recall and severely censured the conduct of some of his subordinates. With Eyre's recall the matter might have ended, but on his return to England, he was entertained at a public dinner where Kingsley praised his conduct; Carlyle, too, commended him as a "just, humane, and valiant man." As the government declined to take further action, a committee headed by Mill and including Tom Hughes, Huxley, and Herbert Spencer, attempted a private prosecution. On the other hand Carlyle became head of the Eyre Defense Fund to which Tennyson and Ruskin contributed. English grand juries refused to indict Eyre and his officers, and the case was dropped; but liberal thinkers noted with satisfaction that the Chief Justice of England had denounced the trial of Gordon as "repugnant to elementary justice." Eyre, an able officer with, so far, a good record, was never employed again; but he was later pensioned by a Conservative government.[20]

Palmerston, the firm opponent of further electoral reform, died just before the Eyre case broke, and Russell succeeded him as Prime Minister. As the author of the first Reform Bill, Russell was eager to add to his reputation by putting a second and more liberal measure through Parliament. A reform was, in fact, long overdue; only one adult Englishman in five had a right to vote and the shift of population (p. 38) since 1832 had emphasized the disparity of electoral districts. An attempt had even been made by a brief Conservative government in 1859 to meet the demand for reform, but the bill which Disraeli

---

[20] Mill states that "as a matter of curiosity" he kept specimens of the abusive letters, mostly anonymous, which he received in this connection, evidence of the sympathy felt with the brutalities in Jamaica by the brutal part of the population at home.

then introduced had failed to satisfy either Whigs or Tories. Now in March, 1866, Gladstone, Russell's leader in the Commons, introduced a fairly liberal reform bill, and, in the debate which followed, paid a well-deserved tribute to the behavior of the working class during the "cotton famine" (p. 64). In spite of his eloquence, however, the bill was defeated by a combination of Tories and conservative Whigs. The government resigned and the Conservatives under Lord Derby and Disraeli took office.

By this time the agitation for reform had reached such a height that it was apparent that action must be taken to avert a crisis like that of 1832 (p. 21). Huge mass meetings in the North demanded manhood suffrage. Bright, the most effective of orators at these meetings, emphasized the fact that an English worker had only to emigrate to Canada or Australia to get the vote denied to him at home. London took up the cry of the North and a crowd, denied access to Hyde Park to plead for reform, broke down the palings and swarmed in.[21] Disraeli, convinced that it was time to act, and determined to "dish the Whigs" and secure for his party the credit of granting the nation's demand, himself introduced a reform bill. Since he could not command a majority in the Commons, he cleverly accepted almost every amendment proposed by the Liberals, and the measure was carried by a joint majority of earnest reformers and well-disciplined Conservatives. In the Lords, where the first Reform Bill had met such stubborn opposition (p. 21), this measure passed unopposed. Lord Derby directed his fellow peers to accept it lest the Conservative

---

[21] Arnold in *Culture and Anarchy* commented on this action as a characteristic example of the English belief in "doing what one likes." A second threat to invade the Park was quieted by the influence of Mill with London workers.

government fall and a succeeding combination of Liberals and Radicals should do something worse. He himself described the measure as "a leap in the dark," but sterner Tories used stronger language. Cranborne, later Conservative Prime Minister as Lord Salisbury (p. 94), denounced Derby's action as a "political betrayal without parallel in our annals," and Coventry Patmore branded 1867 as

> The year of the great crime
> When the false English Nobles and their Jew,
> By God demented, slew
> The Trust they stood twice pledged to keep from wrong.

and Carlyle blasted the new law in the fiercest of his political pamphlets, *Shooting Niagara*.

As a matter of fact the Second Reform Bill did not open the floodgates, as was predicted, to "a multitude struggling with want and discontent." It about doubled the electorate but still excluded large classes of workers, miners, for example, and farm hands, and Mill's dream of "votes for women" (p. 220) had to wait till the next century for fulfillment. In the general election of 1868, the first under the new register, the Liberals won a sweeping victory. Mill remarked that when Disraeli told the workers he had given them the vote, they replied: "Thank you, Mr. Gladstone." Gladstone became Prime Minister and a new era of social and political reform set in.

This time of internal peace and prosperity, 1848-1868, might well be called the golden age of Victorian literature; certainly no other period of Victoria's reign produced so many works that have become English classics.

Two poets, first heard in earlier years, now increased their hold upon the reading public. Tennyson's *In Memoriam*, 1850, won him the Laureateship. His *Maud*, 1855, with its strange notes of passion, shocked many of his readers, but he regained them with the four *Idylls of the King*, 1859, and the homely pathos and sentiment of *Enoch Arden*, 1864, established him as the best loved of English poets. Browning, who had long suffered under the charge of wilful obscurity, regained a hearing with his *Men and Women*, 1855, and touched his highest point in certain parts of *The Ring and the Book*, 1868-9.

Miss Barrett, who had become Mrs. Browning in 1846, presented her husband-lover with the *Sonnets from the Portuguese*, 1850, her one supreme achievement. Her novel in verse, *Aurora Leigh*, 1857, showed the influence of Victorian didactic fiction upon a lyric poet; *Casa Guidi Windows*, 1851, and other later poems appealed to English sympathy with the Italian struggle for liberty.

New voices now made themselves heard. The first of these was Arnold's. In two volumes of poems by A., 1849 and 1852, he gave notice to an unheeding world that a true poet had appeared upon the scene. His place beside Tennyson and Browning was established by the *Poems* of 1853, the first to which he signed his name. The *New Poems*, 1867, closed his brief career as a major Victorian poet. Poems by Dante Gabriel and Christina Rossetti, among them the first form of his *The Blessed Damozel*, appeared in *The Germ* (p. 236), 1850. Dante Gabriel was writing poetry continuously at this time but published little before the *Poems* of 1870. Christina's *Goblin Market* appeared in 1862; her *The Prince's Progress* in 1866. George Meredith's *Poems*, 1851, were at first ignored, but he won a hearing with his sonnet-sequence, *Modern Love*, in 1862.

William Morris dedicated *The Defence of Guenevere* to Rossetti in 1858. His *Life and Death of Jason* and his *Earthly Paradise*, 1868-70, revealed him as, perhaps, the best story-teller in English verse since the time of Chaucer.

Swinburne's poetic plays, *The Queen Mother* and *Rosamund*, 1860, attracted little attention, but *Atalanta in Calydon*, 1865, won him a public that he frightened away by the erotic strains of his *Poems and Ballads*, 1866.

Fitzgerald's *Rubaiyat of Omar Khayyám*, published anonymously in 1859, fell dead from the press. Later it was discovered and praised by the best judges until it became one of the most popular of English poems.

Other ages surpass the Victorian in poetry and drama, but this was, perhaps, the high-water mark of the English novel, and the period from 1848 to 1868 shows it developing in a wide variety of form and purpose.

Dickens added to his immense popularity with *David Copperfield*, 1849, often called his masterpiece. In rapid succession he published *Bleak House*, 1852, *Hard Times*, 1854, *A Tale of Two Cities*, 1859, *Great Expectations*, 1860 and *Our Mutual Friend*, his last long novel, 1864. He left unfinished a mystery story, *Edwin Drood*, at his death in 1870.

Thackeray, who had made his first hit with *Vanity Fair*, 1847, increased his popularity with *Pendennis*, 1848. *Henry Esmond*, his supreme artistic achievement, appeared in 1852, and *The Newcomes*, a novel of contemporary life, in 1855. Later novels, *The Virginians*, 1857, and *Philip*, 1862, seem to show something like a failure of his powers, but he left a historical novel, *Denis Duval*, of real promise, unfinished at his death in 1863.

A third novelist, able to stand beside Dickens and Thackeray, appeared for the first time in this period. Mary Anne Evans, who had earlier devoted herself to philosophical and religious work, suddenly emerged as "George Eliot, novelist" with *Scenes of Clerical Life*, 1858. These three tales were followed by *Adam Bede*, her first long novel, 1859; *The Mill on the Floss*, 1860; *Silas Marner*, 1861; *Romola*, a historical novel, 1862; and *Felix Holt*, a novel of English political life, 1866. Unlike Dickens and Thackeray she lived to continue her work in later years.

George Meredith attracted attention as a novelist with his first long work, *Richard Feverel*, 1859. He continued with *Evan Harrington*, 1861, and with *Rhoda Fleming*, 1865. *Vittoria*, a novel dealing with the Italian Risorgimento, 1867, has already been mentioned, (p. 45). Much of Meredith's best work came in the next period.

Anthony Trollope, the chronicler of Victorian society, attracted little attention at first, but *The Warden*, 1855, opened the popular Barchester series which ran through several volumes to end with *The Last Chronicle of Barset*, 1867. For his later work see below (p. 106).

Several writers of this time employed fiction as an instrument in the cause of social reform. Prominent among them was Charles Kingsley, poet and preacher, whose *Yeast*, 1848, *Alton Locke*, 1850, and *Two Years Ago*, 1857, dealt with social conditions in contemporary England. His historical novels, *Hypatia*, 1853, and *Westward Ho!*, 1855, are, perhaps, better known today. Mrs. Gaskell's first novel, *Mary Barton*, 1848, dealt with the shocking condition of the slums in a manufacturing city and with the struggle of the workers against their employers. *North and South*, 1855, handled essentially the same theme. Her still popular *Cranford* appeared in 1853, and a long novel of social life, *Wives and Daughters*, was left unfinished at her death in 1865. Charles Reade employed *Never Too Late to Mend*, 1853, and *Hard Cash*, 1863, to expose abuses in prisons and insane asylums. His historical novel, *The Cloister and the Hearth*, 1861, is perhaps the only one of his many books that is still read.

Wilkie Collins, a prolific writer of fiction, produced two novels, *The Woman in White*, 1860, and *The Moonstone*, 1868, which still rank as masterpieces of the mystery and detective story.

Apart from fiction this period was distinguished by a number of prose works which affected the life and thought of the Victorian age.

Among the first of these was Macaulay's very popular *History of England*. The first two volumes, appearing in 1848, served to establish the liberal—not to say the Whiggish—view of English history for at least a generation.

In 1848 J. S. Mill published his *Principles of Political Economy*, which promptly became a standard work. His classic essay, *On Liberty*, appeared in 1859.

Carlyle thundered against contemporary social and political conditions in *Latter-Day Pamphlets*, 1850, and then buried himself in his monumental *Frederick the Great*, of which the first two volumes came out in 1858.

This was the time of Ruskin's greatest activity and widest influence. He came to the rescue of the Pre-Raphaelites in 1851 (p. 236) and continued his *Modern Painters* with two more volumes in 1856. He had already begun to turn to an exposition of the moral principles involved in art with *The Seven Lamps of Architecture*, 1849, and followed this line in *The Stones of Venice*, three volumes, 1851-3. He broke into the field of political economy with *Unto This Last*, 1862, and published the lectures, still popular today, *Sesame and Lilies*, 1865, and the *Crown of Wild Olive*, 1866.

Darwin published the epoch-making *Origin of*

Species in 1859. In the long controversy that followed, his champion, Huxley, spoke for the first time in his defense in *Man's Place in Nature,* 1863.

Newman's *Apologia,* perhaps the greatest of English autobiographies, appeared in 1864.

Matthew Arnold turned from poetry to studies in literature and life in his *Essays in Criticism,* 1865, and in social conditions in *Culture and Anarchy,* 1869.

A comparison of this summary of the literature of the mid-Victorian age with the corresponding accounts of the literature of the earlier and of the later period should serve to show the superiority in both quantity and quality of this body of prose and poetry. The period from 1848 to 1868 marks the high tide of Victorianism, and the literature of the time gives it full and satisfactory expression. In literature as in the body politic this epoch deserves the name of the Victorian golden age.

Chapter IV

The Twilight

1868-1892

The break between the central and the final period of the Victorian era is sharper by far than the easy transition of the first into the central period. The years immediately preceding and following 1870 have been called a watershed in Victorian England. The slight difference between the two political parties and the general satisfaction with the established order now give place to bitter party strife and to a firm determination to promote a better social order. Old political leaders have dropped out of the race: Peel died as early as 1850; Wellington, an older man, in 1852; Palmerston in 1865; and Russell retired in 1866. Of the three statesmen who had long led the Liberals, Gladstone alone remained and the history of English politics from 1868 to 1892 is one of a long war between Gladstone and the Conservative Disraeli and Disraeli's successor, Lord Salisbury. New characters appear upon the scene: Parnell, the Irish agitator; Chamberlain, the radical imperialist; and Keir Hardie, the pioneer of international socialism. In the world of letters, too, a change appears. The death of Dickens, 1870, seems to mark the end of an age almost as sharply as that of Scott in 1832. The early Victorians are falling silent; Carlyle, the oldest of them, lived on, but his work was done by 1865; Thackeray died seven years before Dickens; Mill published his last work in 1869; and Darwin put the capstone on his theory of evolution in 1871 with his *The Descent of Man*. Tennyson and Browning, to be sure, worked on till the very end of the period, but neither of them repeated such early successes as *In Memoriam*, 1850, or *The Ring and the Book*, 1868-9. In literature as in politics once the watershed is past we seem to be in a new England.

Some salient features of this final period may be briefly noted. The first, politically the most important, is the steady increase of the democratic element in the government. The Reform Bill of 1867 had created a new class of voters, the urban worker; the later Bill of 1884 doubled the electorate by including the miner and the farm hand. Between these two reforms the secret ballot, an old Chartist demand, was introduced, 1872, which freed the voter from intimidation. One direct result of this growth of the electorate was the increased interest taken by the state in popular education. "We must educate our masters" became the watchword of the once dominant classes as they saw themselves in danger of swamping in a flood of illiterate voters. Hitherto state aid to education had been confined to small grants to voluntary schools, mostly under church control. In 1870 a system of "national" *i.e.* public schools was set up; in 1880 attendance was made compulsory; after 1891 this education was free to all. Looking beyond primary education the state in 1871 forced the universities of Oxford and Cambridge, long dominated by the Church, to open their scholarships, higher degrees, and professorships, except those in the theological faculty, to all scholars regardless of their religious belief.

A new opening of a career to educated men came in 1870 when a position in the Home Civil Service was made dependent upon the result of competitive examinations rather than, as earlier, upon patronage. In the army also promotion now came by merit with the abolishment of the old practice of purchasing commissions.[1]

The leader of the party, now for the first time called Liberal, which put through these reforms was, of course, Gladstone. Thirty years earlier he had been labelled by Macaulay as "the rising hope of the stern and unbending Tories," but England was becoming more democratic and Gladstone moved with the rising tide.

Contemporary with this democratic movement intent upon reform at home, there ran another current directly opposed to it, the spirit of imperialism, aiming at the extension of England's power and prestige abroad. This was essentially the policy of the Conservatives and Disraeli embodied the idea of imperialism. It was he who puchased shares for England in the Suez Canal and joined with France in the Dual Control of Egypt which resulted in the English occupation of that country and the wars in the Sudan (p. 95). Salisbury continued this policy and painted more of the map imperial red by annexing district after district in tropical Africa. The old hesitant attitude toward the self-governing colonies, the readiness to allow them in due time to sever their ties with the mother country, was replaced by a conscious effort to link them up more closely through their recognition of the Queen as the symbol of

---

[1] It was by this practice that such an incompetent as Thackeray's George Osborne became a captain in Wellington's army.

imperial unity.[2] Salisbury urged on the delegates to the first Colonial Congress, meeting in London during the Queen's Jubilee, 1887, a union for imperial defense. This somewhat grandiose conception of Empire appealed strongly to members of the middle class who had once been staunch Liberals.[3] The disruption of the Liberal party over the question of Home Rule for Ireland was mainly due to the conviction that Gladstone's plan was a step toward the dismemberment of the empire, and the seceders from his party called themselves "Unionists." Liberal politicians primarily concerned with social reform were branded "Little Englanders," and "what should they know of England," said Kipling, "who only England know!"

Another notable change in this period is the increasing impact of science upon English thought. The idea of evolution had been in the air before Darwin gave it form and described the process in his *Origin of Species*, 1859. His work evoked a storm of protest from theologians, but by 1871 the worst of the fight was over; the respect with which Darwin's *Descent of Man*, published in that year, was received showed how widely his theory had gained acceptance.

Almost simultaneously with the controversy over evolution came another attack upon orthodox theology. This was the new or the so-called "higher" criticism. Originating in Germany, it slowly made its way to England, where as long as it confined its scrutiny to secular history it was accepted. When it

[2] This spirit found toward the close of the period its uncrowned laureate in Rudyard Kipling.

[3] The Primrose League, founded in 1881, named after Disraeli's favorite flower, conferred a badge of gentility upon even a shopkeeper who joined it. Every gentleman, the League proclaimed, was a Conservative and, conversely, every member of the League was a gentleman.

began to apply its tests to the Bible it was at first ignored. One English clergyman, however, Benjamin Jowett, Professor of Greek at Oxford, was sympathetic with German criticism. His *Commentary on the Pauline Epistles*, 1855, was advanced enough to provoke an orthodox resentment which showed itself in the withholding of the greater part of his professional salary. Undiscouraged, Jowett later joined a group of like-minded scholars in publishing *Essays and Reviews*, 1860, a work that has been called the most important event in the nineteenth century movement of liberal thought in England. Jowett's contribution, *On the Interpretation of Scripture*, was sincerely religious, but he dared to ask why the accepted rules of criticism should not be applied to the text of the Bible, a question rash enough to stamp him as a heretic in the eyes of clergymen who insisted on the literal inspiration of the Bible.[4] The popular success of *Essays and Reviews* provoked a demand for the punishment of the authors. Two of them, Wilson and Williams, ordained clergymen, were tried in a church court, convicted of heresy, and suspended from their posts. They appealed, and the highest English court of justice reversed the sentence, 1884, declaring, *inter alia,* that refusal to believe in eternal damnation, a charge brought against the defendants, was not a penal offense. The final verdict was a decisive and popular victory for freedom of thought and speech even in the field of religion; a wit of the day remarked that "Hell was dismissed with costs."

Before this verdict was rendered, the case of Colenso attracted even wider public attention. A

---

[4] Some of Jowett's associates were even bolder; Godwin rejected the biblical narrative of Creation by an appeal to the discoveries of geology, and Wilson rejected all Jewish history before the reign of Josiah as purely legendary.

brilliant student of mathematics at Cambridge, Colenso had become Bishop of Natal, and his work among the Zulus led him to attempt a translation of the Bible into their language. Disturbed by their questions as to the truth of the Bible story, he began a critical examination of the Old Testament and found that the first five books, generally ascribed to Moses, abounded in precise figures, especially in the story of the Exodus. These figures his mathematical knowledge convinced him were impossible and incredible. It followed, he decided, that these five books were written long after Moses, were based on legend, and lacked historic truth. His conclusions, published in a series of articles, 1862-3, easily understood by the public, were greeted with a shout of rage from the orthodox.[5] The Bishop of Cape Town, claiming to be his primate, deposed him from his see, an act annulled by the Privy Council as *ultra vires*. Thereupon the Cape Town bishop formally excommunicated him, thus handing over a brother bishop to Satan. The publicity given to this example of religious persecution served as a shock to the conventional acceptance of the Bible as infallible.

Chronologically, *Essays and Reviews* and the Colenso case belong to the middle Victorian period, but their consequences become more generally notable after 1868. It was in the decade following 1870 that Arnold turned from literary and social criticism to a long attack upon conventional Protestant theology. Certain effects may be here noted of the twofold assault of natural science and textual criticism upon conventional religion. For many thoughtful persons it sapped the foundation of their faith. Since the Reformation Protestantism had been based upon

[5] Arnold's sneer at Colenso's work as "the critical hit in the religious literature of England" seems unfair since it was highly praised by various Continental scholars.

the conception of an infallible Bible as opposed to the Roman infallible Church. Now science and criticism seemed to have dispelled this conception; henceforth, what truth the Bible contained must be extracted by the exercise of human reason, a task that comparatively few were at once able and willing to undertake. There was consequently a marked decline in this period of professed orthodox believers. Sir Harry Johnston, born 1858, notes in his *Story of My Life*, 1923, the change that had occurred in his lifetime. In 1860, he says, the mass of men unhesitatingly accepted the Bible story and Ussher's chronology; sixty years later they had rejected what he rather rudely calls "theological nonsense." Jowett, a witness of a different type from Sir Harry, confessed, toward the close of this period, 1886: "We shall never return to the belief in facts which have been disproved: *e.g.* miracles, the narratives of creation, and Mt. Sinai."[6] It must not be thought that there was a general apostasy; there remained always a hard core of "fundamentalists" and as late as 1892 Gladstone called on his fellow men to stand with him upon "The Impregnable Rock of Holy Scripture." Yet there was undoubtedly a considerable secession from the orthodox conception of revealed religion. Following the lead of Huxley these seceders called themselves "agnostics," a word of his coinage, and no such social stigma was attached to them as to avowed atheists.[7] On the contrary their unquestioned moral-

---

[6] There is an interesting, somewhat satirical, picture of Jowett in Mallock's *The New Republic*, 1877, where he appears under the name of Dr. Jenkinson as a broad church clergyman.

[7] In this period Charles Bradlaugh, an elected member of Parliament, was repeatedly refused admission to his seat because of his avowed atheism. In *Culture and Anarchy* Arnold calls him "the notorious tribune" of the working class, "who seems to be almost for baptizing us all in blood and fire into his new social dispensation."

ity and intellectual vigor marked many of them as leaders in English philosophy and literature.

For those who remained in the Church new ways were opened. One was that of philanthropic social reform. Abandoning the discussion of dogma the reformers opened Barnardo's Homes for neglected boys, founded university settlements like Toynbee Hall in city slums, and under the leadership of General Booth organized the Salvation Army, 1880.[8] On the other hand there developed within the English Church a vigorous ritualist strain, springing from the Oxford Movement (p. 38), which decorated the former simple service with candles, vestments, and incense. In their reverence of the sacraments the ritualists drew even nearer to the Roman Church. Though denying the authority of the Pope, they were none the less proud to call themselves Catholics and they strongly objected to the term Protestant. This *via media*, however, proved impossible to many emotional minds and there was a steady stream of converts to Rome. This phenomenon was particularly noticeable in the case of the later Victorian poets. Where the pious and mystical Christina Rossetti remained an Anglo-Catholic, a long procession from Patmore to Wilde sought safety under the protection of an infallible church.

During this period there was a marked falling away on the part of the rising well-to-do middle class from the sober *mores* of the early Evangelicals (p. 14). Careless of dogma and contemptuous of ritual, these "Philistines," to borrow Arnold's term, began to indulge in pleasures denied by the earlier strict

[8] William Booth, 1829-1912, brought up in extreme poverty with little education, became the greatest English evangelist since Wesley. His work was specially directed to the submerged urban poor, and his great service was recognized at Oxford by the award of an honorary degree, in 1907.

rule of life, in dancing, card-playing, and the theatre. Family prayers and regular church-going were neglected or abandoned. The old rigid Sabbatarianism was disregarded; museums were opened, excursions organized, and dinner parties given on a day formerly devoted to religious services.[9] Yet these "Philistines" would have been shocked to hear themselves called pagans; they were not, in fact, apostate Julians, only liberal and quite respectable Victorian citizens.

The latter part of the period saw the sudden rise of Socialism in England. Socialism, a word of various connotations, has been defined as the political theory which aims to secure through the action of a central democratic government a better distribution of the national wealth, or, to quote the words of a radical Victorian Socialist, William Morris, its purpose is "to obtain for the whole people duly organized the possession and control of all the means of production and exchange." The immediate cause of the sudden appearance of Socialistic thought in England is, perhaps, to be found in the severe depression of 1878-9 which threw thousands of workers out of employment. Their sufferings roused the somewhat sluggish trade unions of the day to seek a more effective cure for poverty and unemployment. Henry George's widely circulated *Progress and Poverty,* 1879, aroused enthusiastic response, and the Socialist party was organized in 1881-3.[10] It had at first little practical effect; it was not until the Third Reform Bill, 1884, (p. 94) greatly increased the number of

[9] Such liberal clergymen as F. D. Maurice and Charles Kingsley attacked the rigid Sabbatarianism of the Evangelicals; Kingsley advocated the opening of the Crystal Palace and the British Museum to the public on Sunday.

[10] The more radical and revolutionary program of Karl Marx had only a limited response in England. His classic work, *Das Kapital,* was not translated till 1886.

working class voters that Socialism began to play an active part in English politics. In 1888 the Trade Union Congress demanded the nationalization of land, a fundamental Socialist doctrine.

English Socialism assumed various forms, often in bitter conflict with each other. The Social Democratic Federation was Marxist; its leader, H. M. Hyndman, primarily responsible for the Trafalgar Square riot of "Bloody Sunday," looked for an immediate international proletarian revolt. The Fabian Society, on the other hand, a group of students and writers including such figures as G. B. Shaw, the Webbs, and H. G. Wells, believed in slow deliberate action, conducted by propaganda and working through constitutional means. Where the radical Socialists denounced political action, the Fabians pursued it. In 1888 two of their members were elected to the London School Board (p. 135). The Fabian appeal to the intellectual discontent of the age met with considerable success; some ninety local Fabian Societies sprang up in England. The Independent Labor Party founded by Keir Hardie, 1893, grew out of the Fabian propaganda; it increased in political strength until in the twentieth century it was more than once victorious at the polls.

After this survey of the changes which brought the Victorian era from its Golden Age into its Twilight, we may turn to consider the political phases of that final period with special reference to the Irish question which finally wrecked the Liberal party.

When Gladstone heard in 1868 that he was called on to be for the first time Prime Minister, he is said to have exclaimed: "My mission is to pacify Ireland." To this mission, indeed, he devoted his chief energies for the rest of his active life. That distressful country sorely needed a helper armed with the power of the state. During the potato famine (p. 30) Disraeli had described Ireland as suffering under the triple burden of "a starving population, an absentee aristocracy, (*i.e.* of landlords) and an alien Church." Conditions had improved but little since that day; there were, indeed, fewer people in Ireland, but they were still as poor, as hungry, and as resentful of English rule. A series of terroristic attempts, the so-called "Fenian" outrages, had lately called attention to this resentment, but Disraeli had found no better answer than coercion.[11] Gladstone at once set himself to remove its causes. His first blow fell on the "alien Church" which he called one of the branches of the Irish "upas tree." After a bitter struggle with the Lords he succeeded in disestablishing the English Church in Ireland, thus relieving the Irish Catholics from paying taxes to what they regarded as a congregation of heretics. His next move was an attack on "landlordism." At that time the relation between landlord and tenant in both Ireland and England was one of "free contract." In England, where as a rule the landlord was in residence and interested in the welfare of his tenants, this practice was fairly satisfactory, but in Ireland the landlord was usually an absentee, caring only for the rent he could obtain. If the tenant improved his holding, the rent was raised; if it was not paid, he was evicted without compensation. Only in Ulster (p. 98) was compensation for improvements a customary practice. Gladstone's Land Act, 1870, did something to improve these conditions. It allowed the tenant compensation for improvements and, in some cases, for unjust eviction. This was all that could be obtained

---

[11] The Fenian Brotherhood was a secret revolutionary society mainly composed of American Irish. They attempted to invade Canada, 1866, killed a policeman in Manchester, 1867, and in the same year exploded a bomb in London, causing a dozen deaths and many injuries.

in the existing state of English opinion and the Act of 1870 is remarkable less for the actual benefit it conferred than as an early example of state interference with the landlord's "rights." It was the first of a long series of acts by which these were finally abolished in Ireland.

In the same year, 1870, the government assumed for the first time responsibility for providing primary education. It was then estimated that about half the children in England were without schooling, and radical reformers demanded that the state supply primary education, non-sectarian, compulsory, and free. This demand could not then be realized, but Forster, Matthew Arnold's brother-in-law, then Minister of Education, stated that he wished to see "Old England as well taught as New England," and put through an act which set up schools throughout the country in districts where none existed. These schools were put under the control of local boards, supported by grants, and forbidden to give sectarian instruction, a blow at the Church claim to control education.[12] Moreover, any local board might insist on compulsory attendance and pay for the schooling of poor children. Forster's Act was a first step toward general free compulsory education, but it fell short of radical demands.

The year which saw these reforms peacefully accomplished at home witnessed the outbreak and sudden ending of the war between imperial France and Germany. The surprising debacle of the French army, supposed to be the best in Europe, startled England and was the direct cause of army reforms like the abolition of purchase. English sympathies were at first with Germany, in part because of a long-standing distrust of the "faithful ally" (p. 59)

---

[12] English "board schools" are, in general, equivalent to American public schools.

of Crimean days, in part because of the favor with which the court regarded Germans.[13] After Sedan English sympathy was aroused by the heroic and hopeless struggle of republican France against overwhelming military force, and relief poured into starving Paris after the fall of that city. Gladstone himself wished to protest against the German annexation of Alsace-Lorraine, but his fellow ministers convinced him that a protest would be futile. At the outbreak of the war, however, England managed to secure a guarantee of the independence of Belgium signed by both France and Prussia, a pledge which a later German Chancellor rejected, 1914, as "a scrap of paper." Russia took advantage of the fall of France to denounce the clause in the Treaty of Paris (p. 55) neutralizing the Black Sea. Public opinion in England, always suspicious of Russia, protested loudly against this unilateral action, but to no effect.[14] To prevent a possible war, Bismarck, representing the dominant power in Europe, the new German Empire, called a Conference of Powers on the question. Here it was agreed that the prohibitive clause of the Treaty should be annulled, whereupon Russia rebuilt Sebastopol (p. 54) and launched a fleet in the Black Sea. Imperialistic Englishmen sighed for the days of Palmerston, and dissatisfaction with Gladstone's foreign policy led the nation later to support Disraeli's stand against Russia.

The popularity of Gladstone's government was also weakened by its settlement of the Alabama dispute (p. 63). The American claims for reparations were finally submitted to a court composed of arbi-

---

[13] The Queen's oldest daughter had married the Prussian Crown Prince, later the brief-lived Emperor, Frederick III.

[14] The eleventh letter of Arnold's *Friendship's Garland* satirizes the ineffectual protest of England in a parable something in the style of Dean Swift.

trators: one from England, one from America, and three appointed by neutral powers. At first, it seemed as if nothing would come of this early attempt to settle international disputes by arbitration, for America advanced claims for "indirect damages" amounting to a quite impossible sum. Fortunately the American arbitrator, Charles Francis Adams, the American Minister to England during the Civil War, persuaded the court to throw out these claims before adjudicating admitted damages. The English arbitrator was, however, anything but co-operative; in every decision but one he voted against the rest of the court, and when the final award of over fifteen million dollars was made to America, he published his dissent in the *London Gazette*.[15] It does not help a government to have its appointed representative denounce its action.

After 1872 it was clear that the power of Gladstone's government was declining. Reform, apparently, had gone too fast and too far. The government had offended various groups: High Churchmen by the disestablishment of the Irish Church; dissenters by liberal grants to Church schools; labor by restricting picketing; and imperialists by forfeiting English prestige. Disraeli compared the Liberal ministers to a range of exhausted volcanoes where "not a flame flickers upon a single pallid crest." The end came in 1873 when Gladstone's proposed Irish University, open to Protestants and Catholics alike, was rejected by a majority made up of extremists of both religions. In January, 1873, Gladstone appealed to the country, but the General Election gave the Conservatives a majority of over fifty in the Commons. Labor put up thirteen independent candidates,

---

[15] A small sum compared with the astronomical figures of twentieth century finance, but more than twice the price paid by the United States for Alaska.

thus splitting the Liberal party, and two union officials (p. 49) became the first Labor members of Parliament.

Disraeli became Prime Minister, 1874, under the most favorable auspices; he commanded a clear majority in the Commons; the Lords, as always, were Conservative; and he enjoyed the special favor of the Queen, who preferred his clever flattery to Gladstone's ponderous lectures. For his first years of power his motto was, "Rest and be thankful." He did not repeal Gladstone's reforms, but enacted an amendment, the Employers' and Workmen Act, 1875, which conciliated labor. A Public Health Act committed the state to war against unsanitary urban conditions, and a new law protected the lives of British seamen from needless risk in unseaworthy ships. His chief interest, however, was in foreign affairs. In 1875 he bought the shares in the Suez Canal owned by the bankrupt Khedive and set up with France the Dual Control of Egyptian finance. In 1876 his Royal Titles Bill conferred on the Queen the title of Empress of India, and Victoria rewarded him with a peerage so that as Earl of Beaconsfield he could preserve his failing health in the calm atmosphere of the House of Lords. A crisis, however, soon occurred which forced Disraeli to exert all his power.

In 1875-6 revolts in the Balkans against Turkish misrule were suppressed with ruthless cruelty, especially in Bulgaria where thousands were massacred. When the news reached England, the facts were denied or minimized by Disraeli, but it roused Gladstone from the private life to which he had retired. The old champion of freedom who had once denounced the Bourbon rule in Naples (p. 44) now raised his voice against a bloodier tyranny. His pamphlet, *The Bulgarian Atrocities,* which sold like a popular novel, insisted that the Turks clear out, "bag and baggage," from the land they had "desolated and profaned." He followed the pamphlet with a series of public addresses that roused intense feeling. It was well that he did so, for events shortly occurred which almost led England to repeat the mistake of the Crimea. In 1877 Russia, acting as the protector of Christians in Turkey, declared war and pushed her army almost to Constantinople. Disraeli countered by sending a fleet to the Dardanelles and bringing Indian troops to Malta in readiness for action. As in Crimean days a war fever broke out in England, particularly in high society and in the London streets, where it found blatant expression in a song which added a word to the English language:

> We don't want to fight,
> But by *Jingo*, if we do,
> We've got the men, we've got the ships,
> We've got the money too.

London "Jingoism" demonstrated by smashing Gladstone's windows, and for a time it seemed as if war were inevitable, but a strong body of public opinion, finding voice in Carlyle, Ruskin, Browning, and Morris, protested against England's fighting in behalf of the "unspeakable Turk." Finally Disraeli accepted Bismarck's invitation to settle the dispute at a conference of powers in Berlin. There Disraeli and his Foreign Secretary, Lord Salisbury, represented England at the greatest meeting of European statesmen since the Congress of Vienna. Disraeli's diplomacy won a complete victory; the treaty which Russia had forced on Turkey was torn up and replaced by a more lenient one; a neutral Austria was given the right to administer the Turkish provinces of Bosnia and Herzegovinia — one of the causes of World War I — and England occupied the island of Cyprus, later annexed, 1914. Disraeli returned bringing back "Peace with Honor" to be hailed by a grateful people and decorated by the Queen with the Order of the Garter. The summer of 1878 marks the zenith of Disraeli's popularity.

Between Disraeli's return from Berlin and his fall, 1880, British imperialism suffered some startling checks in distant parts of the Empire. In South Africa, the Transvaal, a Boer republic (p. 52), had been annexed, 1877, to protect it from the aggressive Zulus. In 1878 a small British force invaded Zululand only to encounter a disastrous defeat at Isandhlana where the Zulus stormed their camp and massacred the garrison. It mattered little that next year the Zulus were crushed; British prestige had received a fatal blow in the eyes of the Boers who demanded a return of their independence. They were told that this was impossible, and it was left for the next Liberal government to settle the matter (p. 95).

Almost simultaneously imperialism involved England in trouble in Asia. The Viceroy of India felt it necessary to establish British control in Afghanistan in order to check the advance of Russia, "a conquering and aggressive nation."[16] Afghanistan was invaded, and a puppet-king was installed with a British resident to keep him in order. Almost at once the Afghans rose in arms, stormed the Residency, and killed every man in it. In the long war that followed, the British suffered a severe defeat at Maiwand, 1880, and it took all the skill and courage of Lord Roberts to rescue the broken army.[17] Gladstone, who had later to deal with this problem, solved it by abandoning the idea of a British resident in Afghanistan.

---

[16] The words of Sir Bartle Frere to Salisbury in 1874. They are not without significance in the twentieth century.

[17] Celebrated in Kipling's prose and verse as "Bobs Bahadur."

THE TWILIGHT

While Disraeli's government was meeting these reverses abroad it had to contend with a grave depression at home. This affected every branch of commerce and industry, but was particularly hard upon the farmer, and Ireland depending almost entirely on agriculture was the chief sufferer. It became impossible for tenants to pay the rent demanded by absentee landlords, and the years 1877-9 saw the number of evictions doubled, and agrarian crime increased in still greater proportion. Ireland, however, was rapidly becoming able to force attention upon her claim for redress. Parnell, the leader of the Irish party which demanded Home Rule, now began a double attack upon Disraeli's government by obstructing legislation in the Commons and by promoting the Land League to protect tenants against landlords. Trusting to the popularity he had gained by "Peace with Honor" Disraeli dissolved Parliament and called on the nation to condemn the "destructive doctrine" of Home Rule. Gladstone refused to admit this charge and concentrated his fire upon the disastrous results of Disraeli's foreign policy, promising also a further extension of the franchise. He conducted his campaign in a way that marked a new era in English politics, speaking to cheering crowds from the train in which he travelled about the country. To the surprise of Disraeli the General Election resulted in a great Liberal victory. One of the most ominous results, however, was that Parnell came back at the head of over sixty Home Rulers. The latest Reform Bill had increased the number of Irish voters, the secret ballot (p. 75) had secured them from intimidation, and Parnell, the Irish people's choice, was now in command of a party almost large enough to tip the scales in the Commons. Disraeli at once resigned, withdrew from public life, and died a year later, 1881.

The Queen had been so shocked by Gladstone's democratic manner of campaigning that she asked Lord Hartington, a Liberal peer, to become Prime Minister. Hartington, however, informed her that no ministry could be formed without Gladstone and that the old leader of the party would not accept a subordinate post. The Queen gave way; Gladstone became Prime Minister and got a second chance at his "mission to pacify Ireland." It proved an impossible task.

Inasmuch as Gladstone's second administration was largely concerned with the Irish question, we may deal with that phase before passing to other home and foreign issues. He acted at once by stopping coercion and introduced a bill to compensate evicted tenants. It was promptly rejected by the Lords, and Irish landlords renewed their attack; 10,000 evictions were recorded in 1880. The result was a reign of terror in Ireland; ricks were fired and cattle maimed on farms occupied by the successors of evicted tenants; there were cold blooded murders of "traitors" to the cause and of agents who collected rents for an absentee. Parnell himself was opposed to physical violence, but his proposal to treat all enemies as "moral lepers" led to the historic incident of Captain Boycott. When this agent of an absentee tried to evict a tenant, his servants were called out on strike, local tradesmen refused to serve him, and his crops stood ungathered till they were harvested by Protestants from Ulster under police protection.[18] That the Irish peasant had cause to rebel is shown by the comment of "Chinese" Gordon, visiting Ireland about this time: "The people," he said, "are worse off than the Chinese; almost all starved, and living in places where Englishmen would not keep cattle."

[18] This was apparently the first instance of the now too familiar practice of "boycotting."

Yet even a Liberal government was bound to put down a reign of terror and a law was passed suspending all constitutional rights in Ireland.[19]

With Gladstone, however, reform accompanied repression and in 1881 he pushed through the most radical of Irish Land Acts. It practically met the demands of the Land League, granting the tenant the "Three F's": "fair rent, fixity of tenure, and free sale." For political reasons Parnell advised the Irish to reject the offered benefits, whereupon Gladstone, at the end of his patience, arrested him again, threw him into Kilmainham jail without trial, and suppressed the Land League, actions which were followed by a new outbreak of crime.

Now came a sudden turn of the wheel. Parnell got in touch with the government and promised that if relief were given to the poorest tenants, he would co-operate in suppressing crime. His proposal was accepted in the secret, but none the less real, "Kilmainham treaty," and he and his fellow prisoners were set free. Gladstone now appointed Lord Frederick Cavendish, a young liberal nobleman, to carry out this program. Unhappily on the very day of Lord Frederick's landing in Ireland he was murdered in Phoenix Park, Dublin, by a gang of terrorists. Their intended victim, it seems, was his companion, Burke, a hated official, and Lord Frederick died with him because he resisted the murderers with a characteristic English weapon, the umbrella which he carried. This brutal murder had a profound effect on England, but no Englishman was more shocked than Parnell: "I feel as if I had been stabbed in the back," he said. Co-operation was impossible and coercion was resumed. The murderers were betrayed by an informer; they were hanged and he was promptly

[19] Parnell was arrested and tried for conspiracy, but acquitted, and his release was celebrated with bonfires in Ireland.

shot by a surviving member of the gang. The Irish National League, calling for Home Rule outright, took the place of the disbanded Land League, and Irish members of Parliament, joined the Conservative party. In a sudden and unexpected attack they defeated the government and Gladstone at once resigned, June, 1885, to be succeeded by Lord Salisbury, who served as Prime Minister for six months till the General Election in the Autumn.

In spite of his absorption in Irish affairs, Gladstone put through various reforms in this administration. In 1880 primary education was made compulsory; the Married Women's Property Act,[20] another step in the emancipation of women, would have delighted J. S. Mill; and the Ground Game Act, permitting farmers to shoot rabbits destroying their crops, was a blow at the old privileges of the sporting gentry (p. 11). But Gladstone's greatest achievement was the passing of the Third Reform Bill. An extension of the franchise to workers excluded in the 1867 Act (p. 67) had been on the Liberal program since 1880, but it was not till 1884 that Gladstone was able to introduce his bill. It raised the number of voters in Great Britain from about three to five million, a far greater increase than had been effected by the earlier acts. Yet this reform was accomplished with less popular agitation and less aristocratic resistance than either of the others. The bill after an easy passage in the Commons was, indeed, held up for a time in the Lords, and in the outcry, "mend them or end them," which followed their obstruction, the proposal was made, for the first time, to limit their power of veto.[21]

---

[20] It allowed a wife to buy, hold, and bequeath real estate and secured her control of her property and income.

[21] Ten bishops, led by the Primate of Canterbury, voted for the bill. The Church had grown more democratic than in 1832 (p. 21).

The English spirit of compromise, however, prevailed and the Lords accepted defeat.

In foreign affairs Gladstone was from the first embarrassed by difficulties bequeathed to him by Disraeli's imperialism. Roberts soon put an end to the Afghan War (p. 90) and the dreaded Russian advance was checked by pacific diplomacy. In Africa, however, Gladstone was confronted with a situation that involved him in grave trouble and created a suspicion as to his concern for the nation's honor. The Transvaal Boers who demanded the immediate return of their independence (p. 90) were refused with a view of merging their country in a federated South Africa, such as exists today. Thereupon they rose in revolt and annihilated a small English force at Majuba, 1881. In spite of a popular cry for revenge and reconquest Gladstone gave them the terms decided on in his cabinet before the news of Majuba came, independence under the suzerainty — a vague word — of England.[22]

In Egypt the demands of foreign bond-holders, enforced by the Dual Control (p. 76), combined with the extravagance and corruption of the Khedive's court, had brought the country to the verge of ruin. In 1881 a mutinous army led by Arabi Bey seized control of the government, but England and France sent a joint fleet to Alexandria to support the Khedive. This led to an anti-foreign riot in the city costing the lives of many Europeans. English men-of-war then bombarded the forts protecting Alexandria, while the French sailed away, washing their hands of the whole business. An English army defeated Arabi at Tel-el-Kebir, September, 1882, captured and deported him. England now occupied Egypt, announcing that her rule was to be tem-

---

[22] The victory of the Boers and the apparent backdown of England were among the causes of the later, 1899, Boer War.

porary, and gave the country in the main an administration of order and justice such as it had not known since Roman days. So far all was well but Egypt was inextricably involved in the Sudan.[23]

The Sudan, a group of districts on the head-waters of the Nile, had earlier been annexed to Egypt. It was a fertile field for slave-raiding and official oppression when Gordon was sent there, 1873, by the Egyptian government. In two years he stopped the slave-trade and restored order, but on his departure anarchy and oppression again prevailed. Suddenly there appeared a native chief who proclaimed himself the Mahdi, *i.e.* the leader, and preached a holy war against Egypt. Instead of using the English army in Egypt against him the task was entrusted to the Egyptian army under Hicks Pasha. His weak and badly equipped force was wiped out by the Mahdi's troops in 1883 and Egyptian control was reduced to a few scattered garrisons. The English government now called on Gordon to return and secure their safe withdrawal. He accepted the task, but on reaching Khartoum, the center of Egyptian occupation, he decided to reconquer the Sudan and asked for help. It was refused, and he was left to struggle alone against the Mahdi, who besieged him in Khartoum. After long hesitation the government decided to send an English army to rescue him, but its advance force came in sight of Khartoum only to learn that the town had been stormed and Gordon killed two days earlier, January 26, 1885. The army of relief abandoned the Sudan and fell back into Egypt. It had learned by experience the fighting quality of the Mahdi's spearmen who at Abu Klea,

---

[23] The Denshawi incident, discussed in the Preface to Shaw's *John Bull's Other Island,* was an unfortunate exception. For another view of English rule in Egypt see Kipling's story, *Little Foxes.*

1885, actually "broke a British square."[24] It took over a decade of training and frontier fighting to enable an Egyptian army, led by Kitchener, to avenge Gordon in the decisive battle of Omdurman, September, 1898. This victory established the Anglo-Egyptian Condominium of the Sudan, which lasted well into the present century. The news of Gordon's death was received with an outburst of grief and rage. The Queen telegraphed her personal resentment to Gladstone and it was by the slimmest margin that his government escaped a vote of censure. The "too little and too late" Liberal policy was one of the causes of Gladstone's fall (p. 99) and the "desertion" of Gordon was long a matter of reproach to his party.

In the General Election of the autumn of 1885, the first held under the new law (p. 94), the newly enfranchised voters gave the Liberals a majority of 85 or 86 over the Conservatives, but Parnell now commanded a solid block of 86 Irish members, making it possible for him at any time to cast a deciding vote in the Commons. Swinging his party to the support of Gladstone, he overthrew Salisbury's brief administration, January, 1886, and Gladstone became for the third time Prime Minister.

Gladstone's third administration lasted only six months, February-August, 1886, and was wholly concerned with his proposal of Home Rule. Even before he took office it became known that he had been converted to this plan as the only possible means of pacifying Ireland, but a fissure began to open in his party which rent it asunder and destroyed its usefulness for nearly a generation. The

[24] See Kipling's *Fuzzy-Wuzzy*, "a pore benighted heathen, but a first-class fightin' man"; also his *Pharaoh and the Sergeant*, which celebrates the re-organization and disciplining of the Egyptian army by English non-coms.

memory of Irish boycottings, maimings, and political murders was too fresh in the minds of many Liberals for them to acquiesce in handing over the rule of that country to Parnell, "the uncrowned King." Even Gladstone's Cabinet was divided; Chamberlain and Trevelyan, Macaulay's nephew, resigned office. Liberal statesmen like John Bright, leaders of thought like Huxley and Jowett, poets so far apart in politics as Tennyson and Swinburne, were all opposed to the plan.[25] But Gladstone was undismayed; he attributed the opposition merely to the obstinacy of the "classes which have fought uniformly on the wrong side and uniformly been beaten." Working hand in hand with Parnell he introduced the first Home Rule Bill in April, 1886.

This Bill proposed an Irish Parliament in Dublin with power over all local issues. Two features in it excited angry opposition: the exclusion of Irish members from the British Parliament and the inclusion of Protestant Ulster in an otherwise Catholic Ireland. Opposition to the first of these might have been overcome, but there was no answer to the other. The slogan, "Ulster will fight," had already been raised, and the grim determination of the North to resist absorption in Southern Ireland has lasted to the present day. It was — and is — not only a clash of creeds that divided Ireland; racial and economic differences played then — as now — a part. The Northern counties were in the main populated by descendants of the Scotch settled there by James I, the so-called "Scotch-Irish" of American speech; the Southern Irish were Celts who had suffered for centuries under Anglo-Saxon oppression. In the North the manufacturing interest was strong; South-

---

[25] To these names should be added that of Browning, a life-long Liberal — see his sonnet, "Why I am a Liberal" — and a personal friend of Gladstone.

ern Ireland was almost wholly agricultural. The sympathy of many Liberal members with Ulster was so strong, their dislike of Home Rule, which they called "Separation" or "Disunion," was so determined, that Gladstone's bill never reached the Lords. When the final vote came in the Commons, June 8, 1886, 93 old-time Liberals deserted their leader and it was rejected by a majority of 30 over the combination of Gladstonians and Parnellites. Gladstone dissolved Parliament and appealed to the country, but the result was a crushing blow. He had expected the support of what he called "the upright sense of the nation," but the new voters, who less than a year before had backed him, now returned a combined Conservative and Unionist party twice the size of the Gladstonian Liberals. Scotland stood by Gladstone, as Ireland did by Parnell, but England, "the predominant partner," definitely denounced Home Rule. Gladstone resigned and Salisbury again became Prime Minister.

Salisbury's second administration, 1886-92, depended upon Unionist support and this in the main determined its policy at home. In foreign affairs it followed, generally with success, the lines of Disraeli's imperialism. Salisbury had studied diplomacy in Disraeli's school, but he was a steadier statesman than his brilliant master. He avoided war and strengthened the ties of England with Germany and Austria against the so-called "aggressor nations," France and Russia. With Germany he effected an arrangement which was to have disastrous results in the next century; England got a protectorate over Zanzibar, an island off the east coast of Africa, in exchange for Helgoland, a British possession since 1807, which was returned to Germany to become in World War I a fortified harbor for the German fleet. Imperial expansion was most active in Africa where Chartered Companies brought great districts under British control. The leader in this expansion was Cecil Rhodes, best known in America as the founder of the Rhodes Scholarships, whose extraordinary influence with the natives allowed him to push British rule far northwards from the Cape with the aim of ultimately linking a United South Africa with the British-occupied Sudan and Egypt.

The most striking event in the early years of this administration was the Queen's Jubilee, 1887, the celebration of Victoria's fifty-year reign. The "Widow of Windsor," who had long lived in seclusion, came again before the eyes of the people as she drove through London to the thanksgiving service in Westminster Abbey, followed by honoring representatives of nearly every nation. The homage paid to the Queen as the symbol of the spiritual union of all the dominions of the Empire marks the high tide of British imperialism.[26]

Spurred on by the Unionists, the Conservative government put through several measures of social reform. It was high time that the old Whig doctrine of laissez-faire should be discarded and the state should act to better the condition of the "submerged" urban lower class, estimated in the eighties to amount to about one third of London's population. This class, in fact, was becoming stridently vocal in calling attention to its misery. The Trafalgar Square riot on "Bloody Sunday," November 13, 1887, where for the first time in years an English mass meeting of the unemployed was dispersed by soldiers, caused something like a panic in London,

---

[26] It is instructive to compare this homage paid the sovereign by a democratic England with the aristocratic contempt of the royal family at the beginning of Victoria's reign (p. 5). Tennyson as Poet Laureate dutifully composed an ode on the Jubilee.

and the callous indifference of the ruling class began to yield to a recognition of their duty to interfere and improve.[27] The London Dock Strike, 1889, when unskilled labor fought for a wage of 6d an hour was successful largely because of the sympathy it evoked. Cardinal Manning, head of the Roman Church in England, joined hands with John Burns, a labor agitator, to obtain acceptance of the strikers' demands. The Local Government Act, 1888, put the administration of civic affairs into the hands of a popularly elected council, and in London this body set to work to pull down slums and provide clean water. Aristocrats like Lord Rosebery and Labor leaders like Ramsay MacDonald acted together to enforce measures that would have shocked earlier Liberals. A Factory Act, 1891, still further extended state regulation of the working hours of women and children, and the Free Education Act, 1891, put the finishing touch on compulsory primary education.

While social reform advanced in England, conditions in Ireland went from bad to worse. After the fall of Gladstone the policy of coercion was resumed; Balfour, Chief Secretary for Ireland, pushed a stringent Crimes Act through Parliament and jailed without trial Irish members who dared to protest. Parnell escaped arrest, but *The Times*, a strong supporter of the policy of coercion, was determined to ruin him. In 1887 it published a facsimile of a letter with his signature condoning the Phoenix Park murders, and followed this by a series of articles on "Parnellism and Crime" backed by other incriminating letters. Parnell demanded a judicial investigation and three English judges who

[27] William Morris, who had been present at the time, attended the funeral of one of the victims and wrote "A Death Song" in *Poems by the Way*, protesting governmental violence.

conducted it discovered, 1889, that the letters in question were the forgeries of Pigott, a disreputable Irish journalist. Pigott confessed his guilt and committed suicide, and *The Times,* held responsible for the publication of his forgeries, was heavily fined. Cleared of his imputed guilt Parnell now stood on the pinnacle of his power. It immediately preceded his downfall.

In November, 1890, Parnell was involved in a scandalous divorce case; he was charged by his former political ally, Captain O'Shea, with adultery with the Captain's wife. Parnell made no defense and the case was decided against him; evidently he had no conception of its bearing upon his political position. Adultery, however, was regarded with the gravest disfavor in Victorian England, and Gladstone demanded Parnell's withdrawal from political leadership. Parnell refused and appealed to his people, but the Irish Catholic bishops denounced him as "unworthy of Christian confidence," and the majority of his party associates deserted him. After a fierce and hopeless struggle to retain his leadership his health broke down and he died, October, 1891, a ruined man.[28] It was, indeed, most unfortunate that at a time when a form of Home Rule that might have made Ireland a contented member of Great Britain was possible it failed because of a great Irishman's indulgence in guilty passion and his stubborn refusal to yield to the wishes of his people. Instead of Home Rule there exists today the independent Republic of Eire, neutral, if not actually hostile, in World War II to England's struggle for existence.

[28] Joyce's *Portrait of the Artist as a Young Man* presents in the first chapter a picture of a furious family quarrel over Parnell and the priests. There is a detailed and documented account of the Parnell-O'Shea case in Ensor's *England, 1870-1914.*

THE TWILIGHT

The General Election of 1892 was fought on the issue of Home Rule, and the Home Rulers, Irish and English combined, won a majority of about forty members.[29] Gladstone now became Prime Minister for the fourth time. He was over eighty, very deaf and half blind, but he bent all his powers to the final accomplishment of his mission. His Second Home Rule Bill introduced some minor changes, but made no allowance for the angry protest of the Ulster-men now threatened with the rule of the priests who since Parnell's fall had dominated Southern Ireland. The Bill was fiercely debated for months in the Commons; clause after clause was carried by a rigorous application of the closure — "gag rule" the Opposition called it — and finally, September, 1893, the Bill was carried by a majority of 34. In the Lords it was considered for just one week and rejected by a vote of ten to one, 419 to 41.

Gladstone himself wished to dissolve Parliament and appeal once more to the country, but his fellow ministers objected and, indeed, there was little chance that a new election would give him the decisive majority needed to over-awe the Lords. When the Lords rejected the first Reform Bill, 1832, England threatened to break out in revolution; when they turned down Home Rule, England was rather relieved than angered. Gladstone's last speech in Parliament insisted that the conflict between the two Houses must be brought to an end, but he was too old and weary to undertake the fight. He resigned in March, 1894, and Lord Rosebery became Prime Minister. Gladstone's resignation marks the end of the Victorian age in politics as Tennyson's

[29] It is a sign of the growing strength of Socialism that two representatives of that movement won in 1892 seats in the Commons: John Burns and Keir Hardie, later leader of the Independent Labor Party.

death, 1892, had marked it in literature. The Grand Old Man, as he was called, had long carried the banner of Liberalism; when he dropped it, his party was broken and leaderless. They fell from power only a year later and when they returned in 1905 it was in a more radical form, destined finally to give way to the socialistic Labor party. Victorian Liberalism died with Gladstone.

A survey of English literature in this period notes at once the successive disappearance from the scene of the great Victorian writers. It had just opened when England was startled by the sudden death, 1870, of Dickens. He was followed in 1873 by J. S. Mill, and in 1875 by Kingsley. The decade 1880-90 seems to have been especially fatal; George Eliot died in 1880; Disraeli and Carlyle, in 1881. In 1882 Darwin and D. G. Rossetti passed away. Arnold's death, 1888, was followed by that of Browning, 1889, and of Newman, 1890. Tennyson's death in 1892 marks both the end of this period and the close of the Victorian age. Ruskin alone of the earlier Victorians survived till the end of the century, but Ruskin's work had ended more than ten years before.

It must be confessed that the literature of the Twilight presents a decline from the glories of the Golden Age. Some of the older speakers are still present, but their work seems on the whole to lack the inspiration of their earlier utterance. New writers appear, but no novelist enjoys the popularity of Dickens; no graver speaker carries quite the authority and influence of Carlyle. A hasty glance at the actual accomplishment of this period in literature would seem to confirm this statement.

With the exception of Arnold, who deserted poetry for prose after his *New Poems*, 1867, the major Victorian poets are still active. Tennyson completed his *Idylls of the King* in 1872 and turned to the composition of poetic historical drama in a series of plays reaching from *Queen Mary*, 1875, to *Becket* in 1884. Along with these he published from time to time thin volumes of narrative and lyrical verse, ending in his last year with *The Death of Oenone*. Browning was ceaselessly productive, but much of his work was a translation and adaptation of Greek tragedy, along with a group of ratiocinative philosophical poems, interspersed, many of them, with short and lovely lyrics. His last volume, *Asolando*, appeared on the very day of his death. The popularity that had once been denied him came to him at last as Browning Societies sprang up in England and America.

Younger poets who had already appeared now continued their work. Swinburne's *Songs before Sunrise*, 1871, and his *Poems and Ballads*, Second Series, 1878, did much to establish his claim as a true poet. Like Tennyson he contributed to the Victorian fashion of poetic "closet" drama with his *Bothwell*, 1874, and *Mary Stuart*, 1881. The long narrative *Tristram of Lyonesse*, 1882, was his last major work, but he continued writing lyrics and critical literary studies till his death in 1909.

The Earthly Paradise, 1868-70, had established William Morris as a story teller in verse; with *Sigurd the Volsung*, 1875, he turned to the legends and myths of Northern Europe, and continued to explore this field in his prose romances, *The House of the Wolfings*, 1889, and *The Roots of the Mountains*, 1890. Two short prose tales, *A Dream of John Ball*, 1888, and *News from Nowhere*, 1891, are, in a sense, propaganda literature; the second in particular is a lovely dream of a communistic utopia in a future England. Many of the *Poems by the Way*, 1891, sing of a coming social revolution.

Dante Gabriel Rossetti's *Poems*, 1870, was mainly

composed of work written, but not published, earlier. His *Ballads and Sonnets*, 1881, completed his long sonnet sequence, *The House of Life,* and added various new poems. His sister Christina continued her mystical devotional poetry, and a volume of her unpublished poems was edited by her brother William after her death in 1894.

Coventry Patmore's *The Unknown Eros*, 1877, a collection of, perhaps, the finest odes in Victorian literature, marked a great advance over his earlier *The Angel in the House*, 1854.

James Thomson's *The City of Dreadful Night,* 1880, is the most perfect example of the influence of contemporary materialistic science on Victorian poetry.

Some poets whose best work falls in the post-Victorian age make their first appearance in this period. Such, for example, are Yeats with *The Wanderings of Oisin,* 1889, and Bridges, later the Poet Laureate, with *Shorter Poems*, 1890.

After the death of Dickens a group of the older Victorian novelists continued at work. Disraeli completed his fictional studies of English political life with *Lothair,* 1870, and *Endymion*, 1880. George Eliot's *Middlemarch,* sometimes regarded as her masterpiece, appeared in 1871-2, and she closed her career as a writer of fiction with *Daniel Deronda,* 1876. Trollope's series of political social novels from *Phineas Finn,* 1869, to *The Duke's Children,* 1880, falls in this period. His interesting *Autobiography* was published posthumously in 1883.

Erewhon, a satiric scientific romance by Samuel Butler, classical scholar and anti-Darwinian, appeared in 1872. His one novel of lasting importance, *The Way of All Flesh,* on which he had worked from 1872 to 1884 and left unfinished, was not published till 1903. *John Inglesant,* 1881, the only memorable work of J. H. Shorthouse, shows clearly the impact of the Oxford movement on English fiction.

The dominant novelists of this time are Meredith and Hardy. Meredith had already shown his power in *Richard Feverel*, 1859, but his most characteristic works, *Beauchamp's Career*, 1876, *The Egoist*, 1879, and *Diana of the Crossways*, 1885, all belong here. Hardy, on the other hand, was a late beginner; all his best novels from *Under the Greenwood Tree*, 1872, to *Tess of the D'Urbervilles*, 1891, fall in this period. After *Jude the Obscure*, 1896, he abandoned fiction for poetry.

Toward the close of the Victorian age new writers begin to appear. Robert Louis Stevenson brought back romance and adventure into English fiction with *Treasure Island*, 1883, *Kidnapped*, 1886, and *The Master of Ballantrae*, 1889. His best known work, *Dr. Jekyll and Mr. Hyde*, 1886, was an adventure into the field of psychologic fiction. Rudyard Kipling broke into sudden fame with his *Plain Tales from the Hills*, 1888, introducing English readers to an India that he was to exploit for years thereafter. It is with something like a shock of surprise that we find G. B. Shaw, satiric critic of all things Victorian, making his debut in literature with a novel, *Cashel Byron's Profession*, 1886.

Apart from fiction there is a considerable body of memorable prose in this period. Social, political, and religious, it reflects the troubled mind of the later Victorians.

Carlyle's contribution to English literature practically ended with his *Frederick the Great* in 1865, but the posthumous publication of his *Reminiscences*, 1881, called attention again to his work and started the endless controversy over his relations with his wife. Ruskin continued his attack on orthodox political economy in *Munera Pulveris*, 1872, and appealed to the nation at large for a moral and social reform in a series of lectures published under various titles, and in his *Fors Clavigera*, 1871-84, letters addressed to the workmen of England. His autobiography, *Praeterita*, was left unfinished in 1889.

The most important work of J. S. Mill was done earlier, but his *Subjection of Women*, 1869, was to have lasting effect on English social life. His *Autobiography* was published posthumously in 1873.

Newman's *Grammar of Assent*, a plea for faith as opposed to rationalistic logic, appeared in 1870, and his great contribution to humanistic education, *The Idea of a University*, in 1873.

Darwin's *Descent of Man*, 1871, brought his evolutionary theory to its logical conclusion. Huxley, his chief advocate, now became a voluminous writer and speaker; his *Lay Sermons* appeared in 1870, his *Science and Morals* in 1886.

This is the time of Arnold's activity as a critic of orthodox theology in a series of works from *St. Paul and Protestantism*, 1870, to *Last Essays on Church and State*, 1877. He returned to his proper field in *Essays in Criticism*, Second Series, published after his death, 1888.

This summary of the literature of the late Victorian age may suggest the change that is coming over Victorian life and thought. In spite of some brilliant achievements in prose and verse a note of "doubt, hesitation, and pain" seems to be creeping in. Old things are passing away; a new world has not yet come to birth. In literature as in social and political life this period is indeed the twilight of Victorianism.

Part II

SHAPING FORCES OF THE AGE

Chapter I

The Industrial Revolution

The Victorian period which underlies and merges into our own is separated by a wide gap from preceding times, especially in England. In the famous third chapter of his *History of England* Macaulay describes in full and glowing detail the changes that had taken place in England between 1685, the date at which his *History* begins, and 1848, the date of its publication. He notes that about the middle of the eighteenth century this progress became "portentously rapid" and proceeded in the nineteenth with "accelerated velocity."[1] It may be well for the reader to bear these dates in mind: George III became King in 1760, "about the middle of the 18th century"; 1848, the date of Macaulay's statement, marks the close of the first Victorian period.

Macaulay's brilliant rhetoric passes briefly over

[1] With the characteristic optimism of a Victorian liberal Macaulay believed that these changes represented "progress," and that the great body of people were happier in his day than in earlier times. He even sneered at "the demagogues who find it a lucrative trade to expatiate on the distress of the laborer."

the causes and consequences of these changes. We may look into them somewhat more closely.

For centuries up to *ca.* 1760 English life had in the main run along an old established pattern. It was essentially rural; the great majority of Englishmen lived on the land or in villages, deriving a "subsistence" living from small farm and communal agriculture, combined with handicraft production. They submitted quietly to the political dominance of a land-owning aristocracy. After the Civil War of the seventeenth century the supremacy of the state church was acknowledged by most Englishmen, and the Mosaic cosmology, founded on a literal interpretation of the Bible, was accepted by all but a few individual "free-thinkers." By 1848 all this had changed. The bulk of the population had shifted from the country to the town; as small farms were transformed into large holdings by repeated enclosure acts, the "bold peasantry, their country's pride," was driven off the land. Handicraft production transmitted from father to son was crushed by new machine-made large scale production. The long unchallenged dominance of the aristocracy had vanished with the passage of the Reform Bill in 1832. More important still in its effect on literature, the impact of a new critical science was beginning to make the old acceptance of a literal interpretation of the Bible impossible to thinking men, so that the very foundations of religious faith seemed to be challenged.

It must not be supposed from the mention of the date 1760 that at that time a gap suddenly opened between the past and later periods; there was no such swift and violent change in England as later took place across the channel at the time of the French Revolution. It was about the middle of the eighteenth century, however, that the first signs of impending change became apparent and from that time on three factors worked together and successively to revolutionize English life. These three may be conveniently labelled as: the Industrial Revolution; the advance of democracy; and the extension of the scientific method to new fields. Each of these factors demands separate treatment, although, of course, all three were mutually interacting.

* * *

The term, Industrial Revolution, was used by Arnold Toynbee to describe the economic and social changes in England during the reigns of George III and his immediate successors. This seems rather too inclusive a definition; the term might better be limited to the gradual superseding of the traditional method of a single worker's hand-labor product by that of groups of workers, assembled in a factory, tending power-driven machines which produced larger quantities at a cheaper cost, the beginning, in fact, of what we call "mass production." This applies particularly to the manufacture of woolen, cotton, and iron goods.

Woolen goods had long been a staple English product for home use and for export. Home-grown wool was spun into thread and woven into cloth in homes on the age-old hand-worked wheel and loom. Cotton, imported in the raw state since early in the eighteenth century, was spun and woven in like fashion on wheel and loom. Iron, long smelted from the ore over charcoal fires, began in the eighteenth century to be produced in furnaces fed by coal in the form of coke. Since coal and iron-ore fields lay close together in northern and northwestern England, a great impetus was given in this region to the production of iron goods, and iron machines for spinning and weaving soon replaced the old wooden wheel and loom. Later on iron in the form of rails made rapid transport over railroads possible. Power for the new machines was furnished at first by water, but after the invention of the steam-engine, 1765, steam gradually took the place of water-power, and factories moved from villages in the hills where water-power was abundant to cities where coal, easily procurable, was used to produce steam.

It is impossible to fix exact dates for the Industrial Revolution, but Toynbee's phrase, "during the reign of George III," gives at least an approximate date for its beginning, for it was after the accession of George, 1760, that a swift succession of inventions from the spinning-jenny, 1764, to the steam locomotive, 1825, revolutionized all methods of production and transport. Naturally no date can be given for the end of the Industrial Revolution; it is still in progress as shown, among other things, by the increasing shift from hand to mechanized labor in agriculture and by the comparatively recent development of transportation by air.

It must not, however, be taken for granted that the Industrial Revolution runs an unbroken course from *ca.* 1760 to the present time. As a matter of fact it falls into two unequal periods. From its beginning it ran for a time almost unchecked, bringing with it increasing misery to the working class. This was due in part to the indifference of the then ruling class, the land-owning aristocracy, in part to the impotence of local governmental machinery to check and correct abuses. Indifference and impotence alike found a warrant in the orthodox political economy of the age, the dogma of laissez-faire, or non-interference on the part of the state with industrial affairs. After the Reform Bill of 1832, however, there came a recognition of the duty and a consciousness of power on the part of the new rulers of England, the substantial middle class, that led, primarily for humanitarian reasons, to a succession of interferences with industry which culminated in such controls of business as those imposed by Labor governments in England and by the so-called Welfare State in America. The two unequal periods, then, might be said to run, first from 1760 to 1832, and then from 1832 to a still unknown future.

No one single cause can be assigned for the beginning of the Industrial Revolution. The rapidly increasing population of England in the eighteenth century brought on, naturally, a demand for a proportional increase in the supply of food and clothing. The long wars that overlap the end of the century stimulated this demand and quickened the pace of the change. Below these causes lay, however, the prevailing temper of the time. The eighteenth century has long been known as the Age of Reason. Much that had been handed down by tradition was then critically examined and, if unsuitable to present conditions, was calmly discarded. It was a period of scientific rather than of religious thought, and scientific discoveries were promptly turned to practical uses. A long series of mechanical inventions was directly due to scientific research, and in the whole field of production reason prevailed over tradition in a manner and at a rate that would have been impossible in earlier times.

Some of the immediate consequences of the Industrial Revolution have already been noted. Prominent among them was the extraordinary shift in the population from the country to the town. In 1700 the agricultural population of England was double that of the urban; in 1830 at the beginning of the Victorian age the reverse was true. The urban increase was especially swift in the new manufacturing and trading cities; between 1800 and 1831 the population of Glasgow, for example, increased by 161%; that of Manchester by 151%; that of the harbor town of Liverpool by 138%. No provision was made for the proper housing of this rapidly increasing urban population. The newcomers were herded into old houses abandoned by former residents, or, more often, into jerry-built houses rushed up by speculative landlords in the slums that encircled the new factory towns. Living conditions in these houses, built with reckless disregard of sanitary conditions, were no doubt a primary cause of the wave of cholera — regarded by the pious as a judgment of God — which swept over England in the 1830's. The natural result of this shift of population and the intolerable living conditions in the new towns was the emergence of a poverty-stricken urban proletariat hitherto unknown in England. And this class, driven to despair by periods of unemployment and consequent starvation — "clemming," the workers called it — was filled with a bitter anger against the employers whom they held responsible for their misery. Social hatred led to class war marked by sabotage, personal violence, and even murder. Despite repeated efforts in the Victorian age to improve the conditions of the workers, a layer of festering humanity lay below the commercial prosperity of the time. As late as 1885 Engels, long a student of English social conditions, described the East End of London as "an ever-spreading pool of stagnant misery."[2]

One of the most immediate and shocking results of the Industrial Revolution was the vast increase of

[2] Karl Marx, the longtime collaborator of Engels, based his classic work, *Das Kapital*, 1867, on a study of life in English manufacturing towns. Theoretical Marxist Communism is one of the by-products of the Industrial Revolution.

child labor. Children had, of course, long worked beside their parents on farms and in home industries, but with the coming of large-scale production there arose a demand for cheap labor able to perform the comparatively simple task of tending machines, and the demand was met by drafting the children of the new proletariat into factories. The unsanitary conditions under which they worked; the hours of labor often running to twelve and more a day; the use of the stick and whip to keep tired children at work; the pursuit and capture of runaways, like fugitive slaves, are incredible to those unfamiliar with contemporary reports on child labor in early Victorian days. The shocking revelations of these reports stirred the government into action, and the Act of 1833 paid special attention to children, excluding those under nine years from work in factories and setting an eight hour day as the limit of employment for children between nine and thirteen years of age.[3] This was a first step, but there were still many to be taken; ten years later Miss Barrett's *Cry of the Children* voiced the grief and anger of humanitarians over still prevailing labor conditions.

With the expansion of the Industrial Revolution another social class rose rapidly into prominence and power, that of the capitalist employer of labor. The

[3] As early as 1814 Wordsworth noted the darker side of the Industrial Revolution and lamented in particular the imprisonment of country boys in the new factories; *The Excursion,* Book VIII. Frances Trollope's *Michael Armstrong,* 1840, presents a shocking picture of child labor even after the Act of 1833. One of the worst phases of child labor was the employment of young boys, often pauper children from work-houses, in the dangerous practice of chimney-sweeping in the multiplying houses of the new towns. Readers of Dickens will remember that Oliver Twist was only saved from this form of slavery under a brutal master by the intervention of an unusually observant and humane magistrate. The hero of Kingsley's *Water Babies* begins life as a chimney sweeper.

old master craftsman, who took apprentices into his shop and taught them his skills, gave way to the "boss" of big business. In the early days of the change new industries were largely the creation of an exceptionally industrious and intelligent worker, and the man who had built up a business out of nothing naturally regarded it as his private property; he was the owner and the workers were his "hands."[4] He felt no responsibility for their welfare; the only tie between them was the wage he paid — Carlyle's "Cash-Nexus" — and this wage he had the right to fix; "I must be an autocrat," says the wholly honest and upright employer, Thornton, in Mrs. Gaskell's *North and South*. In times of slack business he claimed the right to close his factory regardless of the consequent suffering of his workmen. To combat a strike he could, like Thornton, import low grade, ill-paid Irish workers and call on the military to protect him against consequent mob violence.

There were, of course, exceptions. Owen (p. 34), who rose from a factory hand to become an owner and manager, was profoundly interested in the physical and moral welfare of his employees and played a leading part in the organization of trade unions (p. 36) to protect the worker against the employer. Owen, however, was an outstanding exception; even such an honest and benevolent employer as John Bright, 1811-89, stubbornly opposed state interference in his factories on the ground that they were *his*, and that he was better qualified than any government inspector to guard the safety and well-being of his "hands." Employers as a class justified this opposition to social reform by appealing to the orthodox economic doctrine of laissez-faire.

Throughout the early stages of the Industrial

[4] The ownership of factories by stock companies came considerably later.

Revolution this new class grew in numbers, in wealth, and finally in political power. They brought into politics the energy, the instinct for order, and the practical common sense of their business experience. After the passage of the Reform Bill, 1832, they became in effect a dominant power in English politics. Peel, for example, the ablest statesman of the early Victorian period, was the son of a rich cotton manufacturer. Their wealth often enabled them to invest in landed property, the *sine qua non* of "gentry," to marry into the aristocracy, and to gain entrance into Parliament. An early example of the self-made and dominant employer appears in *Shirley*, 1849, where Robert Moore, risen by intelligence and industry from a worker to an employer, installs labor-saving machinery in his factory against the furious opposition of his workers — the time of the action is in the first decade of the century. Later Josiah Bounderby of *Hard Times*, 1854, a caricature in Dickens' liveliest style, is described as having risen from apprenticeship to become "manufacturer, merchant, banker and what not." Somewhat later Bottles of *Friendship's Garland*, 1871, a typical Arnoldian Philistine, becomes a country magistrate and sends his son to Eton to mingle with the young aristocrats of that old school.[5]

One of the immediate results of this sudden acquisition of wealth by the new capitalists was a crass

[5] Perhaps the best example of such a rise in wealth and power appears in Thackeray's *The Newcomes, Memoirs of a Most Respectable Family*, 1853. This family was founded by Thomas, a weaver in his native village, who came to London, entered the house of Hodson Brothers, merchants and bankers, married the daughter of the partner, and begat the twins, Hodson and Brian Newcome. Hodson remained a London merchant, but Brian entered Parliament and married an earl's daughter. His daughter, the lovely Ethel, was carefully groomed to marry a peer, and the family frowned on her friendship with her artist cousin Clive.

materialism, a frank contempt of ideas and ideals, political or racial, a rejoicing in the "unparalleled prosperity" of England, combined with a smug satisfaction in bodily comforts: well furnished houses, heavily loaded dinner tables, troops of servants and handsome carriages — all, in fact, that money could buy. They accepted blindly the "Gospel of Mammonism" which Carlyle thundered against, that careless neglect of beauty and things of the spirit against which Ruskin raged in vain. Art in England, no longer patronized by a cultured aristocracy, sank to its lowest ebb in 1851 when the Crystal Palace was built to house the first World's Fair and proclaim to the world the triumph of British industry. It is not without significance that the founding of the Pre-Raphaelite Brotherhood, that revolt of youth against Victorian smugness, occurred just about this time, 1848.

It was the flaunting of wealth in the face of misery that more especially provoked the bitter anger of the working class. The old tie that linked landlord to peasant had snapped when the peasant sank into the urban proletariat. Throughout early Victorian literature one hears repeatedly the note of class warfare, most clearly perhaps in Mrs. Gaskell's *Mary Barton* and *North and South,* and in Kingsley's *Yeast* and *Alton Locke*. Disraeli, shrewdest of Victorian politicians, caught that note and echoed it when he added to *Sybil,* his novel of contemporary life, 1845, a second title, *Or the Two Nations*. It was Disraeli, too, who twenty years later put through the Second Reform Bill, 1867, gave the vote to the urban worker, and thus took the first step in making "the two nations" one.

It is easy to denounce the Industrial Revolution as its Victorian critics did, often most volubly and forcibly, but a twentieth century survey can hardly adopt their extreme stand. The Revolution had its good as well as its bad side. It made possible the support of the rapidly increasing population of England, although, it must be owned, with an unfair distribution of its products. It enabled England to confront single-handed a united Europe in the long Napoleonic War. Later in the Victorian age proper, the British navy, a product of the Industrial Revolution, played a brief part in the suppression of the abominable slave trade, and enforced a Pax Brittanica on the high seas. At home the Revolution fostered by canals, toll-roads, railways, and the telegraph the easy and rapid transportation and communication that distinguishes Victorian and later times from preceding ages. Swift and easy communication is not always regarded as an unmixed blessing, but the popular outcry that arises when strikes cut it off today seems to show that it is now regarded as a necessity for the general rather than as a luxury for the rich. Only a few self-sufficient idealists like Thoreau would care to be transported back into the period so highly praised by Macaulay, much less into an earlier pre-Industrial Revolutionary age. And finally we may note that the worst abuses of the Revolution which provoked the anger of humanitarian Victorians were, if not abolished, at least checked by the advance of democracy.

Chapter II

The Advancing Democracy

A characteristic mark of the Victorian age differentiating it from earlier periods of English history and linking it to our own time, is the slow but steady advance of democracy. It may be well before proceeding to establish a more or less acceptable conception of the meaning of this often used and little understood word. It has, we know, different meanings in different lands today. Democracy means one thing in Soviet Russia and the satellite countries, quite another thing in the Western world. The adjective democratic has taken on a wide and variable sense. We speak, for example, of a democratic way of life, or of a politician's democratic manners with some vague general sense of "unostentatious," "popular," or, in the politician's case, "easy-going," "affable."[1] Perhaps a glance at the etymology of the

[1] A modern historian, Muller, in *Uses of the Past*, defines democracy as "an agreement on the right to disagree peaceably about religious or any other belief." It might be noted, however, that a democratic government at Athens put Socrates to death because of his alleged difference from the received religious belief.

word may help to a better understanding of its true meaning.

Democracy is an English spelling of the Greek *demokratia*, a compound of *demos* and *kratos*. *Demos*, originally meaning "country folk," peasantry, came in the Greek city states to mean the common people entitled to participate in the government, the *populus* as distinguished from the gentry, as in the Latin formula, *Senatus Populusque Romanus*. This *demos* did not include all residents in the city state; slaves, women, and alien residents were, of course, excluded.[2] It was, in fact, a sharply restricted body, but it at least included poor men as well as the rich, the common man along with the noble. The Greek *kratos* means first "strength," then "power" or "sovereignty," and *demokratic* meant a government where supreme power or sovereignty resided in the people, or as Blackstone states it, "a government where the right of making laws resides in the people at large."

Ancient democracy, of course, differed widely from its modern form. In the city state laws were made, decisions for war or peace were taken, by the direct vote of the *demos* assembled for that purpose. Something of this sort survives in our "town meetings" where the assembled citizens of a small community vote on local affairs. With the change, however, from the old city state to the modern nation state, such direct control of government became impossible, and its place was taken by "representative government," *i.e.* by "representatives" chosen by qualified citizens to speak for them in a national assembly such as the Congress of the United States. A most important question, of course, is what citizens are legally *qualified* to choose their representa-

[2] Pericles, the leader of Athenian democracy, excluded all who were not born of a citizen father and a free born Athenian mother.

tives. It is on this point, indeed, that the debates on the three Reform Bills in the Victorian age turned. The "advance of democracy" consisted essentially in enlarging the number of qualified citizens by giving the vote to those who formerly could not claim it, in other words by enlarging the *demos*.[3] This was a gradual approach to Lincoln's conception of democracy, a government not only *for,* but *by* the people. In this chapter, henceforth, the word *democracy* will be used only in the political sense.

Whatever we may call the government of England before 1832, it is plain that it was in no sense a democracy. It has been called an aristocracy, but this is a misleading term. Who were the ruling aristocrats? The probable answer would be the well-born English gentry, but this would ignore the presence among the rulers of many merchants and manufacturers, whose wealth enabled them to buy landed property and so to join the ruling class, before 1832 strictly limited to land owners.[4]

The actual rulers of England were the members of the House of Commons; their will became the law of the land. It was checked in theory by the power of the King (p. 4) and in practice by the right of the House of Lords to amend or even to reject a bill passed by the Commons. Actually this right was not often exercised; Wellington who knew successive Parliaments declared: "Nobody cares a damn for the House of Lords; the House of Commons is everything in England and the House of Lords nothing!"

The House of Commons consisted of about 600

[3] The first Reform Bill, 1832, added about a quarter of a million voters to the pre-existing electorate. Figures for later additions are given on pp. 68 and 94.

[4] Brian Newcome, for example, was not wellborn, but he bought land, became a member of Parliament and so one of the voters.

THE ADVANCING DEMOCRACY

members chosen by the vote of properly qualified electors.[5] Generally speaking each English county was represented by two members; each borough, *i.e.* each recognized English town, also by two. By far the largest number of members came from the boroughs, and in spite of the great changes in the distribution of the population already referred to (p. 12), the boroughs had remained unchanged since the time of Charles II, 1660.

The right of an adult male Englishman to vote for his representative depended before 1832 mainly upon his financial status. In the counties the franchise was possessed only by "free-holders," *i.e.* by owners of landed property worth forty shillings *per annum* in rental value; in the boroughs there was a wide variety of qualifications, but in the main it too depended upon the citizen's status. Boroughs were classed as "open" or "closed." In the "open" the elector had the nominal privilege of voting for the man of his choice; in the "closed" he was bound to vote for the candidate supported by the local magnate. Closed boroughs were in fact regarded as private property and were advertised and sold like real estate.[6] Absurd as this system of the closed borough seems, it had the advantage of giving a seat in the Commons to a clever young man, unable to meet the heavy costs of an election, if he were lucky enough to obtain the patronage, and so the nomination, of a closed borough's owner.[7] The brilliant

[5] A brief description of the strangely varied qualifications of the elector is given above (p. 9).

[6] In 1830 the average price of a "closed" borough with secure tenure for the duration of a Parliament was reckoned at about £6,000.

[7] The cost of a contested election in an "open" borough was at times enormous; figures running up to thousands, and even to hundreds of thousands, of pounds are given in Christie's *Transition from Aristocracy*, p. 23.

young Macaulay, for example, got his first seat in the Commons as the representative of a "closed" borough belonging to the Whig Lord Lansdowne; and Peel, the Tory, entered Parliament as the representative of an Irish borough owned by his wealthy father.

Theoretically the House of Commons was a representative body elected to execute the will of the people; actually it was nothing of the sort. In the first place the qualified voters were so few compared with the adult males as to make them incapable of expressing the will of the mass of the people. In the second place these few voters were by no means free to choose their representative. Even in the "open" boroughs, with a few exceptions, the voters were controlled by the influence, often by the shameless bribery, of the local magnate, always a great landlord. Voting in the old parliamentary elections was *viva voce*, or by show of hands, so that the voter's choice was known and controllable. The secret ballot, so familiar to us and actually practised in at least one American colony before the Revolution, was unknown and indeed distrusted in England till after the Second Reform Bill, 1867. The only genuine parliamentary contests were those where two local magnates contended for power.[8]

It seems plain that the government of England before 1832 was an *oligarchy*, the rule of the few, and these few were, with occasional exceptions, the landlords of England. What, then, induced this oligarchic House of Commons to insist, in the face of the King's dislike and the bitter opposition of the Lords, upon a radical change in their own composition? The action of the House in passing the Reform Bill in 1832 dealt a fatal blow to the existing

[8] Cf. p. 9 on the long and costly struggle to control parliamentary elections in Cumberland.

oligarchy and took the first short step toward the democracy that governs England today. Yet this action was not taken because of belief in the virtue of democracy. The Tories, of course, were well satisfied with the *status quo* as was shown by the statement of their leader, Wellington, in 1830.[9] The Whigs, on the other hand, long hesitant in the cause of parliamentary reform, abhorred the very idea of democracy. Burke, their prophet, had denounced "a perfect democracy as the most shameless thing in the world," and even Macaulay, the spearhead of the drive for reform, believed that "purely democratic institutions must sooner or later destroy liberty or civilization or both." It was no belief in democracy as such that finally pushed the Whigs into action, but a growing and even passionate demand spreading through the nation, not so much for democracy, as for such a parliamentary reform as would enable the Commons to execute the will of the people.

Several causes contributed to build up this demand. A prime cause, perhaps, was the Industrial Revolution. This had built up great commercial cities, Manchester for example, in which there was not a single qualified voter because these cities were not recognized boroughs. In them, as in many smaller towns outside of the list of boroughs, successful merchants and intelligent workmen demanded the suffrage denied to them although enjoyed by shepherds who fed their flocks in the fields around the "borough" of Old Sarum. The absurd situation was revolting to the common sense of rational Englishmen.

A second and more immediately effective cause was the crying need of redress in social and economic conditions. The wretched condition of the urban and

[9] See Wellington's statement quoted above, p. 21.

the agricultural proletariat (pp. 12-13) was rapidly becoming intolerable. State interference to redress these conditions was demanded by a small but intellectually powerful body, the Benthamite Radicals, united for this purpose with the humanitarian Evangelicals. Hitherto remedial legislation had either been denied or amended to futility by a House dominated by the landed interest. It was becoming more and more apparent that the first necessary step forward socially was in the direction of parliamentary reform. Sweeping changes in the method of electing members of the House: universal, *i.e.* manhood suffrage, the secret ballot, and others were demanded by the radicals. It was plain, however, that no such changes would be accepted by the House, and it became necessary to concentrate upon a plan of reform that had at least a chance of acceptance. The First Reform Bill, drawn up by a committee of liberal Whig landlords, convinced their party that it could take a step which would identify it with the will of the people and enable it to enact the necessary reforms without opening the floodgates to democracy. It was fondly hoped by most good Whigs that this first would be the final step.

A third and perhaps a most potent cause was the fear of an impending proletariat revolution. Echoes of this fear can still be heard in the letters and diaries of the politicians of that day. The spectre of revolution haunted the minds of men, and there was a widespread belief that the monarchy and, indeed, the whole social order stood on the brink of an abyss. It is hard today to realize how general and, indeed, how well grounded this fear was. In twentieth century England the monarchy is revered, at times almost idolized; then, largely because of the character and behavior of the sons of George III (p. 5), it was either hated or despised. Today the

House of Commons is regarded as an efficient instrument for enacting the will of the people; then, quite naturally, it was looked on as the instrument of one class, the landed gentry, quick to pass corn laws and game laws in their interest, but stubborn to resist all demands for popular reform. And since neither the monarchy nor the Commons could be trusted, revolution seemed to many minds inevitable.

Yet the very idea of an impending revolution was dreadful. The horrors of the French "Terror" were still fresh in men's minds, and even in England the Gordon riot, 1780, had shown the terribly destructive power of the city mob.[10] And if revolution were to break out what was there in England in 1832 to stop it? Except in London there was no civic police capable of dealing with the mob. In default of police the army might be called on, as it had been to put down the Gordon riots, but the English army at that time was small, scattered about the country, and gravely suspected of disaffection. There was a growing sense, at least among the leading Whigs, of the imperative need to avert, rather than await, the dreaded revolution.

The French Revolution of 1830, which overthrew the Bourbon tyranny and established a popular monarchy, exerted a profound influence on contemporary English political thought. It shocked the Tories who saw in it only a rebellion against divinely ordained monarchy, but it inspired the Whigs with hope; France had shown that a revolution was possible without the civil war and atrocities of the earlier period. It stiffened the determination of the Whigs to push through a revolutionary parliamentary reform to prevent a proletariat revolution. This note of prevention is heard most clearly in Macaulay's

[10] See the vivid picture of the sack of London by the mob in Dickens' *Barnaby Rudge*.

speech, March, 1831, during the debate on the Reform Bill. It is an impassioned plea to the House to act while there was still time, not to wait for "the last paroxysm of popular rage," and he warns his hearers that a rejection of the Bill may lead to "the dissolution of the social order."

Such seem to have been the main causes of the action by which in 1832 the House of Commons radically altered its composition, changing it, if not to a democratic assembly, at least to one more representative of and responsible to the will of the people.[11] It is hard to imagine an unreformed House yielding to popular demand and repealing the Corn Law (p. 30) which was believed to be essential to the interest of the landed gentry.

The Reform Bill of 1832, the first step toward a democratic government of England, was not passed without a bitter struggle; an account of the debate in the Commons, of the refusal of the Lords to accept it, and of their final submission has already been told (p. 21). Once passed, however, it was accepted even by the Tories, and the House promptly proceeded to enact several much needed social reforms. There was a general feeling in Parliament that the goal had been attained, and Lord John Russell, the main author of the Bill, got the nickname of "Finality Jack" from his expressed conviction that no further action was needed. As a matter of fact the Victorian compromise in the extension of the suffrage embodied in the Bill lasted for more than a generation.

Yet there could be nothing like a real democracy in England so long as the great majority of the working class remained without the vote. The dissatisfaction of the workers and their determination

---

[11] For the composition of the first House elected after the passage of the Bill, see above (p. 25).

THE ADVANCING DEMOCRACY

to obtain a share in the government found expression in the Chartist movement of the late thirties and the forties. An account of the rise of Chartism and of its collapse in 1848 has already been given (pp. 31-4).

In the eighteen fifties England was at once too prosperous at home and too occupied with the Crimean War and the Sepoy Mutiny abroad to consider seriously any further parliamentary reform. Toward the close of the decade, however, the question was again raised. It is interesting to note that it was Disraeli, shrewdest of Victorian politicians, who in 1859 introduced the first of a series of new reform bills. His suggested extension of the suffrage was, it appears, premature. Even Gladstone, later the champion of democracy, declared the time unripe for a new measure of reform. By 1864, however, Gladstone himself felt that the time had come and declared that every man "not presumably incapacitated," was entitled to the vote. Accordingly, when he became leader of the House in 1866, he introduced a new and liberal reform bill; but after a hot debate it was rejected by a combination of old-fashioned Whigs and stand-pat Tories. This failure led at once to a widespread and threatening popular agitation for reform which gave Disraeli his opportunity. Once more Prime Minister, he introduced and by skillful political management succeeded in passing the Second Reform Bill, 1867. There was no such division along party lines in the Commons as in 1832, and the Tory Lords accepted the Bill without a struggle. It was, in fact, another Victorian compromise, but this time there was no feeling of "finality" in the measure and within a comparatively short time another reform bill was called for.

In the meantime, however, the Ballot Act of 1872 marked another step in the advance of democracy.

It is characteristic of English conservatism that this method of voting which secures the voter from intimidation at the polls was so long delayed. It had been one of the main demands of the Chartists and is regarded today as a prime necessity in popular elections. Yet it was not until the high tide of social and political reform in Gladstone's first administration (p. 75) that it became possible to enforce it by law.

The Reform Bill of 1884 marks the third and final step in the advance of democracy in the Victorian age. This bill, like the earlier ones, was preceded by popular agitation for reform, but this time without the threat of revolution that was heard in 1832 and in a less degree in 1867. The agitation was especially in behalf of the farm laborers left voteless in 1867. Of them, Chamberlain, a keen contemporary observer, declared that they were "the worst paid, the worst fed, the worst clothed, and the worst housed peasantry in the civilized world."[12] They had at last come to realize that only by obtaining the franchise could they secure legislative redress, and as early as 1872 the Agricultural Laborers Union was founded to push their claims. In the early thirties an attempt to organize farm labor had been crushed with cruel severity by a Whig government (p. 13), but times had changed, and this Union was not only permitted, but encouraged, especially by the powerful trade unions interested at this time in securing the franchise also for the still voteless miners.

[12] By way of contrast, Charlotte Brontë — *Jane Eyre,* chap. 34 — calls "the British peasantry the best taught, the best mannered, the most self-respecting of any in Europe." Both statements may be true; Miss Brontë is writing of *women* in the northern hills of England, Chamberlain probably of workers in the Midlands near the great commercial towns.

Gladstone himself introduced the Third Reform Bill, asserting as he did so his belief that the largest possible number of "capable" citizens should have the right to vote. There was, however, one body of citizens that was still to be excluded; a plea in the Commons for Woman Suffrage was killed by Gladstone's emphatic refusal to consider it. Probably he considered women "incapable" citizens. The debate in the Commons on this bill was characterized at the time as "languid." There was a general feeling that a further extension of the franchise was a logical and even necessary consequence of the act of 1867, and the Bill passed the House with little opposition. It was held up for a time by the Lords until the government would promise a redistribution of electoral districts, a measure really demanded by the shift in population since 1832 when the First Reform Bill had arranged them. The delaying action of the Lords provoked an outburst of popular resentment (p. 94), but the matter was soon settled and the Bill became law in December, 1884.

The immediate result of this Third Reform Bill was a great addition to the number of qualified voters. Exact figures vary, but Trevelyan states that this act added more voters to the electorate than the two earlier Bills put together.[13] Whatever the number, the result satisfied the Victorian demand for democracy. It was not until a new world had been created by World War I that the Fourth Reform Bill, 1918, gave England what was practically Manhood Suffrage and granted the vote to a small number of supposedly qualified women. The Fifth Reform Bill, 1928, gave women the vote on the same terms as men. These acts are, of course, outside the scope of this brief account of the advance of democracy in the Victorian age. It is certain, however, that

[13] Cf. the figures given above (pp. 68, 94, and 124).

the 1884 addition to the electorate of great numbers of working men soon resulted in the election of more and more representatives of labor in the House of Commons and made possible the rise of the Labor Party, founded in 1906, which in 1924 assumed the government of England. Since that time political opinion in England has been sharply divided between the Conservative and the Labor Party. The Liberal Party of today is a mere shadow of its Victorian strength. It is, indeed, one of the ironies of history that the law enacted by the greatest of Victorian Liberals should after his death have become the means of destroying the party he so often led to victory.

It would, of course, be wrong to say that popular education in England was a result of advancing democracy. There had always been schools of various sorts in England, and, as a result of the religious revival of the eighteenth century, their number had greatly increased. These schools, however, were all voluntary, supported by voluntary contributions and expecting only voluntary attendance. There were schools conducted by the state church and schools for dissenters, but together they included only a small fraction of the children of school age. The state took no interest whatever in popular education until after the passage of the Reform Bill of 1832. Indeed it is characteristic of governmental indifference that in 1807 a bill providing for the support of primary schools by means of taxes was amended out of purpose by the then oligarchic House of Commons and was rejected altogether by the Lords. In 1832, however, after the first step toward democracy, the state began to show interest in education by making money grants to these voluntary schools; in 1839 it took a further step by insisting on state inspection of these schools to see whether the grants were being properly used.[14] With this for nearly a generation the state's interest in popular education rested. It was not till after the Second Reform Bill, 1867, that the next step was taken in the Education Bill of 1870. It had now become evident that as government was becoming democratic it was a prime necessity to make the *demos* capable of governing; the phrase, "We must educate our masters," seems to have been the inspiring motive in the passage of this bill. Action was all the more necessary since it appeared that about half the children in England, many of them, no doubt, prospective voters, were without any education whatever.

Like most public acts in the Victorian age this bill was a compromise. Radical thinkers demanded state support of a primary education that should be non-sectarian, compulsory, and free. Such action was at that time impossible, but the Bill did something to advance the cause. In fact, like the Second Reform Bill, it took steps which necessitated further steps as a logical and necessary conclusion. It enlarged the grant to Church schools to bring them up to the mark; it founded new schools in districts where none had hitherto existed; it put these new schools under the control of a board elected for that purpose; it forbade the teaching in them of denominational religion; it allowed, though it did not oblige, a board to demand compulsory attendance; and, most important of all, perhaps, it financed these "board" schools by local taxes.[15] While education in these schools was not absolutely free, the cost was trifling, and a poor child could learn the three R's gratis.

[14] It was in this business of school inspection that Matthew Arnold was so long engaged.
[15] Hence the English term "board schools," equivalent in a general way to American "public" schools.

In short this bill paved the way for a further advance in a "democratic" system of primary education. Ten years later, 1880, a bill was passed with little opposition — cf. the debate on the Third Reform Bill (p. 94) — which made attendance compulsory, and so obliged the children of the now enfranchised workers to qualify as future voters. Finally after the Third Reform Bill, 1884, a Tory-Unionist government provided *free* education in both board and church schools. At last what radicals had long demanded was attained, and primary education in England became compulsory, free for all, and, at least in board schools, non-sectarian. If state controlled education was not the immediate result of advancing democracy, at least it followed its advance step by step.

The advance of democracy in the Victorian age had, of course, a marked effect upon the literature of the time. Strange as it may seem to us, the attitude of Victorian literature to democracy is, in the main, rather reactionary than propagandist. We must, however, distinguish between the cause of social reform and that of democracy as defined above. All the great Victorians are champions of social reform from Carlyle with his toast placed in the mouth of Teufelsdröckh, *Die Sache der Armen,* to Morris' prophecy of a coming day "when all shall be better than well."[16] When, however, it comes to democracy, *i.e.* government not only *for,* but *by,* the people, the great Victorians are at best hesitant, at worst frankly and even angrily inimical. They regard democracy as probably inevitable but certainly dangerous and propose various measures for controlling and directing it.

Carlyle, for example, offers Hero Worship, culminating in the leader, or Führer, principle, later

[16] *Poems by the Way,* 1891.

THE ADVANCING DEMOCRACY 137

applied with such disastrous results in continental Europe. In a happier mood he suggests government by "Captains of Industry," apparently "Big Business" converted from private to public gain.[17] Ruskin, Carlyle's disciple, is even more outspoken in opposition. "I am," he begins his autobiography, "a violent Tory of the old school (Walter Scott's school ... and Homer's)."[18] His "only hope of prosperity for England is in discovering and obeying men capable of kinghood." By way of practical experiment he founded St. George's Guild, "an aristocracy electing an absolute chief as Dictator," to whom absolute obedience was the first condition of membership in the Guild.

Arnold, younger and more modern-minded than Carlyle or Ruskin, was more hopeful of the future. He speaks, indeed, of "the encroaching spirit of democracy," but believes that the movement of democracy is an operation of nature which merits neither blame nor praise. Yet he fears that with the growth of democracy "the English people may become *Americanized;*" he italicizes the word to bring out, perhaps, its abhorrent quality. To prevent this dire result he relies on the action of the state; *i.e.* "the nation in its collective and corporate character" — a somewhat cryptic utterance of Burke's, which he elaborates by insisting on "culture" as a means of humanizing man in society and by looking for salvation in a humanized "remnant."

John Stuart Mill is the most democratically minded of the great Victorians, but even Mill feared the dangers attending an unchecked democracy. His

[17] *Past and Present,* Book IV, chapter IV. It would be interesting to compare Carlyle's chapter, *Democracy,* Book III, chapter XIII, with Arnold's essay of that name in *Mixed Essays.*
[18] It might perhaps be noted that neither Scott nor Homer had any experience with democracy.

Representative Government, 1861, insists that the people, the *Demos,* cannot and, in fact, do not *govern,* but can only choose their governors, a condition widely different from the democracy of ancient Athens. Mill's *On Liberty,* 1859, is an immortal plea for individual freedom, threatened now by the danger of a tyrannical majority, a tyranny more to be dreaded, because less resistible, than that of a single tyrant.

It is interesting to compare the attitude of William Morris, youngest of the great Victorians, with those of his elders. He confessed that in the early days Ruskin had been his master, but he soon became a "practical Socialist," preaching the gospel of Socialism in speech and writing. Yet he abhorred the idea, advanced, for example, in Bellamy's *Looking Backward,* of a bureaucratic state Socialism; on the contrary he looked forward to a proletariat revolution which would end the state and establish a society without government and without laws, where all good things were held in common. This, of course, is far from the Victorian, or any other, concept of democracy. It is not, perhaps, too much to say that while Morris retained the idea of a *Demos,* a body which would include women and even children, he utterly rejected the idea of *Kratos,* or sovereignty. In his utopian dream mastery has given place to fellowship.

Various as were the attitudes of the great Victorians toward democracy, they were in the main united in their distrust, often indeed in their scorn, of the Victorian instrument for effecting the will of the people, Parliament and parliamentary government. Carlyle's great hero had sent Parliament packing; the dreamer in *News from Nowhere* sees the Houses of Parliament converted into a receptacle for the city's dung. It is, perhaps, worth noting that the strongest expressions of this distrust are heard before the passage of the Second Reform Bill. They voice the same dissatisfaction with the Victorian compromise of the First Reform Bill that found popular expression in the Chartist movement. After 1867 and the various reforms, political, social, and educational that followed there is less heard of this impatient discontent.[19] Yet a survey of the whole field of Victorian literature reveals at a glance that there is no ardent champion of democracy among the great Victorians, no such inspired singer of its present achievement and future glory as Walt Whitman. The true apostles of democracy in Victorian England are popular journalists like Cobbett, popular orators like John Bright, names worthy of remembrance, but hardly stars in the galaxy of English literature.

[19] An exception must, of course, be made for William Morris, who was impatient of anything but a complete social revolution.

Chapter III

The New Science

A third force which differentiates the Victorian age from earlier periods and links it more closely with our own is the impact of science upon the life, material and mental, of that age. The nineteenth century has been called "the century of science," and the Victorian age covers the greater part of that century. It is in the Victorian age, moreover, that the impact of science upon English life and thought was most widespread and profound.

It may be well to attempt here a more or less exact definition of the familiar, but often misunderstood, word, science. The word "democracy," discussed above, (p. 122) has come in popular usage to have a wide, vague, and, at times, contradictory significance; the word "science," on the contrary, has shifted in recent times to a somewhat restricted meaning. Derived from the Latin *sciere, i.e.* to know, its general meaning is knowledge, in particular the knowledge gained by study. A peasant's inherited knowledge of his plot of ground and of the ancestral tools with which he cultivates it could hardly be dignified by the term science. On the contrary the practice of a modern farmer, acquainted with the mineralogical character of his ground and tilling it with modern instruments, might properly be called "scientific agriculture." As this example shows, the terms "science" and "scientific" tend in popular usage to connote knowledge acquired by the study of natural and technical matters as opposed to knowledge derived from the study of philosophical, historic, and esthetic subjects. Such a limitation of meaning is shown by the practice of some American colleges in granting a degree of Bachelor of Science as opposed to that of Bachelor of Arts. But this is to restrict too narrowly the meaning of science. The field of science is not limited to the study of material and technical matters; it may, and in fact does, deal with things of the mind, with questions of art, history, philosophy, and religion. Science, indeed, might be somewhat loosely defined as knowledge acquired by a study of the true as opposed to the traditional, and the scientific attitude as the pursuit of truth as opposed to tradition. The impact of science upon Victorian life and thought represents a continuous departure from received, *i.e.* traditional, concepts and a strenuous effort to substitute for them ideas more closely allied to what was conceived as the truth. Some notion of the bitterness of this struggle may be caught in a phrase from a letter of Huxley's: there is "no reconcilement possible between free thought and traditional authority." The outcome of the struggle may be seen by a comparison of pre-Victorian England with England at the close of the century.

Pre-Victorian England, so vividly portrayed by Dickens in *Pickwick,* was the old world of stagecoaches, rural inns, and country squires; on sea of the wooden sailing ship. Travel and even internal communication was difficult and infrequent. Existence for all but the well-to-do was a constant struggle against crushing poverty. The mental and moral outlook on life was, on the whole, that fixed in the seventeenth century by the triumph of the Reformation. By the end of the century so much had changed that the observer looks upon a new world, a prelude, indeed, to our world of steam-travel, the automobile, and the airplane; a world of mass production and wide distribution of goods. The old dogmatic conception of life has, with a few exceptions, yielded to a freer, if at times hesitant, belief in man's own control over his future. There have, of course, been changes in England since 1900, but no such revolutionary alteration of life, material and mental, as that experienced by the Victorian age, and this revolutionary change was due in large part to the impact of science upon that period.

This impact of science upon English life really begins before the Victorian period. As has been pointed out above (p. 113), the Industrial Revolution in the eighteenth century was mainly due to technical inventions, especially to the use of steam power in manufacturing and commerce.

These technical inventions were gladly accepted by most Englishmen as forward steps in that "progress of humanity" which was an article in the conventional Victorian creed. The Great Exhibition in Hyde Park, 1851, was designed to proclaim to the world England's pre-eminence in material prosperity. Before this date, however, the first of the so-called "liberating sciences," that of geology, had challenged the conventional English outlook on life. At the beginning of the Victorian era, Englishmen, apart from a group of philosophical skeptics and a small number of avowed atheists, were conventionally orthodox. They regarded the Bible as the literally inspired word of God, and accepted the Seven Days of creation and the Fall of Man as historic facts. Huxley later noted that Milton's *Paradise Lost*, a book found in most English homes, had done much to strengthen popular belief in the Bible story. Bishop Ussher's chronology of the Old Testament, derived from the text of the Bible, and often printed in the margin, fixed the date of the creation at 4004 B.C., and was considered as accurate as a chronology of English kings. Lyell, in his *Principles of Geology*, 1830-33, was the first English scientist to challenge this view. His work went far to show that the age of the earth and man's life upon it far exceeded the brief period allotted by Ussher. From this it seemed to follow that the Bible narrative of the creation could no longer be accepted as historic fact, but Lyell, a conservative thinker, did not press his logical conclusions, and popular orthodoxy remained for a time unshaken.

The second of the "liberating sciences," biology, delivered its attack upon conventional orthodoxy somewhat later, but with considerably greater effect. Its revolutionary idea, evolution, *i.e.* the conception of organic life as due not to a series of special creations but to an orderly process of ascent from the lowest to the highest form, man, is inseparably connected with the name of Charles Darwin. Some vague idea of evolution, however, was in the air long before Darwin. His grandfather, Erasmus Darwin, declared in his *Zoonomia*, 1794-6, "the world has been evolved, not created: it has arisen little by little from a small beginning . . . and so has grown rather than come into being at an almighty word." But Erasmus was regarded as a skillful doctor and a verbose poet rather than as a man of science, and his "confession of faith" fell on deaf ears. A now forgotten, but once popular book—twelve editions appeared in twenty years—*Vestiges of the Natural History of Creation*, 1844, ventured to suggest that "organic creation . . . like the construction of the globe" . . . might be "a result of natural laws," the expression, the author put it, of the will of God. Darwin, who sharply commented on the inaccuracies of the *Vestiges*, thought nonetheless that it had done good service in calling attention to the subject and in dispelling prejudice.[1]

It remained for Charles Darwin to demonstrate the interrelation of various forms of organic life, to point out the transition of one form into another, and to show the cause of this transition in the "struggle for existence," and in the "survival of the fittest." This he did in his *Origin of Species*, 1859, a work that has become a classic in modern thought. Certainly no book so profoundly affected the Victorian outlook on life.[2]

It almost seems as if Charles Darwin (1809-1882) had been destined by heredity and instinctive desire to do the work that made him famous. A grandson of that student of nature, Erasmus Darwin, he neglected the prescribed studies in school and college and early developed a passion for observation and for collecting specimens in the field of natural history. He rejected the life of a clergyman and of a doctor, feeling himself unfit for either. On leaving Cambridge, his friendship with older scientists who had noted his diligent and conscientious habits of observation obtained him a position as naturalist on the ship *Beagle's* surveying voyage. His five-year tour of the world, 1831-6, gave him an unrivalled oppor-

[1] The evolutionary ideas expressed in certain parts of *In Memoriam*, 1850, show Tennyson's acquaintance with the popular conception of evolution in the mid-century. Much of the poem seems to have been written even before the publication of the *Vestiges*.

[2] At the end of the century when a careful poll was taken in England to determine the ten most influential books of the past age, the *Origin of Species* appeared on every list.

tunity for studying nature in various countries and climates. Incidentally it ruined his health; for forty years after his return, we are told, he never knew a single day of normal well-being. In spite of ill health he at once set to work to classify the notes taken on the voyage and to work out a logical explanation of the evolution of organic forms. This was a long and laborious task, its completion was hastened by his receipt, 1858, of an essay from a fellow naturalist, A. H. Wallace, who had hit upon Darwin's own theory of natural selection as the cause of the variation of species. Darwin arranged to have the essay published at once along with an abstract of his own conclusions, and in the next year he brought out his own finally completed work.

The Origin of Species was an instant success; the first edition was sold out on the day of publication. One reason, perhaps, for its popular success was that it seemed to believers in the creed of laissez-faire to justify their opposition to legislative attempts at social reform by showing that the survival of the fittest in the struggle for existence was a natural and unalterable law. On the other hand it provoked bitter opposition since it plainly implied, though it did not assert, the descent of man from lower forms of animal life, a denial of the orthodox belief in the special creation of man.

In addition to his clerical opponents Darwin was attacked by the skeptical, eccentric artist and author, Samuel Butler, 1835-1902, in a series of books, beginning with *Evolution Old and New,* 1879. Butler reverted to the then almost forgotten ideas of the French scientist, J. B. Lamarck, 1744-1829, whose conception of evolution was, to put it briefly, that new wants developed new organs in a creature. Butler's quarrel with Darwin's theory of "natural selection" was that it banished intelligence from the universe and substituted for it the operation of mere chance.³

Darwin's second great work, *The Descent of Man,* 1871, aroused less resentment than *The Origin;* by this time all but the most sternly orthodox had ceased to rail at him as a dangerous heretic. He continued to work and write for another decade, came to be recognized the world over as the foremost naturalist of the age, and at his death was honored by a burial in Westminster Abbey.

Much has been done since Darwin's day, especially by detailed laboratory research, to add to or modify his theory of natural selection. This is no place to discuss later variations of his theory of evolution, but it may be confidently asserted that Darwin laid the foundation of all later biological studies.⁴ His replacement of the conception of "special creation" by that of the continuous development of organic life from the lowest form to man, now generally accepted by thinking men, stands like a milestone marking a stage in the progress of man's attitude to the world about him and to human life.

While the controversy over evolution was still raging in England, a new attack was levelled at conventional orthodox theology. This took the form of historical, or as it was called in reference to its application to the Bible, the "higher" criticism. It was essentially a phase of the developing scientific spirit discarding tradition in the pursuit of truth. It began

---

³ Butler's ideas were scornfully rejected by contemporary scientists as those of an amateur, but they were later revived with what Shaw calls "the advent of the neo-Lamarckians." The reader might consult, perhaps with some degree of scientific skepticism, Shaw's *Preface* to his *Back to Methuselah.*

⁴ Butler, Darwin's lifelong opponent, repeated on hearing of his death what he had formerly written of him: "To the end of time, if the question be asked, 'Who taught people to believe in evolution?' the answer must be that it was Mr. Darwin."

THE NEW SCIENCE

in Germany with a critical study of the sources from which history, especially the history of early Rome, was derived. Niebuhr's epoch-making *Roman History*, 1827-8, showed that the generally received story of early Rome was not factual, but legendary, based at times upon lost ballads.

This attack upon tradition was welcomed in England. Niebuhr's work was translated into English in 1847-51; Thomas Arnold's unfinished *History of Rome*, 1842, and the *Preface* to Macaulay's *Lays of Ancient Rome*, show an English approach to the new scientific study of history.

In Germany, however, this new method soon progressed into a similar study of the Bible, more particularly of those books of the Bible upon which the history of the Jews was based. The text of the Old Testament was no longer regarded as an infallible revelation, but was subjected like the sources of secular history to a critical examination which threw grave doubts upon the factual truth of the biblical narrative.[5] This German shift in the object of historic criticism was at first neglected in England; it would seem indeed as if few English scholars were even aware of it.[6] Later, however, as it became better known, it was angrily attacked, since it evidently denied the received Protestant dogma of "verbal inspiration" of the Bible. An otherwise liberal clergyman, Dean Stanley, declared that "to speak of any part of the Bible as history was an outrage on religion." This opposition culminated in a religious persecution of English adherents of the new method;

[5] Ewald's *History of the People of Israel*, 1845-1859, represents, perhaps, the high water mark of this scientific study of Jewish history.

[6] George Eliot's translation of Strauss's *Leben Jesu*, 1846, seems hardly to have been noted. Browning in *Christmas Eve*, 1850, hears a German professor lecturing on the "Myth of Christ" and expresses his disagreement with the German's conclusions.

examples of this have already been noted, (p. 78). As late, indeed, as 1878, Robertson Smith, a noted popularizer of the higher criticism, was put on trial in ecclesiastic courts for heresy.

Little by little, however, the critical study of the Bible gained scholarly, if not general, acceptance. In 1880, we are told "it was still a heresy to accept the plurality of authorship of the *Book of Isaiah*; in 1890 to a growing group of church-students this has become an indubitable fact."[7]

From the scientific study of the historical books of the Old Testament the higher criticism proceeded to an examination of the New Testament, to a discussion of the sources of the Gospels, and a questioning of the authorship of the Epistles. Generally speaking the results of this examination have been assimilated by liberal theology. The essential truth of the character and mission of the founder of Christianity has emerged clearly from microscopic studies of the New Testament text. A contemporary historian, G. M. Young, attempting a "Portrait" of Victorian England, speaks of the "dethronement of ancient faith by natural science and historical criticism" as one of the two revolutions of that age. The "ancient faith" may indeed have been dethroned; it is no longer possible to prove a dogma by citing, as Bunyan, a typical representative of oldtime orthodox theology, always did, a text of the Old or the New Testament. The Bible is no longer regarded by intelligent readers as a single, sacred, and inspired book, but rather as a collection of many books written by

[7] How widely this new attitude toward the Bible has reached popular levels may be judged by the fact that in a book, *The Essentials of Bible History,* published in 1939 under the auspices of the Yale Divinity School and meant for use in schools and colleges, the author, himself a Professor of Bible History in an American college, dismisses the first chapters of *Genesis* as "folk-lore" rather than history.

many men in various ages, but all bearing witness to the development of religious ideas among a people, apparently peculiarly adapted to that end.

It has been customary to speak of the nineteenth century as a period of war between science and religion. If the term "popular orthodox theology" were substituted for "religion," the statement would, perhaps, be true. It might be noted that in Victorian days this "war" was waged mainly between the extremists: on the one side the fundamentalists who insisted on the verbal inspiration of the Bible and on the dogma derived from that book; on the other the thorough-going materialists who discarded both the form and the spiritual values of religion. Between them stood a body of moderates, liberals accepting the new teaching of science, yet determined to adapt it to a retention of the essentials of a faith in the life of the spirit.

Of these moderates Matthew Arnold is, perhaps, the most striking example. A keen critic of conventional orthodox theology, he was nonetheless a lover of the Bible. His *Notebooks,* recording day by day passages that contributed to his moral and spiritual life, are full of verses literally transcribed from the Bible, and at the height of his campaign against orthodox theology, he prepared a *Bible-Reading for Schools,* 1872. He was not content with the pragmatic morality that satisfied such agnostics as Huxley, but demanded something more, religion, or, as he put it, morality touched by emotion. A famous passage in his *Literature and Dogma* contrasts the bare morality of pagan authors with the emotional force in the sayings of Paul and of Jesus. Beside Arnold stood a quite different type, Charles Kingsley, orthodox clergyman and enthusiastic student of nature. He followed the controversy on evolution with keen interest, called Darwin "my dear and honored master," and declared that his work was "an addition to natural theology." Men like Arnold and Kingsley stood as mediators between the extremists, and it is largely due to them that there is as much of true religion in the world today as there was when the "war," long antedating the Victorian age, began.

The impact of science on the Victorian age was both prolonged and profound. In the beginning it promoted the Industrial Revolution and in so doing changed the whole external mode of English life; in the last period especially it affected traditional beliefs and thus modified man's outlook on life in general. It may indeed well be called revolutionary.

Part III

MAJOR AUTHORS OF THE AGE:

Biography and Collateral Reading

Matthew Arnold

1822–1888

Matthew Arnold, perhaps the most typically upper-middle-class writer of the Victorian age, was the second child and first son of Thomas Arnold, historian, liberal churchman, and headmaster of Rugby School. Matthew was born on December 24, 1822, at Laleham on the Thames River. At the age of fourteen he went to school at Winchester, and then to Rugby. In 1841 he entered Balliol College, Oxford, where he earned a scholarship, and in 1843, like Ruskin before him, won the Newdigate prize, with "Cromwell, a Prize Poem." As an undergraduate he had a reputation for foppish frivolity, but the basic seriousness of his nature brought him the attention of Benjamin Jowett and the friendship of Arthur Hugh Clough, who had been at Rugby with him. Arnold's degree in 1844 was an undistinguished second class, but a year later he won a fellowship at Oriel, one of the most coveted honors Oxford had to offer.

A trip to Switzerland and France followed, made

notable by seeing the great French actress Rachel in every performance she gave for two full months, and by his visit to George Sand, who found him a *"Milton jeune et voyageant."* Back in England in 1847 he became private secretary to Lord Landsdowne, the minister in charge of public education. His new position, although not lucrative, gave him easy access to the cultivated upper-class society in which he took such pleasure all his life. In 1848 he returned to climb the Swiss mountains again, and here he seems to have fallen in love with a French girl, the "Marguerite" of his "Switzerland" lyrics. Little is known of her save what can be inferred from the poems themselves.

His first volume of verse, *The Strayed Reveller, and Other Poems,* appeared in 1849 under the initial "A." Although it contained such favorite poems as "Resignation" and "The Forsaken Merman," the generally unfavorable tone of the reviews caused him to withdraw the edition after only a few copies had been sold. Another trip to Switzerland followed later that year, when he seems to have broken off completely the unhappy association with "Marguerite."

In 1851 Lord Lansdowne made him an inspector of schools, a post which wearied and harassed him for thirty-five years, but gave him sufficient financial security to be married a few months later to Frances Lucy Wightman.

His second volume of poetry, *Empedocles on Etna, and Other Poems,* appeared in 1852, but it, too, was shortly withdrawn, this time to make way for another volume, *Poems,* 1853, the first published under his own name. For the 1853 edition he wrote a preface setting forth his own views on the nature and function of poetry and advising the poet to "choose great actions" and "study the ancients."

Much of the best from his earlier books was reprinted in this volume, besides new poems like "Sohrab and Rustum," "The Scholar-Gipsy," and "Requiescat." Critical and popular reaction was warmer this time, as it was for *Poems, Second Series*, 1855, among which were "Balder Dead" and "Separation."

His old University recognized his growing reputation by electing him Professor of Poetry at Oxford in 1857. The duties were slight, involving only two or three lectures a year on any subject he might choose within the dominion of poetry, and he was, of course, free to continue his work as inspector. Arnold held the chair for two terms of five years each; during this time his attention turned increasingly to the criticism of poetry rather than to writing it. He did, however, publish his metrically experimental, classical-style tragedy, *Merope*, in 1858, and *New Poems*, 1867, which contained "Dover Beach" and the elegies on his father and Clough, "Rugby Chapel" and "Thyrsis." There were subsequent editions of his poems, but this volume, the most popular he ever produced, really marked the end of his creative period in poetry. He wrote poems only occasionally after that time, and his chief work was as critic of literature, education, morals, and culture for his countrymen.

His literary criticism began with the preface to *Poems*, 1853. *Essays in Criticism* appeared in 1865. Many of his lectures at Oxford were published, including *On Translating Homer*, 1861, and *On the Study of Celtic Literature*, 1867. Trips to the Continent in his official capacity as inspector of schools resulted in *Popular Education of France*, 1861, and *Schools and Universities on the Continent*, 1868.

With the close of his Oxford career, Arnold began a full-scale attack on the cultural complacency of the middle class and the religious dogmatism of the nation, with *Culture and Anarchy*, 1869, part of which had already appeared serially in *Cornhill Magazine*. In this he used for the first time the phrases "sweetness and light," meaning beauty and intelligence, and "Philistines," referring to the smug middle class. A collection of satirical letters on British manners, written first for the *Pall-Mall Gazette*, was republished in 1871 as *Friendship's Garland*.

His attacks on conventional theology included *St. Paul and Protestantism*, 1870; *Literature and Dogma*, 1873; *God and the Bible*, 1875; and *Last Essays on Church and Religion*, 1877; the note of finality in the last title pleased his contemporaries, who welcomed his return to literary criticism.

Oxford had conferred the degree of D.C.L. on him in 1870, and in 1883 Gladstone surprised him with an annual pension of £250, which allowed him to retire three years later from the tiring work of his inspectorship. His lectures on a fairly successful tour of the United States, as an apostle of sweetness and light, were published as *Discourses in America*, 1885. He visited Germany in 1885 and returned to America in 1886 to visit his daughter, who had married an American. On April 15, 1888, while in Liverpool to meet his daughter arriving on a visit from America, he leapt over a wall and died suddenly of a heart attack.

BIOGRAPHY AND CRITICISM

There is no satisfactory biography of Arnold. The best insight into his personal life is to be gained from *The Letters of Matthew Arnold to Arthur Hugh Clough*, ed. Howard F. Lowry (London and New York, 1932) and *Letters of Matthew Arnold, 1848-*

1888, ed. George W. E. Russell (2 vols., London, 1895). E. K. Chambers, *Matthew Arnold: a Study* (Oxford, 1947) has much interesting biographical information, but the narrative is broken into separate periods. A good study of Arnold's work is by Lionel Trilling, *Matthew Arnold* (New York, 1939).

PRINCIPAL WORKS

The Strayed Reveller, and Other Poems	1849
Empedocles on Etna, and Other Poems	1852
Poems	1853
Merope. A Tragedy	1858
On Translating Homer	1861
Essays in Criticism	1865
On the Study of Celtic Literature	1867
New Poems	1867
Culture and Anarchy	1869
St. Paul and Protestantism	1870
Friendship's Garland	1871
Literature and Dogma: an Essay towards a Better Apprehension of the Bible	1873
Mixed Essays	1879
Discourses in America	1885
Essays in Criticism, Second Series	1888

A reasonably complete collected edition is *The Works of Matthew Arnold*, Edition de luxe (15 vols., London, 1903-04). A convenient group of selections is included in *Matthew Arnold: Prose and Poetry*, Modern Student's Library, ed. Archibald L. Bouton (New York, 1927); most of the following suggested readings will be found there, as well as a carefully chosen group of Arnold's poetry. For Arnold's own choice of the poems by which he wanted to be remembered, see *Selected Poems* (London, 1878).

SUGGESTED READING

Poems, 1853:
   Preface (reprinted in *Irish Essays and Others*.)

Essays in Criticism:
   "The Function of Criticism at the Present Time."

Culture and Anarchy:
   "Sweetness and Light."
   "Barbarians, Philistines, Populace."
   "Hebraism and Hellenism."

God and the Bible:
   Preface.

Mixed Essays:
   "George Sand."

Discourses in America:
   "Literature and Science."
   "Emerson."

Essays in Criticism, Second Series:
   "The Study of Poetry."
   "Wordsworth."

Charlotte Brontë

1816-1855

Emily Jane Brontë

1818-1848

Charlotte and Emily Brontë were born in Thornton, Yorkshire, but they were undoubtedly of Celtic blood, for their mother came from Cornwall and their father was born in Ireland. Mr. Brontë, an eccentric and domineering clergyman, wrote and published several volumes of undistinguished religious verse and prose. In 1820 he moved his wife and six children to Haworth, a remote and gloomy village on the Yorkshire moors, where Mrs. Brontë died soon after. Her sister came to live at the parsonage to care for the children, but she was no substitute for their mother, and they grew up wild, independent children, devoted to each other and suspicious of outsiders.

Emily and Charlotte and their two elder sisters

were sent in 1824 to the Clergy Daughters School at Cowan Bridge; bad food and poor living conditions aggravated the ill-health of the two eldest girls, who were sent home in 1825 and died there. Charlotte used, and perhaps exaggerated, the horrors of Cowan Bridge in *Jane Eyre*. Emily and Charlotte were removed from school, and their lessons were resumed at Haworth in the company of their brother Branwell, an intelligent and promising boy a year younger than Charlotte, and their sister Anne, two years younger than Emily. The home teaching was sketchy, but the children read widely and wrote cycles of stories set in lands of their imagination.

In 1831 Charlotte went away once more to school, to Roe Head, where she stayed for a year. She returned to the school again in 1835 as an assistant teacher, taking Emily with her, but Emily's health declined as she silently and rebelliously yearned for the freedom of the moors of Haworth, and at last she had to be sent home. After a little more than two years Charlotte left Roe Head, and for the next three years she and Emily worked intermittently as teachers and governesses, the only occupations open to ladies of the time. In 1842 their aunt provided them with money to go to Brussels for nine months to study French in a fashionable school for young ladies, the Pensionnat Héger. Emily hated being away from home and returned to Haworth with joy at the end of their stay, but Charlotte consented to return to Brussels as a teacher the following year, 1843. Without Emily she was lonely, and after falling unhappily in love with her married employer, she left at the end of the year for which she had contracted.

All the Brontës scribbled poetry secretly, and in 1845 Charlotte found and read Emily's manuscripts. To judge by her later emendations of her sister's poems, Charlotte never completely understood them any more than she understood Emily herself, but she at least realized in them the presence of an untrammeled, mystical lyricism which she knew neither she nor Anne possessed. The poems were intensely personal, and Emily was furious at having them read, but after much persuasion she agreed to let Charlotte publish them. To Emily's poems Charlotte added some of her own and Anne's, and in May 1846 *Poems,* by Currer, Ellis, and Acton Bell (the pseudonyms they chose preserved their own initials) was published at the expense of the sisters. Only two copies were sold, and there were but three reviews of the little collection. After this each of the sisters began a novel. Charlotte's book, *The Professor,* based on her Brussels experiences, was refused by a publisher and was not published until after her death. Undiscouraged, she set to work on a new novel, *Jane Eyre,* which was published in August, 1847. This poetic, imaginative story of the love of a young governess for her married employer also has undoubted connections with Charlotte's experiences in Brussels. It was an immediate success with both readers and most of the critics. Emily and Anne had been more successful in getting their first novels accepted, and in December, 1847, a joint book appeared, containing Anne's *Agnes Grey* and Emily's only novel, *Wuthering Heights;* neither work attracted much attention. Like *Jane Eyre,* they were published under the sisters' pseudonyms. As inspiration in her masterpiece, one of the great works of genius in English fiction, Emily drew equally on her own emotional, introverted nature and on the wild and mysterious moorland around her for the story of the passionate Cathy and her savage lover Heathcliff, whose love lasts through their lives and beyond their death and burial in the quiet churchyard on the moors. Both *Jane Eyre* and the still greater *Wuthering Heights* brought to the novel an introspection and an intense concentration on the inner life of emotion which before them had been the province of poetry alone.

In September, 1848, Branwell, whose early promise had degenerated into drunkenness and sloth, died, and in December Emily died of inflammation of the lungs. Anne, who had published a second novel, *The Tenant of Wildfell Hall*, in 1848, failed rapidly after Emily's death, and six months later she died of tuberculosis.

For some years Charlotte continued to live with her father at Haworth, working at her writing. *Shirley*, 1849, was begun before the death of Emily, whose unconventional personality furnished Charlotte with the character for whom the book is named. The story is concerned with the Luddite mill riots in Yorkshire in 1807-12, the setting for which Charlotte knew from her schooldays at Roe Head. For *Villette*, 1853, she returned to her own sad days in Brussels for the tale of a beautifully passionate and tender affection between a plain schoolmistress and an irascible middle-aged professor.

All Charlotte's novels were successful, and she occasionally broke her Yorkshire seclusion for a visit to London, where she was something of a celebrity, once her real identity was known. Among the friendships she formed there was one with Thackeray, to whom she had dedicated *Jane Eyre*. She had several proposals of marriage, but she rejected them until the summer of 1854, when she married her father's curate, the Rev. Arthur Bell Nichols. Her health was already poor, and after a few months of marriage a cold which she caught during pregnancy brought about her death on March 31, 1855, at thirty-nine, the last of the Brontë children.

BIOGRAPHY AND CRITICISM

The strange and secluded life of the inhabitants of Haworth Parsonage has in recent years almost overshadowed their works, and this interest has been reflected in a flood of biographical works, many of them of dubious value. The official biography of Charlotte Brontë by her fellow-novelist, Mrs. Elizabeth Cleghorn Gaskell, *The Life of Charlotte Brontë* (2 vols., London, 1857), is one of the finest pieces of biography in the Victorian period, although it is naturally short on information about Emily, and what is there is somewhat distorted. Easily the most useful of modern biographies of the sisters is by Lawrence and E. M. Hanson, *The Four Brontës: The Lives and Works of Charlotte, Branwell, Emily, and Anne Brontë* (London, 1949), which is accurate, readable, comparatively short, and contains an excellent bibliography; its criticism is sound if somewhat subjective.

PRINCIPAL WORKS

Poems, by Currer, Ellis, and Acton Bell	1846
Jane Eyre. An Autobiography, edited by Currer Bell (3 vols.)	1847
Wuthering Heights. A Novel, by Ellis Bell, in 3 vols. with *Agnes Grey*, by Acton Bell	1847
Shirley. A Tale, by Currer Bell (3 vols.)	1849
Villette, by Currer Bell (3 vols.)	1853
The Professor. A Tale, by Currer Bell (2 vols.)	1857

SUGGESTED READING

Jane Eyre and *Wuthering Heights*.
Emily Brontë. Poems, ed. Philip Henderson (London, 1947), is the only selection of her poetry.

Robert Browning

1812–1889

Browning was born in South London on May 7, 1812; from his father, a clerk in the Bank of England, he inherited his love of music, painting, and poetry, as well as his magnificent good health and open, friendly nature. His mother was of mixed German and Scottish descent, a woman whom Carlyle called "the true type of a Scottish gentlewoman." Since he never attended either public school or university, most of his education was given him at home by tutors. His early poetic enthusiasm for Byron disappeared after he discovered a copy of "Queen Mab" on a bookstall; from that day he became a devoted admirer of Shelley, and later of Keats. By the time he was seventeen he had rejected the career of musical composer in favor of that of poet, and fortunately his approving father could provide him with an allowance, for it was not until he was over fifty that his poetry became at all popular.

His first published poem, *Pauline*, which appeared anonymously in 1833, was subtitled *The Fragment of a Confession*. It was immature, and obviously indebted to Shelley, to whom it carried an invocation, but it foreshadowed Browning's interest in the dark places of a disturbed mind. Except for one or two favorable reviews, it sank without a ripple and was never republished until its author had become famous, and he then acknowledged it with "extreme repugnance."

In the two years following the publication of *Pauline,* Browning travelled on the Continent, visiting St. Petersburg and making his first trip to Italy, "the land of lands" and the country where he lived much of his later life; the subjects of many of his best poems were furnished by his knowledge of Italian life and character. Back in England he published *Paracelsus* under his own name in 1835. This study of a Renaissance alchemist of passionately inquiring intellect caught on with the public somewhat better than did *Pauline,* and it served at least to attract the attention of men of letters of the day, including the great actor Macready. Browning's poetic interest was turning steadily toward drama, and when Macready asked him for a tragedy, he wrote *Strafford,* which held the stage for several days in 1837. Although he wrote several more plays in the next decade, of which *A Blot in the 'Scutcheon* was the most successful, it was clear that his gifts were not for the theater. The slight reputation he had already gained was ruined with the publication in 1840 of *Sordello,* for the complicated plot of the poem and the difficulty of its diction baffled and annoyed both critics and public. Although Browning's style became simpler in later years, it had a frequently elliptical compression, and for a long time he was thought to be unreadable by the general public, who remembered him as the author of *Sordello.*

In 1841 he began the publication of a series of

eight poetical pamphlets, sold for sixpence each, containing lyrics and plays; when completed, the entire series was issued in one volume, *Bells and Pomegranates,* 1846. The general title was meant to indicate "the mixture of music with discoursing, sound with sense, poetry with thought." The first pamphlet, *Pippa Passes,* now his most popular poem, had a cool reception, although a few readers realized that here was the voice of a new and fine poet. In the series first appeared the poetic form of which Browning was to become undisputed master, the dramatic monologue. Into it he could put all his intense study of the workings of the human mind, his innate feeling for the dramatic, and his mastery of the conversational idiosyncrasies which make a character's speech individual. Some of his most famous dramatic monologues appeared in the series, including "Soliloquy of a Spanish Cloister," "My Last Duchess," and "The Tomb at St. Praxed's."

The love story of the Brownings is one of the best-known in English literary history. In 1844 Browning had written to Miss Elizabeth Barrett to praise her poetry and had subsequently been introduced to and had fallen in love with her. Two years later, although she was an invalid (and several years older than he), she eloped with him from the house of her hostile father and went to Italy, where they lived in great happiness for the fifteen remaining years of her life and became the parents of one son. Both of them loved Italy, and their poetry, particularly that of Mrs. Browning, shows their sympathy with the cause of Italian liberation. During the years of their marriage Browning's major works were *Christmas Eve and Easter-Day,* 1850, a poem on the spiritual life of the Christian, and the two volumes of dramatic poems, *Men and Women,* 1855. Here his perfection of the dramatic monologue and his deep absorption in Renaissance Italy and its arts are reflected in poems like "Fra Lippo Lippi" and "Andrea del Sarto." A companion volume, *Dramatis Personae*, 1864, was published after Mrs. Browning's death, although most of its contents were written earlier. Poems like "Rabbi Ben Ezra" and "Caliban upon Setebos" show Browning's increasing preoccupation with philosophical questions.

When his wife died in 1861 Browning returned to England for the sake of his son, and for him he mastered his desire to live in solitude; he edited his wife's papers and plunged into the writing of his greatest work, *The Ring and the Book,* a poem in twelve books which he based upon a seventeenth century murder trial, the records of which he had found in a Florentine market-place in an old parchment-bound volume. As the characters in the poem give their versions of the story, it becomes apparent that what interests Browning in the trial is not its sensational qualities, but the search for truth in conflicting testimony, the development of human relationships, and the intuitive reaction of the noble individual against the evils of society. The poem, a huge receptacle for all Browning's ideas, is probably the finest long narrative poem of the Victorian age. It was published in 1868 and 1869, and with its publication Browning's slowly growing popularity finally matured, and he became, next to Tennyson, the most revered of English poets. During the later years of his life he was given honorary degrees by Oxford, Cambridge, and Edinburgh, and declined invitations to become rector of the universities at Glasgow and St. Andrew's; with mingled amusement and pride he saw Browning Societies spring up in England and America. He was at heart a gregarious man, and after he had recovered from the immediate shock of his wife's death, his friendliness and reputation combined to make him a familiar figure in London social and literary circles.

The advancing years brought no loss of vigor, and Browning continued a large and experimentally varied output. From 1871 to 1878 he wrote a series of poems on classical themes, and translations, inspired partly by his wife's love of Greek literature. Theology and philosophy formed the background of much of the poetry of his later life. Browning has been said to be a "half-Christian," believing always in the divine spark in man which he felt was best nourished by Christianity, although he had little faith in its historical basis. His conjectures on the problematical immortality of the soul are found in *La Saisiaz*, 1878. As the title indicates, the two series of *Dramatic Idyls* in 1879 and 1880 were a return to Browning's earlier manner. His last book, *Asolando*, published on the very day of his death, contained an assortment of lyrics, dramatic monologues, and more clearly philosophical poems.

Today the kind of optimism which Browning displayed has gone out of fashion; it has been called Victorian, but it might be defined more properly as a belief that an ever-present, beneficent power rules the world, and that this power is embodied in man in his struggle for dignity against the forces besetting him. Browning brought to English poetry a fascination with the grotesque, an abounding humor, and a love of fallible man that has hardly been equalled since Shakespeare.

The last few years of his life Browning lived chiefly in his beloved Italy to be near his son, although he avoided Florence, where his wife had died. After his death on December 12, 1889, at his son's palace in Venice, his body was returned to England for burial in Westminster Abbey.

BIOGRAPHY AND CRITICISM

The official biography is by A. L. Orr (Mrs. Sutherland), *Life and Letters of Robert Browning* (London, 1891), although it should be supplemented by W. Hall Griffin, *The Life of Robert Browning* (ed. H. C. Minchin, London, 1910). One of the most stimulating studies of the poet and his work is the entertaining, if somewhat opinionated, contribution to the English Men of Letters series by G. K. Chesterton, *Robert Browning* (New York and London, 1903). A brief biography, correlating Browning's life and works in a critical manner, is by Edward Dowden, *The Life of Robert Browning* (London, 1904). The most authoritative exegesis of the poet's thought is by Sir Henry Jones, *Browning as a Philosophical and Religious Teacher* (Glasgow, 1912). A handy skeleton outline of the poetry for the beginning student is by W. C. De Vane, *A Browning Handbook* (New York, 1935). For anyone interested in the love story of the Brownings, required reading is *The Letters of Robert Browning and Elizabeth Barrett Barrett, 1845-6* (2 vols., London, 1899).

PRINCIPAL WORKS

Pauline: A Fragment of a Confession	1833
Paracelsus	1835
Strafford: an Historical Tragedy	1837
Sordello	1840
Bells and Pomegranates	
Pippa Passes	1841
King Victor and King Charles	1842
Dramatic Lyrics	1842
The Return of the Druses	1843
A Blot in the 'Scutcheon	1843

Colombe's Birthday	1844
Dramatic Romances and Lyrics	1845
Luria; and a Soul's Tragedy	1846
"Introductory Essay" (prefixed to the forged Letters of Percy Bysshe Shelley)	1852
Christmas Eve and Easter-Day. A Poem	1850
Men and Women (2 vols.)	1855
Dramatis Personae	1864
The Ring and the Book (4 vols.)	1868–9
Balaustion's Adventure; including a Transcript from Euripides	1871
Prince Hohenstiel-Schwangau, Saviour of Society	1871
Fifine at the Fair	1872
Red Cotton Nightcap Country, or Turf and Towers	1873
Aristophanes' Apology; including a Transcript from Euripides: Being the Last Adventure of Balaustion	1875
The Inn Album	1875
Pacchiarotto, and How He Worked in Distemper; with other Poems	1876
La Saisiaz: The Two Poets of Croisic	1878
Dramatic Idyls	
First Series	1879
Second Series	1880
Jocoseria	1883
Ferishtah's Fancies	1884
Parleyings with Certain People of Importance in their Day	1887
Asolando: Fancies and Facts	1889

Among the many books of selections from Browning, one of the most complete and readily available is that by Simon Nowell-Smith, *Browning, Poetry and Prose* (London, 1950).

Thomas Carlyle

1795-1881

Thomas Carlyle, eldest and most vehement of the enemies of materialism in the Victorian era, was born in Ecclefechan in the Lowlands of Scotland, December 4, 1795. He was the son of a poor and pious Calvinistic stonemason and his poorly educated but kindly wife. Carlyle's early education was at the village school and at Annan Academy, and when he was fourteen he walked a hundred miles to Edinburgh to begin his studies for the ministry at the University. His four years as an undergraduate were lonely ones, and, despite diligent study, his only academic distinction was in mathematics. Gradually, too, in an atmosphere of rationalism his orthodox religious faith lessened.

In 1814 he left the University without a degree and tried his luck as mathematics master at his old school, Annan Academy. Without any real liking for teaching, he went from Annan to Kircaldy as schoolmaster in 1816, and there met Edward Irving, later famous as the founder of the sect called the Holy Catholic Apostolic Church. Irving opened his heart and library to Carlyle and became his first real friend. To him the unhappy young schoolmaster confided his dissatisfaction with his duties, and the misery of his religious doubt. At last Carlyle severed his slackening ties with the Church of Scotland and gave up all intent of becoming a minister. Although he had broken with orthodoxy, all that he ever wrote showed evidence of his basically religious nature.

In 1818 he went to Edinburgh again, this time to study for the law, which he later dropped, as he had forsaken teaching and the study of theology. For a time he did stultifying hack work for the *Edinburgh Encyclopaedia* and took pupils in mathematics. It was a period of utter despair from which he was suddenly rescued in 1821 by a spiritual rebirth, an instantaneous conversion which overwhelmed him in Leith Walk, Edinburgh. In *Sartor Resartus* he gives an account of the event as the "Baphometic Fire-baptism" of Teufelsdröckh. The temper of his misery was changed from "Fear or whining Sorrow" to "Indignation and grim fire-eyed Defiance."

For some time he had been interested in German literature, particularly in the writings of Goethe, for whose works and personality he had great reverence. His first original work, *The Life of Schiller*, appeared in the *London Magazine*, 1823-4, and the publication of his translation of Goethe's *Wilhelm Meister* followed closely. In 1824 the success of his writings led him to give up his position as tutor to the sons of the wealthy Buller family, the income from which had supported him for two years.

By 1826 he was able to support a wife, and in October he married Jane Welsh, the attractive and talented daughter of a well-to-do Scottish physician. Carlyle had met her five years before through Irving, who had once been her suitor. During the years of their courtship, a long and remarkable correspondence passed between Carlyle and Miss Welsh, whose drily witty letters are some of the best in the English language.

For two years after their marriage the pair remained in Edinburgh, where Mrs. Carlyle became hostess to a circle of the brilliant literary figures then living in the northern capital. Her husband, however, was restive, and he welcomed the change when they were forced by money troubles to move to Craigenputtock, a remote farm belonging to the Welsh family. From 1828 to 1834 they lived in rural seclusion, with Carlyle working hard at his writing, while his wife wore herself out physically in lonely domestic drudgery and wasted her intelligence on household tasks. Occasionally they had visitors, notably the young Emerson and Mrs. Carlyle's relative, Lord Jeffrey, founder and editor of the *Edinburgh Review,* in whose columns Carlyle's essays were appearing. The years at Craigenputtock were lonely but decisive in Carlyle's career. Here he turned to criticism of social and spiritual problems, and, in agony of soul, slowly finished his first great work, *Sartor Resartus,* which appeared serially in *Fraser's,* 1833-4. It is a grimly humorous assertion of his transcendental philosophy in answer to the eighteenth century rationalism prevailing in England.

At last even Carlyle wearied of the seclusion of Craigenputtock, and in 1834 he moved to London, to the Queen Anne house in Cheyne Row, Chelsea, which was his final residence and the one with which his name has ever since been linked. Life here was made difficult by financial troubles, so that Carlyle took to public lecturing, a task he loathed heartily; he stuck to it, however.

Sartor Resartus had only a limited success and was not even republished in England until it had made its way in the United States, but the publication in 1837 of the three-volume history of the French Revolution secured his reputation as a writer, although its sales were slow. Its writing was sadly complicated when he loaned the sole manuscript of the first volume to John Stuart Mill. A careless maid in a friend's house where Mill was visiting burned the sheets as waste paper. Carlyle accepted a small sum of money from Mill to help keep himself and his wife alive and painfully and heroically rewrote what had been destroyed.

The "condition of England question" prompted the publication of *Chartism*, 1840, and *Past and Present*, 1843. *Latter-Day Pamphlets*, 1850, was the last of his indignant examinations of England's social conscience until *Shooting Niagara: and After?*, 1867, warned against the extension of the suffrage in the Second Reform Bill. At the same time that he was interested in social criticism, he devoted an increasing amount of his time to biography and to the study of history as the record of great men. *Heroes and Hero-Worship*, a series of six lectures published in 1841, is his most explicit statement of this doctrine. He edited the letters and speeches of Oliver Cromwell in 1845, and after nearly fourteen years of distasteful research and writing, his enormous *Life of Frederick the Great* was published in six volumes between 1858 and 1865. One of his most polished books, on a smaller scale, was also in the field of biography, the serenely affectionate life of his young friend John Sterling.

Mrs. Carlyle's health had never been strong after their stay at Craigenputtock, and it deteriorated slowly until her sudden death in the spring of 1866, at the very time when her husband was in Edinburgh being installed as Rector of the University which he had attended. Carlyle was broken-hearted, although he had been far from a completely understanding husband. Their life together had been marred by bickering and misunderstanding, by their inability to express their real affection for each other, and by Carlyle's fervent but innocent admiration for Lady Ashburton. After his wife's death Carlyle lived in seclusion, torturing himself with regret for having misunderstood her. During his last years he wrote his own *Reminiscences* and, as a sort of expiation for Mrs. Carlyle's unhappiness while alive, prepared for publication *Letters and Memorials of Jane Welsh Carlyle,* which appeared after his death.

During the last decade and a half of his life Carlyle's gloomy fulminations were heard less frequently, although he had become — except, perhaps, for Tennyson — the most honored writer of the age, the patriarch of Victorian letters. When he died on February 4, 1881, the offer of burial in Westminster Abbey was refused in accordance with his own expressed wishes, and he was buried instead near his parents at Ecclefechan.

BIOGRAPHY

The most interesting biography is by James Anthony Froude, *Thomas Carlyle: a History of the First Forty Years of his Life, 1795-1835* (2 vols., London, 1882) and *Thomas Carlyle: a History of his Life in London, 1834-1881* (2 vols., London, 1884). Froude has been much criticized for his careless editing of Carlyle's papers; another long, carefully documented biography useful for reference and the correction of Froude's errors is by D. A. Wilson, *Life of Thomas Carlyle* (6 vols., London, 1923-34). The best short life is by Richard Garnett, *Life of Thomas Carlyle* (London, 1887). An excellent combination of biography and criticism is by Louis Cazamian, *Carlyle* (Paris, 1913); tr. E. K. Brown· (New York and London, 1932).

PRINCIPAL WORKS

The Life of Schiller, Comprehending an Examination of his Works	1825
Sartor Resartus: the Life and Opinions of Herr Teufelsdröckh Boston, 1836; London,	1838
The French Revolution: a History (3 vols.)	1837
Chartism	1840
On Heroes, Hero-Worship, and the Heroic in History	1841
Past and Present	1843
Oliver Cromwell's Letters and Speeches: with Elucidations (2 vols.)	1845
Latter-Day Pamphlets	1850
Life of John Sterling	1851
The History of Friedrich II of Prussia, called Frederick the Great (6 vols.)	1858-65
Reminiscences, ed. J. A. Froude (2 vols.)	1881

Of the several editions of the collected works, the most complete is *The Works of Thomas Carlyle*, Centenary Edition, ed. Henry D. Traill (30 vols., London, 1896-9).

SUGGESTED READING

Sartor Resartus:
- "The World in Clothes," I, 5
- "The World out of Clothes," I, 8
- "The Everlasting No," II, 7
- "Centre of Indifference," II, 8

"The Everlasting Yea," II, 9
"Organic Filaments," III, 7
"Natural Supernaturalism," III, 8

The French Revolution:
"To Arms!", I, V, 4
"Give Us Arms," I, V, 5
"Storm and Victory," I, V, 6
"Not a Revolt," I, V, 7
"Death of Mirabeau," II, III, 7
"Place de la Révolution," III, II, 8
"The Whiff of Grapeshot," III, VII, 7
"Finis," III, VII, 8

On Heroes, Hero-Worship, and the Heroic in History:
"The Hero as Poet. Dante: Shakespeare."
"The Hero as King. Cromwell, Napoleon: Modern Revolutionism."

Past and Present:
"Midas," I, 1
"Morrison's Pill," I, 4
"Plugson of Undershot," III, 10
"Labour," III, 11
"Reward," III, 12
"Democracy," III, 13
"Captains of Industry," IV, 4

Charles Dickens

1812–1870

Unlike most of the great Victorian writers Charles Dickens came of the lower middle class. He was born in Portsea on February 7, 1812, the son of a Navy pay office clerk whose lovable, improvident nature was later made famous in the person of Micawber. Charles' education was haphazard, but he supplemented it with constant reading, particularly of the eighteenth century novels in his father's small library. When Charles was still a child his father was transferred to London, where the expenses of a large family so overtaxed the resources of Mr. Dickens that he was at last committed to the Marshalsea, a debtors' prison. Charles, then twelve, was left to look after himself and, with the help of a relative, found a job pasting labels on bottles in a blacking warehouse. The shame of his poverty and the menial work which he did so haunted him that he later concealed this period of his life from the knowledge of his own wife and children.

Thanks to a legacy, Mr. Dickens was soon able to leave prison, and Charles returned to school for three more years. At fifteen he began working as a lawyer's office boy, studying shorthand and reading at the British Museum in his spare time. His skill at shorthand got him employment reporting debates in the House of Commons for the daily newspapers.

His first published sketch appeared in the *Monthly Magazine* in 1833, when he was twenty-one, and a series of his stories and sketches followed in that magazine and in the *Evening Chronicle;* they were collected in 1836 as *Sketches by Boz,* for which he took his pseudonym from a family nickname. In this year he married Catherine Hogarth, daughter of the owner of the *Evening Chronicle.*

At the time of his marriage he was writing a series of humorous stories to accompany illustrations of Cockney sporting life. The artist's death after the appearance of the first number left Dickens a freer hand to develop the richly comic adventures of the Pickwick Club in the English countryside. The sales of the *Pickwick Papers* were slow at first, but they jumped with the introduction into the story of the engaging Cockney servant, Sam Weller, and by 1837, when its publication in numbers was completed, Dickens at twenty-five had risen in a year from obscurity to a position of popularity unequalled in England before or since.

His industry was tremendous, and before *Pickwick* was finished, *Oliver Twist,* 1837-8, began to appear in a monthly magazine. This, his first true novel, has a carefully worked out plot, in contrast to the picaresque series of incidents in *Pickwick.* Its picture of the evils of the workhouses created under the New Poor Law (p. 26) and the descriptions of the criminal slums of London in which young Oliver lived brought Dickens a new class of serious reader interested in social reform. While *Oliver Twist* was still appearing Dickens started publishing *Nicholas Nickleby,* 1838-9. It begins as an exposé of the cruelty and neglect of boarding schools in Yorkshire, but it owes its vitality to the high spirits in which Dickens created such comic characters as the provincial theatrical troupe of Mr. Crummles, and Mrs. Nickleby, for whom Dickens' mother in her less agreeable moments furnished the model. All Dickens' major novels were published either in numbers, like *Nicholas Nickleby,* or in installments in magazines, which frequently accounts for the episodic quality of his work.

In 1840 Dickens began a weekly paper, *Master Humphrey's Clock,* patterned on the *Spectator* and *Tatler.* The readers' interests were less in the familiar essays than in the stories which Dickens was providing; gradually the paper became only the framework for the publication of two novels, *The Old Curiosity Shop,* 1840-41, and *Barnaby Rudge,* 1841. In the former the interest today is in the humorous characters, but Dickens' contemporaries loved the pathos of the sufferings and death of Little Nell, who was created in the image of Dickens' sister-in-law, who had died in 1837, and to whom he was devoted. *Barnaby Rudge,* his first historical novel, is set in the period of the Gordon anti-popery riots of 1780.

His first trip to America, in 1842, began with an enthusiastic and uncritical reception which slowly soured as Dickens began to speak out against slavery and the American publishers' piracy of English books. He, in turn, was disgusted by the crudeness of life and manners in America, and in particular by his own lack of privacy there. His *American Notes,* published on his return to England, provoked great resentment in the United States. In his next novel, *Martin Chuzzlewit,* 1843-4, he once more used his observations on the trip to draw the ludicrous characters of the American episodes of the book, and again there was trans-Atlantic protest. The novel is concerned with the evils of the love of money, but Dickens embroidered the tale with the humor of some of his most comic characters, such as the old nurse Sara Gamp and the hypocritical Pecksniff. His first and best Christmas book, *A Christmas Carol*, 1843, failed to sell as well as he expected. Both his family (he had five children by this time) and his expenses were increasing, so he spent 1844-5 in Italy to economize and to rest. He had always had a great love for the stage, and on his return to England he began to act in private theatricals, an activity which took increasing amounts of his time and overtaxed his energies. He returned to the Continent for several months in 1846, and in Switzerland began *Dombey and Son*, 1847-8, which was a great financial success; most critics, however, agree that this study of middle class pride and the decline of the merchant house of Dombey is hardly one of his best works.

David Copperfield, 1849-50, however, pleased everyone. Many of the events of its hero's childhood and his romance with Dora are clearly reminiscences of Dickens' youth. The mellow vein of memory provided a range of characterization he never surpassed, and such creations as the marvelous Micawber and the cringing Uriah Heep have made it the most perenially popular of his novels.

In March, 1850, Dickens began a weekly family magazine, *Household Words*, from which he excluded politics and anything which would shock his readers. The magazine sold well, and in it he printed many of his own works, as well as those of such writers as Mrs. Gaskell, Bulwer Lytton, and Wilkie Collins.

Bleak House, 1852-3, a satire on the abuses of the Court of Chancery, shows Dickens at his best in handling complex narrative and interlocking plots, but the prevailing mood of somberness was new to his readers. *Hard Times*, 1854, is an earnest attack on the vulgarity and materialism of the rising middle class industrialists. In *Little Dorrit*, 1855-7, the most vivid scenes are those in the debtors' prison, remembered from his father's stay in the Marshalsea; the satire on bureaucracy, however, the scenes on the Continent, and the contrived mystery woven into the plot show Dickens at his gloomiest and in his least successful vein.

His wife bore him ten children, and their marriage had been an amicable one even if there was no deep understanding between them. In 1857 Dickens seems to have fallen in love with a young actress, and the following year he announced his formal separation from his wife. The news shocked his readers deeply, and Dickens unwisely tried to defend his position publicly. Because his publishers, who controlled both magazines, refused to let him republish in *Punch* the defense which he had printed in *Household Words*, Dickens left them to start a new and similar magazine, *All the Year Round*. Its first number in 1859 contained the beginning of his historical novel of the French Revolution, *A Tale of Two Cities*. The story of redemption through devotion shows his ability at handling pure narrative, and it has always been one of his most popular novels, although it lacks his characteristic humor.

By this time his reputation was great. His concern for the oppressed poor, his sentiment (which sometimes slipped into sentimentality), his flair for narrative, often melodramatic, and, above all, his invention of comic character, combined to make him more popular than any other English novelist has ever been. His royalties were large, but the expenses of a big family, the upkeep of a country house, and his private philanthropy kept him pressed for money. After the separation from his wife, he began to give public readings from his works to increase his income. He had a natural talent for acting, and his reading tours were enormously successful, but the addition of this strain to his already heavy load of writing undermined his health.

Great Expectations, 1860-61, is told in the first person by Pip, a young man who learns through adversity to discard his own superficial snobbishness. Because of the unity of interest, centered on the chief character, and the credible quality of its romantic story, many critics have called it the best of his novels. Its immediate successor was *Our Mutual Friend,* 1864-5, which is set in the early 1860's, one of the few times when Dickens used a contemporary setting. The characterization is as carefully developed as any Dickens created, but the plot, centered on a young man who watches the effect of his supposed death upon society, is so loosely constructed that the book is hardly one of his major successes.

In spite of repeated warnings about his health, he continued his public readings. Late in 1867 he sailed for America, where he stayed four months. He and his hosts let bygones pass, he complimented the Americans on their progress, and they turned out in such numbers to hear his readings that he made nearly £20,000 on his tour. With his system dangerously weakened by his American trip he continued the high pressure of his readings on his return to England, until he was forced by his physician to stop. In the autumn of 1869 he began his last book, *Edwin Drood,* a mystery, of which the first number appeared in April, 1870. While working on the still unfinished story at his country house, Gads Hill Place, on June 8, 1870, he suffered a stroke of apoplexy and died a day later. After a funeral service which was as simple as possible to conform with his own wishes, England entombed her favorite novelist in Westminster Abbey.

BIOGRAPHY AND CRITICISM

Although the original biography by John Forster, *The Life of Charles Dickens* (3 vols., London, 1872-74) reflects perhaps too much of Forster himself and is too reticent on the subject of Dickens' marriage, it remains the standard from which other lives derive or depart; a one-volume edition with useful notes and introduction was prepared by J. W. T. Ley (London, 1928). The biography by A. W. Ward, *Charles Dickens* (London, 1882), in the English Men of Letters series, is a convenient, brief life; a more modern, if somewhat gossipy, study is by Una Pope-Hennessy, *Charles Dickens, 1812-1870* (London, 1945). A recent and authoritative biography is the admirable one by Edgar Johnson, *Charles Dickens; His Tragedy and Triumph* (2 vols., New York, 1952). The correspondence is published in the Nonesuch Dickens edition, *The Letters of Charles Dickens*, ed. Walter Dexter (3 vols., Bloomsbury, 1938). Perhaps the best criticism of his work is by George Gissing, *Charles Dickens* (New York, 1924).

PRINCIPAL WORKS

[Since practically all Dickens' works were published serially, the date of their publication in book-form is sometimes at variance with that given in the text for their original appearance.]

Sketches by Boz (2 vols.)	1836
The Posthumous Papers of the Pickwick Club	1837
Oliver Twist; or, the Parish Boy's Progress (3 vols.)	1838

The Life and Adventures of Nicholas Nickleby 1839
The Old Curiosity Shop 1841
Barnaby Rudge; a Tale of the Riots of 'Eighty 1841
American Notes for General Circulation
 (2 vols.) 1842
A Christmas Carol 1843
The Life and Adventures of Martin Chuzzlewit 1844
Dealings with the Firm of Dombey and Son 1848
The Personal History, Adventures, Experiences,
 and Observation of David Copperfield the
 Younger 1850
Bleak House 1853
Hard Times. For These Times 1854
Little Dorrit 1857
A Tale of Two Cities 1859
Great Expectations (3 vols.) 1861
Our Mutual Friend (2 vols.) 1865
The Mystery of Edwin Drood 1870

SUGGESTED READING

Pickwick, David Copperfield, and Great Expectations

Mary Ann Evans Cross
("George Eliot")
1819-1880

Mary Ann Evans was the daughter of a prosperous estate agent at Warbury, Warwickshire, where the future novelist was born in 1819. From the age of five until she was sixteen Mary Ann (or Marian, as she later signed her name) was educated at boarding schools at Attleborough, Nuneaton, and Coventry. As a girl she was shy and awkward, plain, and a little priggish; because social intercourse was difficult for her, she threw herself into hard and concentrated study. Her great interests were music — she played the piano well all her life — and religion, in which she was moving away from the conventional Anglicanism of her childhood, through a fervent and emotional evangelicalism, to the rationalism of her adult life.

When she was eighteen, after the death of her mother and the marriage of an elder sister, Mary Ann took charge of her father's house, at the same time keeping up a rigorous course of study, reading Greek and Latin, as well as German and Italian. In religion she became more and more intolerant of the exclusive claims of any single sect, and for a time alienated her father by refusing to attend church with him. During 1844-6 she worked at her first book, a translation from the German of *Leben Jesu*, a critical examination by Strauss of the life of Christ, for which many orthodox Christians felt deep resentment.

After her father's death in 1849 she visited the Continent and lived for some months in Geneva. On her return to England she became assistant editor of the *Westminster Review*, a journal of philosophical liberalism edited by John Chapman. She moved into Chapman's household as a guest, but after two years Mrs. Chapman's jealousy made her feel obliged to leave. She was always dependent emotionally, and this aspect of her nature showed itself in her unreturned devotion to Chapman.

At this time she found most of her friends in the liberal and rationalist intellectual leaders of London; among them was the philosopher, Herbert Spencer, who remained her close friend for life. Through him she met George Henry Lewes, a journalist and miscellaneous writer whose home had been broken by his wife's infidelity. Lewes and Miss Evans fell in love, but he could not free himself to marry her, because of the strictness of Victorian divorce laws. In July, 1854, they left England to travel in Germany, quietly announcing to their friends their intention to live as man and wife henceforth. In spite of its having no legal status, they always regarded their association as a true marriage; Miss Evans called herself "Mrs. Lewes" and was a devoted stepmother to Lewes' three sons. Their return to England after a year in Germany brought them some unhappiness, because they were frequently snubbed socially for the irregular nature of their relationship.

In 1856 she read Lewes a sketch of rural life she had written; in spite of feeling that it was dramatically weak, he admired it greatly and encouraged her to continue writing fiction. Her first published story, "Amos Barton," appeared in *Blackwood's Magazine*, followed by two other tales, "Mr. Gilfil's Love Story" and "Janet's Repentance," and the three stories were collected in *Scenes of Clerical Life*, 1858, published under the masculine pseudonym of "George Eliot." The following year she published her first novel, *Adam Bede*, a rural tragedy played out among the non-conformists in country scenes remembered from her Warwickshire childhood. After the publication of *Adam Bede* the identity of the author leaked out gradually in spite of her efforts to conceal her real name. The first two works of fiction had brought her a critical reputation as one of the most powerful of contemporary writers. Her preoccupation was always with the serious consideration of the moral position of the individual in the universe, but her psychological insight into the development of character, her flair for country scenes and speech, her fine sense of fun, and the narrative interest of her novels gave her a general popularity not common to didactic novelists.

From this time on, the story of her life is chiefly the history of her writing. *The Mill on the Floss*, 1859-60, tells of the love, estrangement, and eventual reconciliation of the daughter and son of a country miller. The early sections of the book are the most clearly autobiographical of all her writing. *Silas Marner*, 1861, last and shortest of the rustic novels, is set in the period before the Industrial Revolution, and has for its theme the influence of his fellow men in first crushing a poor hand-loom weaver and then restoring him to happiness.

After the great success of the early novels, she

spent a decade in experimentation, not always with happy results. A trip to Italy, where she worked diligently at research in Renaissance politics, preceded the writing of her historical novel, *Romola*, set in the time of Savonarola. Her genius for psychological development of character is shown strikingly in the study of progressive degeneration of Romola's husband, Tito. An estimate of her popularity is afforded by a rival publisher's offer of £10,000 for the copyright of the novel, which appeared in *Cornhill Magazine*, 1862-3. *Felix Holt*, 1866, the complicated story of a young radical in the 1830's, is in the tradition of Disraeli's political novels. Her major poetical work, *The Spanish Gypsy*, 1868, a blank verse drama, showed that her real talent lay in prose.

A return to scenes she knew more intimately produced the long "study of provincial life," *Middlemarch*, 1871-2, set in one of the new towns of the industrial North. This is the book on which her reputation rests with modern readers, and some critics have called it the greatest of Victorian novels. *Daniel Deronda*, 1876, is a study of Jewish racial consciousness. By this time she had achieved a position of respect never approached by any other English woman writer. Even today, among all the Victorian women novelists, only the Brontë sisters seem her equals; in the study of aspiration and nobility in the mind of woman she has no rival.

The great sales of George Eliot's books insured financial security for herself and Lewes, and allowed him the leisure to win a name of his own as a philosophical and scientific writer and critic. Their increasing reputation put them well above mean gossip, so that during the last years of their life together the circle of friends who visited them included many of the most famous and respected of their contemporaries. Lewes' death in 1878 put an end to their long and happy relationship; in her grief Miss Evans leaned heavily on John Cross, who was more than twenty years her junior. The friendship deepened, and in May, 1880, they were married. Seven months later she caught a chill at a concert and died after four days of illness, on December 22, 1880.

BIOGRAPHY AND CRITICISM

The official life is *George Eliot's Life as Related in Her Letters and Journals,* Arranged and Edited by Her Husband [J. W. Cross], (3 vols., Edinburgh and London, 1885). A recent and complete, if rather long, biography is by Lawrence and Elisabeth Hanson, *Marian Evans and George Eliot: a Biography* (London, New York, and Toronto, 1952). Short biography is combined with critical evaluation by Gerald W. Bullett, *George Eliot, Her Life and Books* (London, 1947) and Joan Bennett, *George Eliot; Her Mind and Her Art* (Cambridge [England], 1948); of these the former is particularly useful for biography, and Mrs. Bennett's book contains what is probably the most perceptive criticism of the novelist yet written.

PRINCIPAL WORKS

The Life of Jesus Critically Examined (translation). By Dr. David Friedrich Strauss (3 vols.)	1846
Scenes of Clerical Life (2 vols.)	1858
Adam Bede (3 vols.)	1859
The Mill on the Floss (3 vols.)	1860
Silas Marner: the Weaver of Raveloe	1861
Romola (3 vols.)	1863

MARY ANN EVANS CROSS ("GEORGE ELIOT") *191*

Felix Holt the Radical (3 vols.)   1866
The Spanish Gypsy, a Poem   1868
Middlemarch, a Study of Provincial Life
    (4 vols.)   1871–2
Daniel Deronda (4 vols.)   1876

SUGGESTED READING

Scenes of Clerical Life, Silas Marner, Middlemarch.

Thomas Hardy

1840-1928

Thomas Hardy, last and one of the greatest of Victorian novelists, was born in Dorset on June 2, 1840, in the center of the Wessex country which later figured in his works. Both his mother and his father, who was a builder, came of Dorset stock, and Thomas early learned to love the country ways and speech around him. He was a precocious boy but reserved; because his health was delicate he was educated at home until he was eight, and then in the village schools and in the nearby town of Dorchester. At sixteen he was apprenticed to a local architect who specialized in "restoring" Gothic churches, but at least as much of his study was devoted to Greek as to architecture. In 1862 he left for London to continue his work as an architect, an occupation he practiced until his marriage.

In the meantime he had found what was to be the chief love of the rest of his life: poetry. He tried unsuccessfully to publish his poems, but even after they were rejected he continued writing them. In 1867 poor health forced his return to Dorset, where his work as an architect supported him so that he could write in his leisure. Hoping that it would sell better than poetry he turned his hand to fiction, and after his return to Dorset he began his first novel, *The Poor Man and the Lady*. He submitted it to George Meredith, then a reader for Chapman and Hall, who advised him to concentrate on plot. Hardy, completely humble about his own talents, promptly and regrettably destroyed the manuscript. *Desperate Remedies*, 1871, his first published book, is a contrived, melodramatic murder story, the result of following Meredith's advice; it had bad reviews and failed to earn its publication costs. The first of his many novels of country life, *Under the Greenwood Tree*, 1872, shows in a pleasant little idyll how deeply Hardy understood rustic ways. *A Pair of Blue Eyes*, 1872-3, is a romantic tragedy which alternates between Cornwall and London, between peasantry and upperclass society, and once more it is in the rustic scenes that the real interest lies. The success of these last two novels brought a commission to write a serial for the *Cornhill Magazine; Far from the Madding Crowd*, published anonymously in 1874, was Hardy's first masterpiece, a story of fortitude and of suffering brought about by the capriciousness of a country girl. After this, most of his novels made their first appearance in periodicals.

Hardy still preferred poetry to fiction, but he felt compelled to write stories to support himself, for he had married and given up architecture in 1874, encouraged by his success with *Far from the Madding Crowd*. His next work, *The Hand of Ethelberta*, 1875-6, is a "society" novel in which the reader misses the elemental strength of the Wessex tales. In *The Return of the Native*, 1878, he looked again to the land as a source of his power; the two major "characters" are Eustacia Vye, who broods with a tragic passion over the heath on which she lives, and the heath itself, which symbolizes the blind forces of nature against which she rebels.

The Trumpet-Major, 1880, is a light-hearted love story of the period of the Napoleonic Wars, written with little of Hardy's characteristic irony. *Two on a Tower*, 1882, shocked his audience with the frankness of its treatment of sexual passion in a woman. Over the pages of *The Mayor of Casterbridge*, 1886, hangs the shadow of an inexorable fate hounding a man to miserable death by means of the flaws in his own character, but for all its gloom it is one of Hardy's most powerful novels. *The Woodlanders*, 1886-7, is the quietly beautiful story of a simple countryman, unable to marry the girl he loves, who has risen above him socially.

At the same time that his novels were appearing Hardy was writing short stories, and, although they were hardly so successful, many of them are worth ranking beside his longer works. *Wessex Tales*, 1888, *A Group of Noble Dames*, 1891, and *Life's Little Ironies*, 1894, are the major collections.

His novels culminated with the two greatest, *Tess of the D'Urbervilles*, 1891, and *Jude the Obscure*, 1896. The second part of the title of *Tess* is *A Pure Woman*, to show what Hardy thought of his heroine, who is seduced, abandoned, and finally driven to murder for which she is hanged. Through it all she remains his most lovable woman character, cruelly tormented by fate and innocent of any intention to sin. *Jude* shows the horrible decline of a man and woman drawn together by sexual desire and torn apart by the disaster it entails. Both novels were badly bowdlerized for serial publication, but even so, they shocked British prudery and Hardy was terribly abused for being "filthy."

Partly because of the reception of *Tess* and *Jude*, partly because he had always preferred poetry to prose, Hardy announced in 1896 that *Jude* was his last novel, and turned with relief to the writing of vigorously intellectual and experimental lyrical poetry which many critics think is at least as great as his novels. His career is thus divided sharply between his Victorian novels and his post-Victorian poetry, which lies outside the scope of this book. One poetic work, however, requires attention, his gigantic "epic drama," *The Dynasts,* published in three parts in 1903, 1906, and 1908. This tremendous work, set in the Napoleonic Wars, is the capstone of his career and shows most clearly his idea of the Immanent Will working itself out in human affairs.

In 1914, two years after the death of his first wife, he remarried, this time to a woman much younger than himself with whom he spent a happy old age. The public had long since stopped calling his last novel "Jude the Obscene" and his final years were full of honors; he succeeded Tennyson and Meredith as president of the Society of Authors. He died of a cold on January 11, 1928, and his ashes were placed in Westminster Abbey, but his heart was buried with his first wife in Dorset.

BIOGRAPHY AND CRITICISM

Florence E. Hardy's two volumes, *The Early Life of Thomas Hardy, 1840-1891* (London, 1928) and *The Later Years of Thomas Hardy, 1892-1928* (New York, 1930), provide the most complete information about her husband's life; the bulk of both volumes is compiled from his own writings. Carl J. Weber, *Hardy of Wessex; His Life and Literary Career* (New York, 1940) is excellent critical biography for general use. For criticism alone, Henry C. Duffin, *Thomas Hardy: A Study of the Wessex Novels, the Poems, and the Dynasts* (Manchester, 1937) provides detailed accounts of almost all Hardy's work, while David Cecil, *Hardy the Novelist: An Essay in Criticism* (London, 1943) is confined to an urbane examination of the major novels.

PRINCIPAL WORKS

Desperate Remedies. A Novel (3 vols.)	1871
Under the Greenwood Tree. A Rural Painting of the Dutch School (2 vols.)	1872
A Pair of Blue Eyes. A Novel (3 vols.)	1873
Far from the Madding Crowd (2 vols.)	1874
The Hand of Ethelberta (2 vols.)	1876
The Return of the Native (3 vols.)	1878
The Trumpet-Major. A Tale (3 vols.)	1880
A Laodicean, or the Castle of the De Stancys. A Story of To-Day (3 vols.)	1881
Two on a Tower. A Romance (3 vols.)	1882
The Mayor of Casterbridge: the Life and Death of a Man of Character (2 vols.)	1886
The Woodlanders (3 vols.)	1887
Wessex Tales; Strange Lively and Commonplace (2 vols.)	1888
Tess of the D'Urbervilles: a Pure Woman Faithfully Presented (3 vols.)	1891
A Group of Noble Dames	1891
Life's Little Ironies. A Set of Tales. With some Colloquial Sketches entitled A Few Crusted Characters	1894
Jude the Obscure	1896
Wessex Poems and Other Verses	1898
Poems of the Past and Present	1901
The Dynasts. A Drama of the Napoleonic Wars (3 pts.)	1903–08
Time's Laughingstock, and Other Verses	1909

*The Famous Tragedy of the Queen of
   Cornwall at Tintagel in Lyonness*   1923

SUGGESTED READING

Under the Greenwood Tree, The Return of the Native, and *Tess of the D'Urbervilles. Selected Poems of Thomas Hardy,* ed. G. M. Young (London, 1940), is a good introduction to his poetry.

Thomas Henry Huxley

1825-1895

Huxley was born in Ealing, a village near London, on May 4, 1825. For two or three years he attended the school at which his father was a master, but when he was ten the family moved to Coventry, interrupting his formal education. In 1841 he went to London as apprentice to a London physician, and the following year earned a scholarship to study medicine at Charing Cross Hospital, from which he was graduated with highest honors.

Medically qualified in 1845, when he was only twenty, Huxley applied for appointment as a surgeon in the Royal Navy. At the end of 1846 he left England on H.M.S *Rattlesnake,* bound to explore the dangerous seas around Australia. During the four-year cruise Huxley spent most of his time investigating the morphology of marine invertebrates, particularly of jellyfish. The value of his research on this then little known subject was recognized by his election in 1851 as a Fellow of the Royal Society, and the following year he received the Society's medal. After his return to England he had a long leave of absence from the Navy to arrange for publication of the notes made during his voyage, and in this period he became intimate with many of the most famous scientists of the day, of whom the most important was Darwin. In 1854, when he was unable to get further leave from the Navy, Huxley resigned in the hope of earning his living by lecturing, for he had already determined to make his career in teaching and research rather than in the practice of medicine. He failed to get a chair in various universities in Canada, Ireland, and Scotland, but in July, 1854, he was appointed lecturer on natural history at the Royal School of Mines in London, and in August he became naturalist to the Geological Survey and lecturer in comparative anatomy at St. George's Hospital. With the income from these positions he could afford to marry, and he sent immediately to Australia for his fiancee, Henrietta Heathorn, whom he had met while he was with the *Rattlesnake*. Three sons and four daughters were born to the marriage; Huxley's two greatest talents have reappeared in his grandchildren: scientific ability in the person of the distinguished biologist Julian Huxley, and literary skill in the novelist Aldous Huxley.

In 1855, the year of his marriage, Huxley's interest in popular education led him to begin a series of free "People's Lectures" for London working-men. Within three months the hall, which held 600, was crowded to capacity on lecture-nights. One of the talks which indicated at this early stage the direction his thinking was taking was "On the Educational Value of Natural History Sciences," stating the applicability of a single method of study to all sciences, and their value as moral and intellectual discipline. Through a common interest in science and popular education, he became friendly with the Broad Churchmen F. D. Maurice and Charles Kingsley and lectured at their newly founded Working Men's College.

For some years Huxley had been investigating the theories of evolution then current; at last he found his answer in Darwin's theory of "natural selection." From the publication of *The Origin of Species* in 1859 until his own death Huxley worked untiringly as "Darwin's bulldog," spreading Darwin's ideas at the expense of time for his own research. His bent was toward teaching, and it may be said truly that he became science master to Victorian England, lecturing, debating, writing in support of Darwin with a persuasiveness and clarity that his master lacked, and advocating general education in the sciences. National attention was first fixed on him at a meeting in 1860 of the British Association for the Advancement of Science, where the Bishop of Oxford asked sneeringly whether Huxley claimed descent from an ape on his grandfather's or his grandmother's side. Without rancor Huxley replied that if he had to choose he would prefer descent from an ape to kinship with an able man who sought to discredit truth by appeals to religious prejudice. The remark made Huxley famous and advanced the cause of evolution immeasurably in the popular mind. In his lectures on "Man's Place in Nature" Huxley extended the Darwinian theory to include the appearance and development of man on earth as purely natural phenomena, a logical extension of Darwinism, but one from which orthodox England shrank for fear it would undermine Christianity.

In spite of the enormous amount of time required for his lecturing and writing, Huxley kept his place as one of the leading workers in the field of morphology and natural classification, and each year he published one or more of the results of his investigations in biology and paleontology.

Huxley was reared in the Anglican Church, but soon lost his belief in the historical accuracy and literal interpretation of the Bible. His own purely rational approach was that the truth of religious doctrine was neither demonstrated nor demonstrable. To clarify his position as one who could verify physical phenomena but who had no special *gnosis*, or direct knowledge of things spiritual, he invented the term "agnostic" to describe himself. He was abused by many of the orthodox for his frank statement of his agnosticism, but his personal integrity was so great that he was able to retain close friendship with many liberal churchmen.

Huxley was always interested in the English educational system and worked hard to broaden its limits, whether in elementary schools or in the universities. His best known work on education is *Lay Sermons*, 1870, in which he advocated the place of science in general education, rather as a discipline for the mind than as preparation for specific scientific professions. For him the scientific approach was the one sure way to deal rationally with any subject, avoiding what seemed to him the dangers of vague emotion and prejudice, whether the problem was one of natural science or of religion and philosophy. Almost inevitably this led him into controversy with Matthew Arnold, the devoted advocate of a classical education; both men agreed on the necessity for "liberal education" but differed on its definition and the means by which it could be achieved. One of the most able statements of the scientific point of view is Huxley's "Science and Culture," to which Arnold replied with "Literature and Science."

Huxley was a member of the London School Board, and in 1872 was installed as Rector of Aberdeen University. He was invited to America in 1876 to give the inaugural lecture at Johns Hopkins University, the "Address on University Education." His sense of public responsibility and the breadth of his knowledge fitted him as an adviser to the government on problems of science and education; as a public servant he served on four royal commissions. He was professor of the Royal College of Surgeons and of the Royal Institution, and was elected president of the Royal Society. Honorary degrees and foreign decorations poured in on him, and in 1892 Gladstone made him a privy councillor.

He was forced to retire in 1885 because of bad health from which he had suffered since childhood. In his retirement he continued his prolific writing; although he was modest about his own literary powers, the simple, forceful quality of his writing, lucid but uncondescending on difficult subjects, made him one of the finest of English writers of expository prose.

In 1895 he died of influenza. Because of his religious views there was no church service, but the burial service was read by an old friend, a broad church Anglican clergyman.

BIOGRAPHY

The standard biography is by Huxley's son, Leonard Huxley, *Life and Letters of Thomas Henry Huxley* (2 vols., London, 1900). A short and informative modern life, designed for the general reader, is by E. W. MacBride, *Huxley* (London, 1934).

PRINCIPAL WORKS

Evidence as to Man's Place in Nature   1863
*An Introduction to the Classification
   of Animals*   1869

Lay Sermons, Addresses, and Reviews	1870
Critiques and Addresses	1873
American Addresses	1877
Hume	1879
Science and Culture and Other Essays	1881
Essays upon Some Controverted Questions	1892
Collected Essays (9 vols.)	1893-4
The Scientific Memoirs of Thomas Henry Huxley, ed. Michael Foster and E. Ray Lankester (5 vols.)	1898–1903

SUGGESTED READING

Lay Sermons:
    "A Liberal Education; and Where to Find It"
    "The Origin of Species"
    "On the Physical Basis of Life"
    "On a Piece of Chalk"
American Addresses:
    "Address on University Education"
Science and Culture:
    "Science and Culture"
Essays upon Some Controverted Questions:
    "Agnosticism and Christianity"

All but the last two readings are included in the selections in *Essays* by T. H. Huxley, ed. Frederick Barry (New York, 1929).

Charles Kingsley

1819–1875

Charles Kingsley, the first child of a large family, was born in Holne, Devonshire, on June 12, 1819. His father was an Anglican parson who held clerical posts in the Fens of East Anglia and at the picturesque fishing-village of Clovelly, Devonshire, during Charles' childhood; both Devon and the Fens occur repeatedly in his son's writings.

Charles was educated at home and in private schools before entering Magdalene College, Cambridge, in 1838. His preparation had been good, and in his first year he gained a scholarship, but in general he found sports and occasional dissipation more congenial than hard, systematic study. Only six months of drudgery just before his examinations enabled him to graduate with a first class degree in 1842. During his undergraduate days he was oppressed by religious doubt, but in his last year at Cambridge he recovered his faith and decided to give up the study of law to go into the Church. A few months after his graduation he was ordained to the country parish of Eversley, Hampshire, where he lived almost without interruption the rest of his life.

As a clergyman his sympathies were with the Broad Church party, and he was unalterably opposed to both High Church Anglicanism and Roman Catholicism. He felt the clergyman's duties to be as much concerned with the living conditions and bodily health of his parish as with their souls.

During his first summer vacation Kingsley had fallen in love with Frances Grenfell, but they were unable to marry until 1844, five years later, because of his poverty and the disapproval which the wealthy Grenfells felt for him. He became the father of four children, of whom one, Mary, inherited her father's literary bent and became a novelist under the pseudonym of "Lucas Malet."

Kingsley had begun a prose life of St. Elizabeth of Hungary during his courtship, intending it as a wedding gift for his wife. After their marriage he reworked the material, and in 1848 he published his first important work, *The Saint's Tragedy*, a poetic drama dealing with the struggle in St. Elizabeth — "the only healthy Popish saint" — between her own natural affections for husband and children, and the asceticism taught by the medieval Church.

The political aspirations of the Chartists appealed to Kingsley's sympathies at the same time that he deplored their occasional violence. The failure of the Chartist meeting at Kensington Common in 1848 was the signal for him and his friends, F. D. Maurice, Thomas Hughes, and J. M. Ludlow, to inaugurate the Christian Socialist movement in an attempt to instill Christian ideals into popular political thinking, and to make the Church a force for the cure of social evils. To the periodicals published by the group he contributed many papers, and during the same period published his first two novels, both embodying the principles of the Christian Socialists. *Yeast*, a study of the conditions among poor agricultural laborers, appeared in installments in *Fraser's Magazine* in 1848 and was republished as a book in 1851, after the success of *Alton Locke*, 1850. This latter book is the supposed autobiography of a young poet and tailor who is driven into Chartism by the miserable working conditions of his trade. One of the central characters is an old Scotsman, a sketch from life of Kingsley's friend, Thomas Carlyle, to whom he was much indebted in his thinking. Kingsley's crusading talents were always best in championing an unpopular cause, and after 1852 he withdrew from active participation in the Christian Socialist movement, when he felt that its principles had been safely planted in the English social consciousness.

His next novel, *Hypatia*, 1853, is the story of the clash between early Christianity and dying paganism in fifth century Alexandria. *Westward Ho!*, 1855, the most popular of his novels, is laid in the Elizabethan England he loved so well, at the time of the Spanish Armada. In spite of its setting in the past, the novel's chief characters are recognizably the athletic, God-fearing young Victorian men whom Kingsley so obviously admired that his critics called his religion "muscular Christianity." The novel had large sales, but many reviewers criticized it for its bitter anti-Catholic bias.

Since boyhood he had been interested in the zoology of the seacoast, and in 1855 he published his first scientific work, *Glaucus, or the Wonders of the Shore*. Its success with amateur scientists inspired a long succession of magazine articles and short books on scientific subjects, chiefly geology. It was his scientific curiosity and the deep humility with which he regarded external nature as the almost unexplored handiwork of God which allowed him to accept the conclusions of Darwin and Huxley in later years, and to defend them against those Christians who felt their faith shaken by the new evolutionary theories.

Two Years Ago, 1857, tells of the cholera epidemic in a Devonshire fishing village, brought on by the insanitary living conditions of the inhabitants. Turning from the novel to poetry, he published *Andromeda and Other Poems* in 1858; his real facility in light verse and ballads made the volume immediately popular, and the title poem remains one of the most successful attempts at hexameters in English.

Clerical advancement was slow for him because his outspoken attacks on social abuses caused many Englishmen to regard him as a symbol of dangerous radicalism, although his political theories were actually conservative enough. Fortunately, the Queen enjoyed his poetry, and the Prince Consort admired his social work — and his liking for the German people. In 1859 the Queen appointed him one of her chaplains, and in the following year she made him Regius Professor of Modern History at Cambridge, a post he held until 1869. His historical scholarship was inadequate for the chair, but his lectures were popular with the undergraduates for their enthusiasm and because of his instinctive sympathy with youth. When the Prince of Wales came to Cambridge in 1861, his father chose Kingsley as his tutor in history.

The income from his Cambridge chair allowed him to spend less time on the continual novel-writing which was undermining his health, so that he produced only two works of fiction during this period. *The Water-Babies*, 1863, is a charming fable for children. The Fens of his childhood furnished the background for his last novel, *Hereward the Wake*,

1866, the adventures of the outlaw who led the last English resistance against William the Conqueror.

In 1864 Kingsley rashly accused Newman of holding truthfulness to be a virtue unnecessary for Roman Catholic priests; in answer Newman wrote his *Apologia pro Vita Sua*. Kingsley was merely incautious in expressing a common Victorian Protestant prejudice, but he was far less skilled in controversy than his opponent, and his reputation suffered accordingly.

To recuperate from an illness he took a long sea voyage in 1869-70, visiting the West Indies. The record of the trip, taken from his letters home, was published in 1871 as *At Last*. His only trip to the United States was a lecture tour in 1874, which dangerously weakened his health. He contracted a severe case of pleurisy in the Rockies, and after his return to England he suffered another attack, from which he died at Eversley on January 23, 1875.

BIOGRAPHY

The official biography, *Charles Kingsley: His Letters and Memories of His Life*, Edited by His Wife [F. E. Kingsley] (2 vols., London, 1877), is long and unsatisfactory. A good shorter life is by Margaret Farrand Thorp, *Charles Kingsley, 1819-1875* (Princeton and London, 1937), which contains an extensive bibliography of Kingsley's works.

PRINCIPAL WORKS

The Saint's Tragedy; or, the True Story of Elizabeth of Hungary	1848
Alton Locke, Tailor and Poet (2 vols.)	1850
Yeast: A Problem	1851

Hypatia: or, New Foes with an Old Face
(2 vols.)   1853
Westward Ho! or, the Voyages and Adventures of Sir Amyas Leigh (3 vols.)   1855
Glaucus; or, The Wonders of the Shore   1855
The Heroes; or, Greek Fairy Tales for My Children   1856
Two Years Ago (3 vols.)   1857
Andromeda and Other Poems   1858
The Water-Babies: a Fairy Tale for a Land-Baby   1863
Hereward the Wake, "Last of the English" (2 vols.)   1866
At Last: a Christmas in the West Indies (2 vols.)   1871
Prose Idylls, New and Old   1873

SUGGESTED READING

Alton Locke and *Westward Ho!*

George Meredith

1828-1909

The first ten years of George Meredith's life were spent in Portsmouth, where he was born on February 12, 1828. His father had inherited the family business, a prosperous tailoring and naval outfitting shop, but had little success in managing it; his mother died when George was five. He attended boarding schools in Southsea and Portsmouth, and during 1843-4 he studied at a Moravian school near Coblentz on the Rhine, but he attended neither English public school nor university.

When he returned to England he was articled to a London solicitor, through whom he became acquainted with a group of literary men who issued the *Monthly Observer,* to which he became a contributor. One of his new friends was Thomas Love Peacock's son, who introduced him to his sister Mary Ellen Nicolls, a witty and beautiful widow some years older than Meredith, whom she married in 1849. Meredith became acquainted with the group of intellectuals with whom his wife's family was friendly, and from them he absorbed his radical political thinking. The elder Peacock influenced him greatly in style and literary theory, particularly in the use of comedy and laughter as correctives for man's faults.

Meredith gave up the law, and both he and his wife worked hard at writing, occasionally in collaboration. The bulk of his work at this time was poetry, some of which Dickens published in *Household Words*. His first book, *Poems*, published in 1851 with a dedication to Peacock, contained little of permanent value except the first version of "Love in the Valley"; among the few favorable reviews were those by W. M. Rossetti and Charles Kingsley. Through the rest of his life Meredith wrote and published several volumes of poetry at the same time that his novels were appearing. His first two novels, youthful pieces, were an Oriental fantasy, *The Shaving of Shagpat*, 1855, and *Farina: a Legend of Cologne*, 1857, a burlesque Gothic novel which owed much to Peacock's style. The reviews of *Shagpat* were favorable, but both novels sold poorly.

A son was born to the Merediths in 1853, but their marriage was unhappy and full of the quarrels of two headstrong people. In 1858 Mrs. Meredith eloped with a painter who later deserted her; she died alone and friendless in 1861. In spite of her requests, Meredith neither visited her in her illness nor attended her funeral. After her death he began the fine series of sixteen-line poems, "Modern Love," published in 1862, which tells the tragic story of a marriage not unlike his own.

Before his wife's death his first full-length novel, *The Ordeal of Richard Feverel*, probably the most popular of his works today, appeared in 1859. It is the brilliantly satirical and epigrammatic story of the conflict in a young man between instinct and a too rigidly systematic education, of the antithesis between young, passionate love and the pressure of society. In his later years Meredith learned to tell a story more economically and more obliquely, but he never surpassed the psychological insight into character he displays in Richard and his father, nor did he ever improve upon the beauty of the lyrical, romantic intensity of the love story of Lucy and Richard. *Feverel* was well received, but a second edition was not printed for nineteen years. To support himself Meredith began writing leading articles for the *Ipswich Journal,* a Conservative newspaper which he served well in spite of his own professedly radical opinions.

Evan Harrington began its serial appearance in 1860 in *Once a Week.* Much of this study of social snobbery is autobiographical, and members of the Meredith family appear as thinly disguised characters; the central figure is a young man who is ashamed of his family's tailoring business. This candid likeness to the author's own life is surprising because he later seemed to grow ashamed of his commercial background and became mysterious and secretive about his family.

In 1860 he began work as literary adviser to Chapman and Hall, the publishers for whom he worked for thirty-five years. During the early 1860's he travelled abroad frequently. For a time he had rooms in Chelsea in the celebrated Bohemian menage on Cheyne Walk which he shared with D. G. Rossetti and Swinburne.

His second marriage, in 1864, was to Marie Vulliamy, who lacked the intellectual gifts of his first wife, but had the stability her husband needed. During the Austro-Italian War of 1866 he went to Italy and Austria as correspondent for the *Morning Post* and in 1867-8 served as editor of the *Fortnightly Review.* That year he moved to a cottage at Box Hill, Surrey, where he lived the rest of his life. He was strong and vigorous and spent long hours tramping the Surrey hills which are reflected in the lovingly drawn natural backgrounds of many of his novels.

The year of his marriage, 1864, he published *Emilia in England* (later called *Sandra Belloni*), which has for its heroine a young half-Italian singer, one of the splendid women whom Meredith created so convincingly; once more snobbery and sentimentalism are his targets. The sympathy which he shared with many of his contemporaries for the Italian Risorgimento runs through *Vittoria*, 1867, the sequel to *Emilia* and his only historical novel; for its background he drew on his Italian experiences as a correspondent the previous year. Between these two novels, in *Rhoda Fleming*, 1865, he turned to a rustic setting for the melodramatic story of two sisters whose characters are developed through their suffering when one of them is seduced and deserted.

Several of his best novels were yet to come. *Harry Richmond*, 1871, is the extravagant story of an unscrupulous and conceited father who nearly ruins his son's life by his social pretensions. Meredith's own favorite novel, *Beauchamp's Career*, 1876, is concerned with the life of an aristocratic and idealistic Radical politician; Beauchamp's mentor, Dr. Shrapnel, is Meredith's portrait of Thomas Carlyle. *The Egoist*, 1879, takes its name from the insufferably pompous Sir Willoughby Patterne, whose progressive humiliation furnishes the plot. *Diana of the Crossways*, 1885, was the first of Meredith's novels to gain wide popularity; its story deals with the political and personal indiscretions of an Irish authoress whose life parallels that of the beautiful writer, Mrs. Caroline Norton.

By now Meredith had an established reputation

for originality, but his satirical outlook and his glancing, indirect methods of exposition kept him from general popularity; indeed, he has always been the least read of the great Victorian novelists. From this time forward his novels became increasingly obscure; although he was contemptuous of his critics and said that such later novels as *One of our Conquerors*, 1891, and *The Amazing Marriage*, 1895, were deliberately made tortuous as a "revenge," he was nonetheless bitter that the books sold poorly.

Two of his most enduring successes were in other literary forms. His essay on the corrective power of laughter, *The Idea of Comedy and the Uses of the Comic Spirit*, delivered as a lecture in 1877, is the classic statement of the idea in English. Of his several books of poetry, perhaps the finest is *Poems and Lyrics of the Joy of Earth*, 1883. A less successful venture, *The Sentimentalists*, his only comedy for the stage, was pieced together from fragments and produced for a few performances after his death.

In his old age England belatedly recognized him as one of her great men of letters; he was elected president of the Society of Authors at Tennyson's death, and in 1905 he received the Order of Merit. He died at Box Hill on May 18, 1909, and his ashes were buried beside his wife in Dorking.

BIOGRAPHY AND CRITICISM

Meredith's own reticence about his private life is reflected in the scarcity of adequate biographical material. The first attempt at a complete biography was by S. M. Ellis, *George Meredith, his Life and Friends in Relation to his Work* (New York, 1920). J. B. Priestley's contribution to the English Men of Letters series, *George Meredith* (New York, 1926), is a good and comparatively short study of both life and works. The poet Siegfried Sassoon, *Meredith* (London, 1948), is frequently very perceptive, but his critical judgments are highly personal. Easily the most satisfactory book on Meredith is the latest one, by Lionel Stevenson, *The Ordeal of George Meredith: a Biography* (New York, 1953); as the title indicates, Stevenson is more concerned with the author's life than with a critical assessment of his work.

PRINCIPAL WORKS

Poems	1851
The Shaving of Shagpat. An Arabian Entertainment	1855
Farina: a Legend of Cologne	1857
The Ordeal of Richard Feverel. A History of Father and Son (3 vols.)	1859
Evan Harrington (3 vols.)	1861
Modern Love, and Poems of the English Roadside, with Poems and Ballads	1862
Emilia in England [*Sandra Belloni*] (3 vols.)	1864
Rhoda Fleming. A Story (3 vols.)	1865
Vittoria (3 vols.)	1867
The Adventures of Harry Richmond (3 vols.)	1871
Beauchamp's Career (3 vols.)	1876
On the Idea of Comedy and the Uses of the Comic Spirit	1877
The Egoist. A Comedy in Narrative (3 vols.)	1879
Poems and Lyrics of the Joy of Earth	1883
Diana of the Crossways. A Novel (3 vols.)	1885
A Reading of Earth (poems)	1888
Lord Ormont and his Aminta. A Novel (3 vols.)	1894

The Amazing Marriage (2 vols.)   1895
A Reading of Life, with Other Poems   1901

SUGGESTED READING

The Ordeal of Richard Feverel and *The Egoist*. Of his poetry the volume containing "Modern Love" is the most generally appealing.

John Stuart Mill

1806-1873

John Stuart Mill was the eldest of nine children of James Mill, the Scottish Utilitarian philosopher and radical reformer. The elder Mill, determined to make his son into a logician and thinker in his own pattern, educated John in their London home instead of sending him to either school or university. He was a bright boy who responded well to the impossibly rigorous system; he began learning Greek at three, Latin at eight, and by the time he was twelve he was proficient in mathematics and several modern languages and had read closely most of the major works of the classical authors. In later years he referred to the atheistic quality of his education as making him "one of the very few examples in this country of one who has not thrown off religious belief, but never had it."

When he was fourteen he went for a year to France, where he lived with the brother of Jeremy Bentham, the great Utilitarian thinker with whom James Mill had been long and intimately associated. To the end of his life Mill felt a close affection for the French and their culture. After his return to

England he found employment in the India House, where his father was an important official. He was advanced steadily in his work, which supported him well and left him ample time for study and writing.

He had, of course, been well indoctrinated with Utilitarianism, the political and economic doctrine of Bentham and his father, which was founded on a belief in "utility" or "the greatest good for the greatest number" as the basis of moral and political action. When he was sixteen he founded the Utilitarian Society, composed of several friends of like views who met for discussion and the reading of essays, and about the same time he wrote his first published article, a defense of his father's economic theories.

The machine-like regularity with which Mill had worked his mind and body suddenly came to a stop with a "spiritual crisis" or nervous breakdown when he was twenty-one. He asked himself the question: " 'Suppose that all your objects in life were realized; that all the changes in institutions and opinions which you are looking forward to, could be completely effected at this very instant: would this be a great joy and happiness to you?' And an irrepressible self-consciousness distinctly answered, 'No!' " Slowly he came to see that his own happiness was dependent upon much that was not material and to value the cultivation of feelings and emotions which had been left out of his stern upbringing. Particularly he learned to value the effects of music and of poetry, especially that of Wordsworth. At the same period, through the influence of some of his friends, he began to study the transcendental philosophy of Coleridge and Goethe. To this period Mill probably owed the inspiration for his greatest service to Utilitarianism, the widening of its borders and the humanizing of its doctrines.

In 1830 he visited Paris and there, under the influence of the French philosophers, worked out for himself a compromise between the philosophical determinism of the Utilitarians and the free will without which he could see no prospect of mankind's improvement. For some years he had been contributing to the magazines of the philosophical radicals, notably the *London Review*, of which he was editor, and the *Westminster Review*, which had been founded by his father and Bentham; when the two *Reviews* merged he became editor of the new journal in all but name. His first major work was the *System of Logic*, 1843, followed in 1848 by *Political Economy*, of which one of the most provocative chapters is that in which Mill champions the working classes and speaks, almost prophetically, of their increasing power.

When he was twenty-four Mill had met Mrs. Taylor, a married lady with whom he fell in love. The pair spent much time together and were married in 1851, two years after the death of Mr. Taylor, who seems to have countenanced the intimate friendship during his own lifetime. Mill's wife discussed his work with him and made helpful suggestions; he later declared that it was due to her intellectual influence that his mind came to final ripening. He retired from the India House in 1856; three years later he was left a widower when his wife died in southern France.

During the period of his married life Mill was writing continually, but he published nothing of importance until 1859, the year after his wife's death, when *On Liberty* appeared, dedicated to her. This long, carefully written essay, with which Mrs. Mill had helped, is one of the noblest statements of English liberalism; it attempts to set the limits of domination of society over the individual, to show that "the only purpose for which power can be rightfully exercised over a member of a civilized community, against his will, is to prevent harm to others."

In *Considerations on Representative Government*, 1861, he expressed his belief in the necessity of free institutions. The same year he also published *Utilitarianism*, the statement of his own philosophical belief in an enlarged, more optimistic form of Benthamism.

By this time he was the most respected of English liberals, admired and liked even by those who most profoundly opposed his doctrines. His growing reputation led to his being asked to stand for Parliament for Westminster in 1865. After his election he served capably for three years, helping in the passage of the Reform Bill of 1867 and advocating Irish reform and woman suffrage.

He was defeated in the election of 1868 and retired to his home in southern France, where he had been living half of each year to be near his wife's grave. Her daughter was his constant companion in his late years. In 1869 he published *On the Subjection of Women*, perhaps the most influential single force in the ultimate political emancipation of women in England.

During the last ten or fifteen years of his life Mill was working on his *Autobiography*, which was not published until after his death. In an age notable for fine autobiographies this stands out as one of the best, a record of the history of Mill's mind rather than of the intimacies of his private life. During the same period he was also working on *Three Essays on Religion*, which were also published posthumously. In the last of the essays Mill showed that he had moved from the atheism of his youth to a position of admiration for Christ and Christianity and of reserved judgment about the supernatural and an after-life.

On May 8, 1873, he died at Avignon as simply as he had lived, and with his death the voice of the most eloquent defender of political freedom in Victorian England was stilled.

BIOGRAPHY AND CRITICISM

The most satisfactory biographical sources are Mill's own *Autobiography* (London, 1873) and *The Letters of John Stuart Mill*, ed. Hugh S. R. Elliot (2 vols., London, 1910). Critical biographies are by Alexander Bain, *John Stuart Mill. A Criticism: With Personal Recollections* (London, 1882) and W. L. Courtney, *Life of John Stuart Mill* (London, 1889). A useful critical study whose nature is indicated by its title is by Emery Neff, *Carlyle and Mill: Mystic and Utilitarian* (New York, 1926).

PRINCIPAL WORKS

A System of Logic, Ratiocinative and Inductive	1843
Principles of Political Economy (2 vols.)	1848
Thoughts on Parliamentary Reform	1859
On Liberty	1859
Considerations on Representative Government	1861
Utilitarianism	1863
Auguste Comte and Positivism	1865
On the Subjection of Women	1869
Autobiography	1873
Three Essays on Religion	1874

SUGGESTED READING

On Liberty and *Autobiography*.

William Morris

1834–1896

William Morris was born in Walthamstow in suburban London, March 24, 1834, the eldest son of prosperous middle class parents from whom he seems to have inherited none of the love of art which guided his own life. In his boyhood, living in Epping Forest, and later at school at Marlborough, he acquired the close knowledge of nature which inspired so much of his mature poetry and decoration, and from early reading and a precocious interest in medieval architecture he developed a deep love of the middle ages. When he went to Exeter College, Oxford, in 1853 he was an ardent Anglo-Catholic intending to be ordained, but during his Oxford days he gradually lost interest in the church and turned to literature and art. At Exeter he formed an intimate friendship with the future painter, Edward Burne-Jones, whom he saw almost daily for the rest of his life, and with him became part of an undergraduate circle known as "The Brotherhood," formed of friends with artistic interests similar to his own. During a long summer vacation he went with Burne-Jones to France, where his first acquaintance with

French Gothic architecture rekindled the passionate enthusiasm with which he had read "The Nature of Gothic" in Ruskin's *Stones of Venice*. After taking an undistinguished degree, Morris stayed on in Oxford as pupil to an architect, but when he realized that this was a false start he moved with Burne-Jones to a studio in London, there to begin a new life as a painter, since he had been convinced by his friend Rossetti that painting was the only career for a man devoted to art.

Meanwhile, Morris, who had begun writing poetry at Oxford, helped the other members of the Brotherhood to found the *Oxford and Cambridge Magazine*. To this magazine, for which Rossetti wrote several poems, Morris contributed the bulk of the poetry and prose, as well as much of his private income, but the publication lasted only a year. In 1858 he published *The Defence of Guenevere and Other Poems*, which contained not only the treatment of the Arthurian theme in the title poem but a number of lyrics and monologues concerned with the chivalric code of the late middle ages, showing the influence of both Rossetti and Browning. In spite of the freshness of the poetry, the sale of the volume was a complete failure.

With Rossetti, Burne-Jones, and others he worked in 1857 on the ill-fated murals of the Oxford Union; the paintings quickly faded, but a more permanent result of the Oxford visit was the love he found there for Jane Burden, a dark beauty who later became Rossetti's favorite model. After his marriage to her in 1859, Morris began building in Kent his beautiful home known as the Red House from its rosy brick. In despair at the ugly furnishings then available, he turned to decorating the house himself, designing everything down to the smallest detail; he had never felt completely at home as a studio painter, but in decoration he found the art form with which his name was afterward linked. His success with the Red House led naturally to the formation in 1861 of the firm of decorators and manufacturers which bore his name; it was devoted to supplanting hideous Victorian furnishings with things of good taste. Morris himself worked on everything he produced, designing, painting, even dyeing and weaving with his own hands. One of the most important parts of the business was the supply of stained glass windows for churches that were being built during the height of the Gothic revival.

Business affairs forced Morris to return to London in 1865, and there he once more found time to write poetry, which he had neglected since his marriage, and to project an ambitious scheme for a series of narrative poems based on medieval and classical themes. One of these, *The Life and Death of Jason,* soon outgrew the volume for which it was intended, and was published separately in 1867. In this retelling of the story of the Golden Fleece Morris made no attempt to capture the Greek spirit, but instead followed Chaucer in looking at classic myth through medieval eyes. Unlike *Guenevere, Jason* was a great success with the public. The rest of the series of narrative poems followed in three volumes, *The Earthly Paradise,* 1868-70. Part of the charm of the volumes lies in the lovely lyrics on the change of the seasons and the English countryside which separate the longer poems. In his metres, the narrative framework, and the abundant life and profusion of detail one is reminded again of Morris' master, Chaucer. Poetry came easily to Morris, although it was always carried on concurrently with his other work, and he once said of his verses, "Well, if this is poetry, it's very easy to write."

Among the classical and medieval myths in *The*

Earthly Paradise were two Icelandic tales which were indicative of Morris' growing interest in Northern sagas. In 1870 he collaborated on a prose translation of the Volsunga saga, and the following year he made his first journey to Iceland. His translation of the *Aeneid* followed in 1875, and the next year he published what he considered his finest poetic work, *Sigurd the Volsung,* a long epic based on the Volsunga saga.

Morris moved in 1871 to a fine old house on the upper Thames, Kelmscott Manor, which he shared for a time with Rossetti. His love of England's old architecture prompted his founding of the Society for the Protection of Ancient Buildings in 1877. Like Ruskin, Morris discovered that his love of medieval art and his dissatisfaction with Victorian aesthetic taste brought him to the belief that sound art could only come of a healthy society. For all his love of the past, he was the most socially and politically conscious of the great Victorian poets. In 1883 he joined the Democratic Federation, an association of working-men's clubs with socialist leanings. When the group broke up in quarrels the next year, Morris became one of the leaders of its successor, the Socialist League. He seems to have been more interested in a humane desire to raise the status of the working man than in actual socialist doctrine, but to the cause he contributed money, speeches, and his own writing, chiefly in the League's journal, *The Commonweal.* Many of his "Chants for Socialists" are poor, but his power as story-teller informs two of his finest works, the socialist prose romances, *The Dream of John Ball,* 1888, notable for its recreation of the medieval setting, and *News from Nowhere,* 1890, an enchanting Utopian dream-picture of a future England where the dreariness and abuses of the Industrial Revolution are wiped out and happy craftsmen and lovely women live in rural peace and beauty.

Morris' verse translation of the *Odyssey* appeared in 1887, and his love of Northern stories was shown again in the prose romances of the Gothic tribes, *The House of the Wolfings*, 1889, and *The Roots of the Mountains*, 1890. *Poems by the Way*, 1891, contains much of Morris' best revolutionary poetry, including "The Day is Coming."

The last of Morris' many careers was as founder of the Kelmscott Press. Just as he had become one of the few masters of narrative verse in English since Chaucer, so he now became one of the finest printers since Caxton. The greatest of his works in that field, quite fittingly, was the Kelmscott edition of Chaucer, 1896, which was illustrated by Burne-Jones.

Two months after the publication of the Chaucer, Morris, worn with the work and the interests of twenty lesser men, died at Hammersmith, October 3, 1896, and was buried at Kelmscott.

BIOGRAPHY AND CRITICISM

J. W. Mackail, *The Life of William Morris* (2 vols., London, 1899) is the most complete source of biographical information, although it should be supplemented by the work of Morris' daughter, May Morris, *William Morris: Artist, Writer, Socialist* (2 vols., Oxford, 1936). A good short biography with sound criticism is by Arthur Clutton-Brock, *William Morris, His Work and Influence* (New York and London, 1914). One of the fullest treatments of Morris as socialist is by Lloyd Wendell Eshleman, *A Victorian Rebel: The Life of William Morris* (New York, 1940) [published in England as Lloyd Eric Grey, *William Morris: Prophet of England's*

New Order (London, 1949)]. Literary style and sound biography characterize Esther Meynell, *Portrait of William Morris* (London, 1947). In the English Men of Letters series, Alfred Noyes, *William Morris* (London, 1926) deals chiefly with criticism of the major poetry.

PRINCIPAL WORKS

The Defence of Guenevere and Other Poems	1858
The Life and Death of Jason	1867
The Earthly Paradise: a Poem (3 vols.)	1868–70
Love is Enough, or the Freeing of Pharamond. A Morality	1873
The Story of Sigurd the Volsung and the Fall of the House of the Niblungs	1876
Hopes and Fears for Arts: five Lectures	1882
Signs of Change: seven Lectures	1888
A Dream of John Ball and A King's Lesson	1888
A Tale of the House of the Wolfings and all the Kindreds of the Mark	1889
News from Nowhere, or an Epoch of Rest	1891
Poems by the Way	1891
The Water of the Wondrous Isles	1897
The Sundering Flood	1898

An excellent selection from the voluminous prose and poetry is contained in *William Morris*, ed. G. D. H. Cole (Bloomsbury, 1934).

John Henry Newman

1801–1890

The future cardinal was born in London, February 21, 1801, first of the six children of John Newman, a prosperous banker of Dutch extraction, and his wife Jemima. The second of the three sons, Charles, became an avowed atheist in later life, and the youngest brother, Francis William, a Unitarian; they all came, however, from a sober Evangelical home. When he was fifteen John experienced an intense religious conversion about which he said, "I am still more certain than that I have hands or feet."

From a private school at Ealing Newman entered Trinity College, Oxford, in December, 1816, two months before his sixteenth birthday. At this time he was intended for the bar, although he dropped the idea before graduation in favor of becoming a clergyman. In 1818 he won a college scholarship, but it was his only academic distinction. He over-prepared for his final examinations in 1820, broke down, and took a comparatively poor degree instead of receiving the high honors he had expected. Undismayed, in 1822 he tried for and won a fellowship at Oriel College, then the center of intellectual life of Oxford.

In June, 1824, he was ordained in the Anglican Church and became curate of St. Clement's, a little church in Oxford, retaining at the same time his fellowship at Oriel. Four years later he became vicar of St. Mary's, the University church, and for fifteen years he preached there to large congregations attracted by the ascetic charm of his manner and the brilliance of his sermons.

By the time that he went to St. Mary's, however, he had travelled far from the Evangelicalism of his boyhood and had become increasingly high church in practice and belief. In the University his friends included several men who later took part in the Oxford Movement, notably Pusey, Keble, and Hurrell Froude. With Froude, Newman took a trip to Italy in 1832; he loved the city of Rome, but at this time he still thought its religion "polytheistical, degrading, and idolatrous." During his travels he wrote many of the poems which were later included in *Lyra Apostolica,* and on the return journey he composed the well-loved hymn, "Lead, Kindly Light." After a long illness in Sicily he returned to Oxford in July, 1833, just in time to hear the opening gun of the Oxford Movement, Keble's famous sermon on "National Apostasy," which proclaimed the need for a return to sacramental religion and a belief in the apostolic succession of the Anglican clergy. Keble's words struck deep into the heart of Newman. In September he began the long series of "Tracts for the Times," which he edited and many of which he wrote himself. More important, however, were his four o'clock sermons at St. Mary's, the spell of which has been recorded by many of his listeners. Matthew Arnold left a famous impression of "that spiritual apparition, gliding in the dim afternoon light through the aisles of St. Mary's, rising into the pulpit, and then in the most entrancing of voices, breaking the silence with words and thoughts which were religious music, subtle, sweet, mournful."

Yet at the very time his influence was greatest in Oxford, doubt was assailing him, and he began to feel a likeness in their relations with Rome between the Church of England and certain early heretics. The happiness he had known since coming to St. Mary's was at last shattered. In February, 1841, he published Tract XC, an attempt to show that the Anglican thirty-nine articles of faith were not incompatible with Catholic teaching, and that they only opposed Roman error. The resulting uproar forced the Bishop of Oxford to stop the Tracts, and it showed clearly the Protestant character of the rulers of the Established Church. From then on Newman was but a step from deserting Anglicanism, although he was not yet ready to accept the claims of Rome. The next year, 1842, he retired to a life of monastic simplicity in Littlemore, near Oxford, and in 1843 he resigned the living of St. Mary's and his fellowship at Oriel, yet he still hesitated, wanting to be sure of his convictions. Early in 1845 he began an "Essay on the Development of Christian Doctrine," and during its writing all his doubts vanished. In October he knelt before a priest at Littlemore and made his submission to Rome.

The next year he was ordained in Rome and became a member of the semi-monastic order of Oratorians. In 1847 he returned to England to introduce the order there, and founded an oratory at Birmingham.

At this time Protestant England was alarmed over the supposed threat of "Papal Aggression," and applauded an apostate Dominican named Achilli, who ranted against Rome. Newman was sued for libel in 1851 when he spoke bluntly of the moral turpitude of Achilli. He was fined £100, but the costs of the trial, about £14,000 were defrayed by popular subscription, most of the money coming from Roman Catholic admirers, although part of it was given by Protestants who deplored Achilli and his methods.

In 1852 Newman went to Dublin at the invitation of the bishops of Ireland to become Rector of the new Catholic University. After a series of lectures, later printed as *The Idea of a University,* 1852, he was installed, but the indifference, if not open hostility, of both clergy and laity made him resign his post in 1858 to return to England. While still in Dublin he wrote his second novel, *Callista,* 1856; his first, *Loss and Gain: the Story of a Convert,* had been published in 1848 after his own conversion.

In the years immediately following his return from Dublin, Newman attempted to establish an oratory at Oxford and to promote a new English version of the Vulgate Bible; both schemes failed, but he did succeed in establishing a Roman Catholic public school at Edgbaston, near Birmingham, in 1859.

His greatest fame and his finest work both resulted from the slanderous and unsupported statement which Charles Kingsley made in a magazine article in 1864, that "Truth for its own sake had never been a virtue with the Roman clergy. Father Newman informs us that it need not, and on the whole ought not to be." After an exchange of letters and pamphlets in which he easily made Kingsley look ridiculous, Newman vindicated his own religious sincerity by writing at great speed, often with tears in his eyes, his beautiful spiritual autobiography, *Apologia pro Vita Sua,* 1864. Many of his fiercest opponents were moved by its honesty and simplicity, and his honor was once more bright in his own country; the unpopularity he had suffered after his conversion was almost completely swept away. Shortly after the Kingsley affair, Newman wrote his finest poem, "The Dream of Gerontius," published in 1866.

In 1877 he was elected an honorary fellow of his old college, Trinity, and two years later his adopted church, which had long viewed his convert's zeal with some suspicion, rewarded him with a cardinal's hat. The rest of his life he lived in contented retirement at Edgbaston, looked on by his countrymen as a living symbol of the toleration and mutual respect which he had, almost single-handed, created between the Anglican and Roman Catholic churches of England. He died in quiet serenity at Edgbaston on August 11, 1890.

BIOGRAPHY AND CRITICISM

The best source for Newman's life before his conversion is his own *Apologia;* for his later life, the authorized biography, Wilfred Ward, *The Life of John Henry Cardinal Newman* (2 vols., London, 1912), is detailed, if not particularly readable. A good short biography is by J. Elliot Ross, *John Henry Newman* (London, 1933). An excellent survey of Newman's works is given by Charles F. Harrold, *John Henry Newman: an Expository and Critical Study of his Mind, Thought and Art* (London, 1945).

PRINCIPAL WORKS

The Arians of the Fourth Century   1833
Lectures on the Prophetical Office of the Church, Viewed Relatively to Romanism

and *Popular Protestantism* (republished as
part of *Via Media*, 1877)   1837
*An Essay on the Development of Christian
Doctrine*   1845
Loss and Gain: the Story of a Convert   1848
*Lectures on the Present Position of Catholics
in England*   1851
The Idea of a University   1852
Callista: a Sketch of the Third Century   1856
*Apologia pro Vita Sua: Being a Reply to a
Pamphlet Entitled "What, then, does Dr.
Newman Mean?"* (revised as *History of my
Religious Opinions*, 1865)   1864
Verses on Various Occasions   1868
An Essay in Aid of a Grammar of Assent   1870

The complete collected works (41 vols., 1874-1921) are published by Longmans, Green and Co.

SUGGESTED READING

Parochial Sermons:
  "The Invisible World"

Sermons Bearing on Subjects of the Day:
  "Wisdom and Innocence"

Essays Critical and Historical:
  "John Keble"

Lectures on the Present Position of Catholics in England:
  "The Protestant View of the Catholic Church"

The Idea of a University:
  "Knowledge its Own End"

"Knowledge Viewed in Relation to Learning"
"Knowledge Viewed in Relation to Religion"

Apologia pro Vita Sua:
"History of my Religious Opinions up to 1833"
"History of my Religious Opinions from 1841 to 1845"
"General Answer to Mr. Kingsley"

"The Dream of Gerontius"

Historical Sketches:
"What is a University?"

Dante Gabriel Rossetti

1828-1882

Dante Gabriel Rossetti, painter and poet, was born in London, May 12, 1828, the second child of Gabriele Rossetti, a political refugee and a profound student of Dante; the half-Italian Mrs. Rossetti was a deeply religious Church of England woman. These two modes of thought dominated the children of a bilingual family. The oldest, Maria, died an Anglican nun; the youngest, Christina, became "the only mistress of sacred verse" in English. Much of the early work of Dante Gabriel shows the influence of Christian tradition and through all the changes of his life he held to the faith of Dante in the love that "moves the sun in heaven and all the stars."

Rossetti's schooling was brief and unsatisfactory; his true education was at home where he read widely in English, French, and German, and along with the other children scribbled English and Italian verse and prose. He early decided to become a painter, and in 1842 entered the first of several art schools where he worked for some six years with growing impatience of their formal discipline. In 1848 he became apprentice to the painter Ford Madox Brown and later joined the young Holman Hunt in preparing a picture for exhibition.

Rossetti was all his life a successful professional artist; his living depended on the sale of drawings and paintings; from his poetry, although it circulated in manuscript and occasionally appeared in ephemeral magazines, he never received a penny till the publication of his first volume, the *Poems* of 1870. Yet painting and poetry went hand in hand with him; he wrote poems on his own paintings and at times painted pictures on themes he had already treated in verse. His first painting, "The Girlhood of Mary Virgin," and his first published poem, two sonnets on that picture, appeared together in 1849.

In 1848 Rossetti, Hunt, the young painter Millais, and a few other kindred souls, founded a group which they called the Pre-Raphaelite Brotherhood. Its aim was a protest against the academic conventionality of English art, along with a return to the serious subjects and truth to nature of earlier painters. To the paintings they exhibited they affixed the mystic initials, P. R. B., which aroused the wrath of conventional artists and critics. Two years later the group started a periodical, *The Germ,* to give expression to their ideas on literature and art. It failed after only four numbers, but it included a number of Rossetti's early poems and a prose tale, "Hand and Soul," which embodied his ideals and aspirations as a painter.

About this time Rossetti met and fell in love with Elizabeth Siddal, a delicate girl who had served as model for several of the Pre-Raphaelite painters. Their marriage was long delayed because of his poverty and her ill-health, but under Rossetti's influence she developed a certain talent for drawing and poetry. Ruskin, who had defended the Pre-Raphaelites against the early attacks of the press, admired Elizabeth's drawings, gave her a pension of £150 a year, promised to buy all Rossetti's paintings that he approved of, and subsidized the publication of his projected volume of translations from the early Italian poets.

In 1857 Rossetti went to Oxford with Ruskin. Fascinated by the bare walls of the new Oxford Union, he enlisted a group of young artists to decorate them with paintings. The attempt failed and the work was left unfinished, but a more important result of his visit was the friendship that he formed with the Oxonians: Burne-Jones, William Morris, and the young Swinburne. A little later Morris and Swinburne dedicated their first volumes of verse to Rossetti. He contributed three of his own poems to the *Oxford and Cambridge Magazine*, among them "The Burden of Nineveh," one of the few poems that show his awareness of the brutal materialism of mid-Victorian England.

Rossetti and Miss Siddal were married in May, 1860, but after the birth of a dead child she sank into a state of nervous depression aggravated by insomnia for which she took laudanum as a sedative. In the following year she died of an overdose of the drug. The coroner's jury pronounced a verdict of accidental death, but Rossetti seems to have felt that he was in some measure responsible for her death, and in a fit of remorse he enclosed in her coffin the manuscript volume of poems he had been collecting for publication.

During his short married life his volume of translations, *The Early Italian Poets,* had appeared. It was well received by a few scholars but did little to acquaint the public with Rossetti's original genius. After his wife's death he seems to have abandoned for a time all thought of poetry; he rented Tudor

House in Chelsea and devoted himself entirely to painting.

About 1867 the lovely Mrs. Morris began to sit for him, and she may have inspired a fresh burst of poetic composition, for he now began to write again and resumed the idea of publication. Late in 1869 Mrs. Rossetti's grave was opened and the buried manuscript retrieved. In 1870 he published his first volume of poems, which contained practically all that he had yet written, with a careful revision of much early work.

The *Poems* achieved an instant and unprecedented success; readers were quick to recognize a new and fresh voice in contemporary poetry. Late in 1871, however, a minor Scotch poet, Robert Buchanan, savagely attacked Rossetti as the leader of the "fleshly school of poetry" in an article in the *Contemporary Review,* and he redoubled his onslaught in a pamphlet published in May, 1872. Rossetti had replied with an exposure of his critic's unfair methods (*Athenaeum,* December, 1871), but under the renewed attack his mind failed. He suffered delusions of persecution and in June, 1872, attempted suicide. The blow fell when he was least able to resist it; he had formed the habit of taking chloral for insomnia and he suffered from nephritis until his death. The drug habit, of which he was cured just before the end of his life, was probably responsible for the persecution mania which persisted as long as he took the drug. After recovering from his attempted suicide, he spent two years at Kelmscott Manor, a country house which he shared with Morris. In 1874 he published a new edition of his translations (now renamed *Dante and his Circle*) and began again to write poetry.

In 1881 Rossetti published his *Ballads and Sonnets* along with a new edition of the *Poems.* He shifted the sonnets of "The House of Life" from the *Poems* into the new volume to complete the sonnet cycle, and among other minor revisions he omitted one fine sonnet, "Nuptial Sleep," to comply with Victorian standards. In addition to the added sonnets the new volume contained several long narrative poems, among them "The White Ship" and "The King's Tragedy." *Ballads and Sonnets*, like the *Poems*, was a distinct success, and several thousand copies were sold at once.

Throughout his life Rossetti had exercised a dominant influence on his circle of friends and after his death he was the inspiration of the post-Victorian esthetic school. The most sensuous of Victorian poets, his awareness of bodily beauty is always linked with his recognition of the soul's beauty that alone gives it true significance; at his best this painter of fair ladies attains the high utterance of a true ethical poet.

In December, 1881, he suffered a paralytic stroke, and on April 9, 1882, he died of nephritis at the seaside resort of Birchington, where he was buried in the little graveyard.

BIOGRAPHY AND CRITICISM

Elisabeth Luther Cary, *The Rossettis: Dante Gabriel and Christina* (New York and London, 1900) is chiefly valuable for the large number of reproductions of Rossetti's paintings. For a short biography and concise criticism, the student would be well advised to turn to A. C. Benson, *Rossetti,* English Men of Letters series (New York, 1904). The most complete of the biographies, although it is definitely unfavorable to its subject, is by Oswald Doughty, *A Victorian Romantic: Dante Gabriel Rossetti* (London, 1949). A healthy corrective to some of the romanticizing about the poet is contained in the study by his niece, Helen Rossetti Angeli, *Dante Gabriel Rossetti: His Friends and Enemies* (London, 1949).

PRINCIPAL WORKS

The Early Italian Poets from Ciullo d'Alcamo to Dante Alighieri 1100-1200-1300 in the Original Metres together with Dante's *Vita Nuova* [republished as *Dante and his Circle*, 1874]	1861
Poems [revised edition, 1881]	1870
Ballads and Sonnets	1881

The standard edition of the poetry is the *Complete Poetical Works*, ed. W. M. Rossetti (7 vols., London, 1898-1901); *Dante Gabriel Rossetti: an Anthology*, ed. F. L. Lucas (Cambridge, 1933), contains a carefully chosen selection of the poems.

John Ruskin

1819-1900

John Ruskin was born in 1819, the only child of a prosperous wine merchant and his middle-aged wife, both of whom were of good Scottish middle class stock, inflexibly puritanical in their Evangelical religion. Most of Ruskin's childhood was spent in and near London, studying at home during the winters and travelling through England and Scotland in the summers when he and his mother accompanied Mr. Ruskin on business trips. When he was fourteen the family made an expedition to France, Germany, Switzerland, and Italy, the first of the frequent trips to study Continental art and scenery which he made during the rest of his life.

His early education was largely under the restrictive supervision of his mother, who was sure that her precocious son was a genius. Determined that he should become a bishop, she not only taught him the customary elementary subjects, but made him work long hours at repeated, detailed readings and memorizations of the Bible, to which he later claimed that he owed his sense of language and the basis of his own prose style. In 1837 his mother accompanied him to Oxford when he was matriculated at Christ Church; she settled there during the time he was an undergraduate, and his father completed the family circle on weekends. Although he won the Newdigate prize for English verse, Ruskin's Oxford career was undistinguished, largely because of a two-year gap in his studies when he was threatened with tuberculosis; he did not receive his B.A. degree until 1842.

While he was still an undergraduate Ruskin had a disappointing love affair with a young French girl, the daughter of one of his father's partners, but he was not seriously in love again before 1848, when he married Euphemia ("Effie") Chalmers Gray, a pretty and lively girl nine years his junior. The two were ill-matched; the marriage was never consummated and was annulled in 1854 at the suit of his wife, Ruskin making no defense. A year later she married the painter Millais, formerly an intimate friend of Ruskin.

In 1840 Ruskin became acquainted with J. M. W. Turner, the great English painter, whom he had long admired, several of whose pictures already hung in the Ruskin home. Three years later, under the signature "A Graduate of Oxford," Ruskin published the first of the five volumes of *Modern Painters*, a work growing out of a defense of Turner's later, impressionist style. The book's success was immediate, and its author's identity soon became known. At twenty-four he found himself already celebrated and on his way to becoming one of the most influential art critics England has ever known. During the years of his married life, he undertook a defense of the paintings of the Pre-Raphaelites. Turning increasingly to the study of architecture, he published *The Seven Lamps of Architecture*, 1849, and between 1851 and 1853 the three-volume *Stones of*

Venice, books which helped the Gothic revival in English architecture. Their equation of art and morality won an enthusiastic response from such men as Carlyle, while their exuberant, ornate style assured Ruskin's place as the foremost of the Victorian "word-painters." His critical powers were always far in advance of his own ability in painting and drawing, but in 1854, after the disastrous end of his marriage, he took charge for four years of the drawing classes at the Working Men's College in London, along with D. G. Rossetti, Ford Madox Brown, and Edward Burne-Jones.

Ruskin's popularity as lecturer and writer on art was increasing rapidly, but his own interests were turning more and more toward social questions. The transition from his insistence on the essential morality of art to insistence on a society in which it could develop was a natural one. His first attack on the prevailing political economy of the Manchester School began as a series of essays, later published in book form as *Unto This Last*, in the *Cornhill Magazine* in 1860, but Thackeray, the editor, was obliged to halt their publication because of the hostility which the surprisingly outspoken bitterness of the first four installments aroused. In 1862-3 he contributed a further attack on political economy to *Fraser's Magazine*, then under the editorship of J. A. Froude, and once more public abuse caused the cessation of the serial publication of the essays, republished as *Munera Pulveris* in 1872. The popularity of his other writings suffered by contagion from the essays, and Ruskin's influence went into a decline for some years. Even his father, an orthodox follower of the Manchester School, abandoned his habitual overindulgence and reproached Ruskin, perhaps the first disturbance in the unity of the family.

In 1864, at the death of his father, Ruskin inherited a considerable fortune. By the end of his own life he had given away his whole inheritance in benevolent and charitable gifts, and lived on the income from his writings, which averaged £4,000 a year — more than $20,000 — for many years before his death; it was, however, his father's wealth which had originally allowed him to devote his whole time to writing. In 1871 he began *Fors Clavigera,* a series of monthly letters addressed to the workmen of England, in which he poured out his views on art, education, social reform, and religious belief. What the workers got out of it is problematical, but many of the more intelligent young men took to it kindly.

Ruskin was elected the first Slade Professor of Art at Oxford in 1869. His lectures were enormously popular with the undergraduates, and he entered actively into University life, establishing a drawing school and endowing a drawing master for it, and supervising the unsuccessful building by undergraduates of a model country road near Oxford. In 1871 he founded the Guild of St. George, a society devoted to the replacement of modern manufacture by handicraft, to the reclaiming of barren land for agriculture, and to the mental and moral education of boys and girls: all to be done under the absolute control of Ruskin as master of the Guild. Into this vain attempt to revive an ideal medievalism he poured a great part of his own fortune.

For some years he had been living under the threat of mental breakdown, probably brought closer by the death in 1875 of Rose La Touche, a girl thirty years younger than he, whom he had loved unhappily for more than fifteen years. In 1879 he was forced by a complete mental collapse to give up his Oxford professorship. He recovered sufficiently to resume the Slade lectures in 1883-4, but again broke down and definitely resigned his post in 1885.

Ruskin ranks with Carlyle as one of the major Victorian prophets. When he retired from public life in 1885 he felt that his mission had completely failed, but an address presented to him by a group of Ruskin societies on his eightieth birthday testifies to the continuing influence of his ideals. These ideals may be summarized as: a) the moral value of the love of beauty in nature and in its recreation in art, and b) the duty of the state to promote the welfare, physical, mental, and moral of all its citizens.

After his retirement, Ruskin's life was darkened by intermittent insanity; in moments of lucidity, however, he worked at his autobiography, *Praeterita*. The last chapter of this charming and uncompleted work was written in 1889, after which he sank into complete isolation from the world at Coniston in the Lake District, where he died of influenza on January 20, 1900. Interment was offered in Westminster Abbey, but he was buried as he had wished, in the Coniston churchyard.

BIOGRAPHY AND CRITICISM

The standard lives are by William G. Collingwood, *The Life of John Ruskin* (London, 1900) and Sir Edward T. Cook, *The Life of John Ruskin* (2 vols., London, 1911). A more recent critical biography is by Reginald H. Wilenski, *John Ruskin: an Introduction to Further Study of his Life and Work* (London, 1933). A new light was thrown on Ruskin's married life by the publication of many hitherto unknown letters in *The Order of Release* (London, 1947). This important book by Sir William James, which was published in America under the title of *John Ruskin and Effie Gray*, needs to be checked by J. H. Whitehouse, *The Vindication* of *Ruskin* (London, 1950). Much of James's material is embodied or used by Peter Quennell, *John Ruskin: the Portrait of a Prophet* (London, 1949).

PRINCIPAL WORKS

Modern Painters (5 vols.)	1843–60
The Seven Lamps of Architecture	1849
The Stones of Venice (3 vols.)	1851–3
Pre-Raphaelitism	1851
Unto This Last	1862
Sesame and Lilies	1865
The Crown of Wild Olive	1866
Time and Tide, by Weare and Tyne	1867
Lectures on Art	1870
Fors Clavigera (8 vols.)	1871–84
Praeterita (28 pts.)	1885–9

The only complete edition of Ruskin's tremendous literary output is the monumental *Works of John Ruskin*, Library Edition, ed. Edward T. Cook and Alexander D. O. Wedderburn (39 vols., London, 1903-12). A well-chosen group of readings is given in *Selections and Essays*, Modern Student's Library, ed. Frederick W. Roe (New York, Chicago, 1918), in which will be found most of the following suggested readings.

SUGGESTED READING

Modern Painters:
    "Of the Received Opinions Touching the 'Grand Style,'" III, IV, 1
    "Of the Pathetic Fallacy," III, IV, 12
    "The Mountain Glory," IV, V, 20, i-x
    "The Two Boyhoods," V, IX, 9

The Seven Lamps of Architecture:
   "The Lamp of Memory"
   "The Lamp of Obedience"

The Stones of Venice:
   "St. Mark's," II, 4
   "The Nature of Gothic," II, 6, i-lxxviii, cvi-cxiv

Unto This Last:
   "The Roots of Honour"
   "The Veins of Wealth"

The Crown of Wild Olive:
   "Traffic"

Lectures on Art:
   "Inaugural"

Praeterita:
   "Herne-Hill Almond Blossoms," I, 2
   "Papa and Mamma," I, 7

Algernon Charles Swinburne

1837–1909

Swinburne, the only one of the great Victorian writers who came of an aristocratic family, was born in London, April 5, 1837. His father was an admiral and his mother, daughter of the Earl of Ashburnham, was a woman of artistic taste who read French and Italian to her children. He was a delicate, undersized boy, and even as a man he had a tiny, nervously moving figure which had never grown to full physical stature. He had an active boyhood at his homes on the Isle of Wight and in Northumberland, climbing, riding, swimming, always within sight and sound of the sea, the "green-girdled mother," the most constantly recurrent image in his poems. He read widely, beginning Shakespeare when six and the other Elizabethan and Jacobean dramatists at Eton, which he entered in 1849. Here, too, he read the classical authors, particularly the Greeks, who were to become the other dominant literary influence on his poetry. He withdrew from Eton at sixteen and after two years of private tutoring went to Balliol College, Oxford, in 1856. He continued his reading in several languages and began writing seriously, but his genius was late in maturing, and few of his early poems gave promise of his later talents. At Oxford he made his first contact with the Pre-Raphaelites and became a friend of both Rossetti and Morris. Like that earlier undergraduate Shelley, at the University he first felt the passionate devotion to political and personal liberty which was so important in his later writing. One is constantly reminded by his republicanism and agnosticism of the great Romantic poets; for them the French Revolution fired the imagination, for Swinburne the Italian Risorgimento lit the spark. And, like Byron, he was to defy social decorum. A growing susceptibility to alcohol combined with his outside interests to keep him from his formal studies, until at last he was suspended, and in 1860 Jowett advised him to leave Oxford without a degree.

He moved to London and there renewed his friendship with Morris, Rossetti, and Meredith. To Rossetti he "affectionately inscribed" his first published work, two historical verse tragedies, *The Queen Mother and Rosamond,* 1860, which appeared in a volume that was completely ignored by his contemporaries. In London his excessive drinking continued, and at frequent intervals he had to be carried off to the country by his family to recover his health. On one trip of recuperation to Italy he met the elderly Landor, whom he idolized for his liberal tendencies and for his series of verse tales on Greek mythology, *The Hellenics.* On his return to England Swinburne finished his own verse tragedy in the Greek manner, *Atalanta in Calydon,* which he dedicated to Landor. On its publication in 1865 the reading public instantly recognized a new genius; Ruskin called it the "grandest thing ever done by a youth — though he is a Demoniac youth." Later the same year he published *Chastelard*, first of his trilogy of plays on Mary, Queen of Scots. With England still excited by his first success, great attention naturally centered on his volume of *Poems and Ballads*, 1866, a collection containing such lyrics as "Laus Veneris," "Dolores," and the beautiful "Triumph of Time," written after the disappointment of his only love affair in 1862. All the metrical beauty, rich in alliterative and anapestic verse, for which he was famous, was there, but there was also a strong pagan, anti-Christian undertone, and open sexuality of an unpleasantly sadistic sort. Writing in the *Saturday Review*, John Morley spoke for the conservative critics when he called Swinburne the "libidinous laureate of a pack of satyrs." Taking fright, his publishers withdrew the book from sale, but critics like Ruskin had found in the power of Swinburne's imagination the beginning of a new poetic age, and a more courageous publisher finally undertook to reissue the book.

Although Swinburne became notorious by the erotic freedom of *Poems and Ballads*, his next works showed an interest in a deeper, more permanent form of liberty: political revolution. His enthusiasm for Mazzini and the Italian Risorgimento dominated *A Song of Italy*, 1867, and *Songs Before Sunrise*, 1871, and his pamphlet of political verse, *An Appeal to England*, 1867, demonstrated his radicalism in domestic politics. During this period he began a novel, *Lesbia Brandon* (unpublished until 1952), and became a regular contributor to the *Fortnightly*, in which his memorial to Baudelaire, "Ave atque Vale," appeared in 1868. The poem was reprinted in the second series of *Poems and Ballads*, 1878, a fit successor to the first volume in melody and richness, but with a muted sensuousness.

For several years Swinburne's life had been one

of dissipation, with a consequent deterioration in his health. By 1879 his breakdown was complete and death near when his friend Theodore Watts-Dunton established him in a suburban villa in Putney, where he spent the last thirty years of his life. The external history of the rest of his years is one of little change: a quiet existence, guarded jealously from undesirable acquaintances and prevented from dissipation.

Swinburne "in his early work . . . was a poet of amazing promise, and . . . in his later work he was a great man of letters." During the Putney years there were frequently beautiful pieces in the many volumes he published, but his lyric impulse had slackened. Perhaps the finest work of the period was his retelling of the old Tristram legend in *Tristram of Lyonesse*, 1882. The third series of *Poems and Ballads*, 1889, is notable for its ballads written twenty years earlier.

In his mature years Swinburne returned to his interest in the verse drama. *Bothwell*, 1874, and *Mary Stuart*, 1881, complete the trilogy begun with *Chastelard*; *Erechtheus*, 1876, like *Atalanta*, was modelled on the Greek drama; and a half dozen other plays show his indebtedness to the Elizabethans.

After 1868 Swinburne published several volumes of literary criticism, to which he brought a poet's sensibility and the scholar's diligence in research, although he lacked the ideal critic's impartiality. He published monographs on such dramatists as Chapman, Jonson, and Shakespeare (perhaps his most enduring critical work), and among the moderns he studied Blake, Charlotte Brontë, Dickens, and Victor Hugo.

But in spite of all his other accomplishments, it was the loss of one of her greatest lyric poets, a magician in rhythm and sound, revolutionary and daring, which England felt when Swinburne died in Putney of pneumonia on April 10, 1909.

BIOGRAPHY AND CRITICISM

The standard biography, *The Life of Algernon Charles Swinburne,* by the poet's friend Sir Edmund Gosse (London, 1917), devotes little time to the latter part of Swinburne's life. Harold Nicolson in *Swinburne,* English Men of Letters series (New York, 1926) blends biography and criticism concisely. Perhaps the other most satisfactory critical biographies are by T. Earle Welby, *A Study of Swinburne* (New York, 1926) and Samuel C. Chew *Swinburne* (Boston, 1929).

PRINCIPAL WORKS

The Queen Mother and Rosamond	1860
Atalanta in Calydon	1865
Chastelard	1865
Poems and Ballads	1866
A Song of Italy	1867
William Blake	1868
Songs Before Sunrise	1871
Bothwell	1874
George Chapman	1875
Essays and Studies	1875
Erechtheus	1876
A Note on Charlotte Brontë	1877
Poems and Ballads: Second Series	1878
Songs of the Springtides	1880
The Heptalogia [parodies]	1880
A Study of Shakespeare	1880
Mary Stuart	1881
Tristram and Other Poems	1882

A Century of Roundels	1883
Marino Faliero	1885
A Study of Victor Hugo	1886
Locrine	1887
Poems and Ballads: Third Series	1889
A Study of Ben Jonson	1889
The Sisters	1892
Astrophel and Other Poems	1894
Rosamund: Queen of the Lombards	1899
The Duke of Gandia	1908
Charles Dickens	1913
Posthumous Poems	1917
Lesbia Brandon	1952

Swinburne's *Complete Works* are edited by Edmund Gosse and T. J. Wise (20 vols., London, 1925-7). The same editors have compiled a useful anthology of his poetry, *Selections from A. C. Swinburne* (London, 1919); another anthology with an excellent introduction is *Selections from Swinburne*, ed. William O. Raymond (New York, 1925).

Alfred Tennyson

1809-1892

Alfred Tennyson was born on August 6, 1809, fourth of the twelve children of George Tennyson, Rector of Somersby, Lincolnshire, a man of education and considerable poetic talent. Like most boys of the period, Alfred began his education at home; under his father's thorough tutelage he studied the classics by memorizing and constantly repeating Latin and Greek verse. When, at seven years, he left home to join his two elder brothers at the grammar school in Louth, he already knew the odes of Horace by heart. He disliked leaving home and hated the school and its tyrannical discipline; in later life he said that all he had learned there was the beauty of the sound of *"sonus desilientis aquae."* In 1820 he returned to Somersby to study once more with his father. For eight years Alfred and his brother Charles worked hard together on their home studies and read widely in both the classics and English literature. By the time he was fifteen he could write fluent Greek and Latin verse.

Mr. Tennyson's children inherited both his tendency to melancholia and his poetical talents; not only Alfred, but also the two elder sons, Frederick and Charles, later achieved reputations as poets. They all scribbled poetry constantly as boys, and in 1827 Alfred and Charles published *Poems by Two Brothers* — actually it contained four by Frederick, too — a volume made up chiefly of conventional Byronic imitations. They received ten pounds in payment and an equal sum in credit for the purchase of books from the publisher-bookseller. The volumes received no critical attention, and the sales were small.

At Trinity College, Cambridge, where Tennyson matriculated in 1828, he became a member of the "Cambridge Conversazione Society," better known as "The Apostles," a small and brilliant group devoted to discussions of questions political, religious, and literary. Perhaps the most gifted of the members was Arthur Hallam, a wealthy and cultivated Etonian two years Tennyson's junior. Despite the contrast in their backgrounds, perhaps because of it, the two soon became the closest of friends. In 1830 they took a summer excursion to the Continent, the first long trip Alfred had ever made; the natural beauty of the country, particularly that of the Pyrenees, was a moving emotional experience to him. Hallam was a frequent visitor at Somersby and there fell in love with one of Alfred's sisters, Emily, to whom he became engaged. The prospect of family ties strengthened the friendship of the young men. Although their intimacy had only a few years remaining before Hallam's death, its memory was to stay with Alfred the rest of his life.

Tennyson won the Chancellor's medal for English verse in 1829 with his poem "Timbuctoo," but when he had to leave Cambridge without a degree in February 1831, he regretted the loss of little but the companionship of the Apostles. His father was critically ill, and when he died a few weeks later, Alfred was left to act as head of the family.

"Timbuctoo" had been published at Cambridge, but Tennyson's first independent volume, *Poems, Chiefly Lyrical*, did not appear until 1830. It was followed two years later by *Poems*. The reviewers were moderately kind to the first volume, although "Christopher North" (John Wilson) criticized it condescendingly in *Blackwood's*. A brutally cruel notice of the 1832 volume by J. W. Croker in the *Quarterly Review* so completely stopped its sales and so crushed the thin-skinned poet that he published little more for ten years and remained agonizingly sensitive to reviews for the rest of his life.

In 1833 he was overwhelmed by the news of Hallam's sudden death while visiting in Vienna with his parents; it took Alfred years to recover from the blow.

At the wedding of his brother Charles in 1836 Tennyson renewed his acquaintance with the exquisitely fragile Emily Sellwood, whom he had met some years before. They fell in love, but Tennyson's family responsibilities and poverty prevented their marriage. The Sellwoods disapproved of Alfred and his family, and in 1840 they forbade any further correspondence between him and Emily, a ban which lasted for ten years. In an attempt to relieve his poverty Tennyson invested in 1841 in a scheme for mechanical wood-carving; the failure of the venture swept away both his own slender means and most of those of his family.

The publication in 1842 of *Poems* in two volumes finally established his reputation. The first volume contained revised versions of the best of his works from the 1830 and 1832 editions, and the second was made up of such memorable new poems as "Ulysses" and "Locksley Hall." Three years later his position was recognized by a civil list pension of £200 per year given by Sir Robert Peel, on whom Arthur's father, Henry Hallam, had pressed the poet's merits. Despite his popularity, *The Princess* was coolly received in its first edition in 1847, but as Tennyson reworked it and inserted a series of beautiful songs and lyrics into later editions, it became in time one of his most popular works.

The real turning point of his life was the year 1850, when he was forty-one. In June he and Emily Sellwood began a long and happy married life, less than a fortnight after the publication of *In Memoriam*, the great elegy on which he had been working during the seventeen years since Hallam's death. Its overwhelming success and Prince Albert's admiration of it led the Queen in November to offer him the position of Poet Laureate left vacant by Wordsworth's death. To celebrate the appointment, he attended the Queen's levee in court dress borrowed from Samuel Rogers, which Wordsworth before him had worn on a similar occasion.

His first poem as Laureate, the *Ode on the Death of the Duke of Wellington*, is one of his finest, but its reception was not altogether favorable. In 1855 the new strains of his "monodrama," *Maud*, provoked almost universally hostile criticism, but after the publication in 1859 of the first four of the *Idylls of the King* he became the object of public adulation of a sort known to no other English poet. His work commanded increasingly high prices, and in 1871 he was offered £1,000 by a New York editor for "any poem of three stanzas."

For more than a decade after 1875, when he published his first blank verse drama, *Queen Mary*, Tennyson continued experimenting in writing for the stage, a medium for which he had no particular aptitude. The most successful of his plays are those dealing with English historical subjects, *Queen Mary, Harold,* and *Becket.* Both *Becket* and *The Cup* had long runs on the stage, perhaps because Irving produced them and played the leads with Ellen Terry. The last few years of his life Tennyson dropped his dramatic writing and returned to the earlier lyrical strain for which he is best known today.

The University of Oxford conferred the degree of D.C.L. on him in 1855, and in 1864, 1873, and 1874 he was offered a baronetcy, which he repeatedly declined. Both the Queen and Prince Albert admired his work, and after the latter's death Tennyson dedicated the second edition of *Idylls of the King* to his memory. He became increasingly intimate with the Queen, and in 1883 she offered him the title of baron, the first peerage ever given a poet for his work. He accepted and became the first Lord Tennyson the following year.

His peaceful old age was saddened by the death of his second son, Lionel, in 1886, and by the loss of many of his best friends. He lived in retirement at his houses on the Isle of Wight and near Haslemere. The last two years of his life he was a semi-invalid, but he continued writing and completed work on his last volume, *The Death of Oenone,* just before his death. He died of heart failure in 1892 and was buried in the Poets' Corner of Westminster Abbey, next to Robert Browning, as the choir sang "Crossing the Bar" and Lady Tennyson's musical setting of "Silent Voices." With his death the Victorian era of letters came to a close.

BIOGRAPHY AND CRITICISM

The two standard biographies, both of which are long and detailed, are by Tennyson's son, Hallam

Tennyson, *Alfred, Lord Tennyson; a Memoir* (2 vols., London, 1897) and by his grandson, Charles Tennyson, *Alfred Tennyson* (New York, 1949). A shorter work which is both critical and readable is by Harold G. Nicolson, *Tennyson; Aspects of his Life, Character and Poetry* (Boston and New York, 1923). A good study of Tennyson's poetry is by Paull F. Baum, *Tennyson Sixty Years After* (Chapel Hill, 1948).

PRINCIPAL WORKS

[The following list is of first editions; many of the poems included were much altered in subsequent editions.]

Poems by Two Brothers	1827
Timbuctoo	1829
Poems, Chiefly Lyrical	1830
Poems	1832
Poems (2 vols.)	1842
The Princess	1847
In Memoriam	1850
Ode on the Death of the Duke of Wellington	1852
Maud, and Other Poems	1855
Idylls of the King	1859-85
Enoch Arden, and Other Poems	1864
Ballads, and Other Poems	1880
Becket	1884
Tiresias, and Other Poems	1885
Locksley Hall Sixty Years After	1886
Demeter, and Other Poems	1889
The Death of Oenone, and Other Poems (published posthumously)	1892

Although there are several collected editions of the works, none is complete and definitive; perhaps the most useful is the Eversley Edition, ed. Hallam Tennyson (9 vols., London, 1907-08). A convenient, nearly complete one-volume edition is *The Poetic and Dramatic Works of Alfred Lord Tennyson*, Cambridge Edition, ed. W. J. Rolfe (Boston and New York, 1898). Two useful modern volumes of selections are *The Best of Tennyson*, ed. Walter Graham (New York, 1940) and *A Selection from the Poems of Alfred Lord Tennyson*, ed. W. H. Auden (Garden City, 1944).

William Makepeace Thackeray

1811-1863

Thackeray was born in Calcutta, July 18, 1811, the only child of an Englishman in the Indian Civil Service and his young wife. In 1817, after his father's death, he was sent to England to a succession of preparatory schools which he hated, and then to public school at the Charterhouse, where he was made even more miserable by bullying and flogging. After six years he left to enter Trinity College, Cambridge, in 1829, where he remained for a little more than a year. He enjoyed the University more than the Charterhouse, but in both places his achievements were social rather than academic. At Cambridge he wrote for the *Snob*, an undergraduate journal to which he contributed a burlesque of Tennyson's prize poem, *Timbuctoo;* he formed lasting friendships with Tennyson, Edward Fitzgerald, translator of the *Rubáiyát*, and William Brookfield, debated at the Union, spent a great deal of money, and left without a degree.

Having a comfortable income from his father's estate, he could afford to take an active part in the society he always enjoyed so much, and to travel.

The year he left Cambridge he spent some months in pleasant dilettantism at Weimar, where he was introduced to Goethe. On his return to London he began to study for the bar, but the law was distasteful to him, and he abandoned it after a year's desultory work. He lost a considerable sum of money in 1833 by buying and editing a short-lived paper, the *National Standard*. Extravagance and unwise investments dissipated the rest of his inheritance, and by 1834 he was compelled to earn his living. He always had a flair for drawing, so he decided to study painting in Paris, but this was no more successful than his other ventures, although he did become a competent cartoonist and later illustrated several of his own works. When the *Pickwick Papers* were appearing in 1836 he applied unsuccessfully to Dickens for employment in illustrating them.

On the strength of eight guineas a week which he was earning as Paris correspondent for the *Constitutional*, a Radical newspaper of which his stepfather was director, Thackeray married an Irish girl, Isabella Shawe, in August 1836. Three daughters were born to them, of whom two survived; the eldest, Anne, later Lady Ritchie, became a novelist and essayist. After the birth of her third child Mrs. Thackeray's mind became progressively more deranged until in 1842 she had to be confined; she survived her husband more than thirty years without recovering her sanity. In the wreck of his marriage Thackeray was left to supervise the rearing of his daughters. While his wife lived he was not free to remarry, of course, and the rest of his domestic life was frequently sad and lonely.

The *Constitutional* failed some months after Thackeray's marriage, and he turned to hack-work for several journals, including *The Times*. To the new *Fraser's Magazine* he contributed his first important success, *The Yellowplush Correspondence*, 1837-8, the fictional memoirs of a pushing and self-important footman, of which the theme was one he later used frequently: the ridiculousness of pretension. Reviews, sketches, and novels followed in *Fraser's*, notably *Catherine*, 1839-40, written to satirize such "Newgate Calendar" novels of crime as *Oliver Twist* and Harrison Ainsworth's *Jack Sheppard*; *The Great Hoggarty Diamond*, 1841, a story of corruption and speculation in business; and *Barry Lyndon*, 1844, the supposed autobiography of an eighteenth century Irish adventurer, which covers his career from rascally youth to death in prison. To the newly founded *Punch* Thackeray began contributing in 1842, and the "Snob Papers," printed there and later collected as *The Book of Snobs*, 1848, made his reputation as a social satirist.

At the same time that he was working on the "Snob Papers," he was engaged on a long novel; his first masterpiece, *Vanity Fair*, 1847-8, appeared in monthly installments. Its setting is England during and after the Napoleonic Wars, but its panoramic view of folly and vanity is universal. Becky Sharp, the unscrupulous governess whose adventures dominate the book, is generally recognized as one of the most vividly drawn characters in the English novel. Hard on the heels of *Vanity Fair* came the publication in numbers of *Pendennis*, 1848-50, the history of an amiable and extravagant young man whose early career is a clear parallel to Thackeray's own.

Thackeray was always gregarious, and he loved the easy life of the upper classes, with whom he was friendly but who were frequently the butts of his satire. His wife's incurable illness made him still more dependent upon his friends' hospitality. For several years after her breakdown he found comfort in the home of one of his closest Cambridge friends,

William Brookfield; gradually he fell deeply but innocently in love with Mrs. Brookfield. In the autumn of 1851 Brookfield wisely insisted that his wife see less of his friend. The loss of a companionship on which he had depended heavily was one of the most severe emotional blows of Thackeray's life.

In an effort to forget his hurt and to make his daughters financially secure he began lecturing, although he suffered much embarrassment in speaking in public; his six lectures on the English humorists of the eighteenth century were so well received that he decided to repeat them in America. Before sailing he published *Henry Esmond,* a historical novel for which his studies of the humorists had provided the background. It is set in the period of history he loved best, the reign of Queen Anne, but the love story of Esmond and Lady Castlewood is in part a reflection of his own feeling for Mrs. Brookfield. Perhaps because it was the only one of his novels not published serially, *Esmond* has a finish and structural organization greater than any of his other works. Unlike Dickens, he enjoyed his American visit in the winter of 1852-3, quite aside from the £2500 which he took back to England with him.

His delightful fairy-tale, *The Rose and the Ring,* was published in 1855 at the same time that *The Newcomes* was appearing in numbers. The central character of *The Newcomes* is another view of Thackeray himself as a young man of good instincts which are thwarted by his own shortcomings; Clive's struggles to establish himself as an artist and the trials of his first marriage are reminiscent of Thackeray's early manhood. The real interest of the book, however, is in the characterization of Clive's capriciously charming sweetheart, Ethel, and of the honorable and guileless old Colonel Newcome.

In 1855 he went once more to America, this time

to give a set of lectures which were published as *The Four Georges*. After his return he stood unsuccessfully as Liberal candidate for Parliament in the city of Oxford in July, 1857; in his advocacy of the extension of suffrage he anticipated the Reform Bill of a decade later.

The last of his great novels, *The Virginians*, 1857-9, continues the fortunes of the Esmond family in the persons of the American twin grandsons of Henry Esmond, in a setting divided between the fast and fashionable society of England and America of the Revolution.

By this time his popularity rivalled that of Dickens, with whom he was friendly if not intimate; their only quarrel was healed just before Thackeray's death. The sentimentality which he shared with Dickens over scenes of suffering, and the occasionally maudlin quality of his "good" women are tempered in his work with a satirical, sometimes cynical, view of society which perhaps has more appeal today than in his own time. Thackeray had considerable skill in parody, of which his best example is the burlesque of his contemporary writers in the series of "Mr. Punch's Prize Novelists," republished as "Novels by Eminent Hands," 1856. He never thought of himself as a poet, but some of his light verse, such as "The Ballad of Bouillabaisse," is among the best of its kind.

A huge salary tempted him into becoming the first editor of the *Cornhill Magazine* in 1860, a task he performed adequately, although he was not well fitted for the position. His editorial standards of taste were those of his age; he once rejected a poem by Mrs. Browning because it contained "an account of unlawful passion felt by a man for a woman." His own reputation (and the prices paid by *Cornhill*) helped him get such contributors as Arnold, Tennyson, Trollope, Ruskin — and his own daughter Anne. To the magazine he contributed his last three novels: *Lovel the Widower*, 1860, a short fictionalized version of an earlier unsuccessful two-act play; *The Adventures of Philip*, 1861-2, the last in the series of young heroes molded in the image of Thackeray's early life; and the unfinished *Denis Duval*, 1864, a historical romance in which he returns to his beloved eighteenth century. He also wrote for *Cornhill* the finest work of his late years, the amusing series of gossipy, familiar editorial essays, *The Roundabout Papers;* like most of his finest work they are mellowly reminiscent and autobiographical.

The ill health from which he had suffered for more than ten years ended in his sudden death at Kensington, London, in December, 1863.

BIOGRAPHY AND CRITICISM

Thackeray's own injunction to his daughter on biography, "Let there be nothing of this when I am gone," has resulted in a paucity of details of his life until comparatively recently. The dam broke, however, with the publication by Gordon N. Ray of his edition of *The Letters and Private Papers of William Makepeace Thackeray* (4 vols., Cambridge, Mass., 1945), which is the primary source of biographical information. Of the biographies written since then, the most satisfactory is by Lionel Stevenson, *The Showman of Vanity Fair* (New York, 1947). An admirable, if somewhat too admiring, critical work is by George Saintsbury, *A Consideration of Thackeray* (London, 1931). Biography and criticism are combined by John W. Dodds, *Thackeray: a Critical Portrait* (New York, London, Toronto, 1941).

PRINCIPAL WORKS

[Since practically all Thackeray's works were published serially, the date of their publication in book-form is sometimes at variance with that given in the text for their original appearance.]

The Yellowplush Correspondence	1838
The Irish Sketch Book. By Mr. M. A. Titmarsh (2 vols.)	1843
Vanity Fair. A Novel without a Hero	1848
The Book of Snobs	1848
The History of Samuel Titmarsh and the Great Hoggarty Diamond	1849
The History of Pendennis. His Fortunes and Misfortunes, His Friends and His Greatest Enemy (2 vols.)	1849–50
The History of Henry Esmond, Esq., a Colonel in the Service of Her Majesty Q. Anne. Written by Himself (3 vols.)	1852
The Luck of Barry Lyndon (2 vols.)	1852
The English Humorists of the Eighteenth Century. A Series of Lectures Delivered in England, Scotland, and the United States of America	1853
The Newcomes. Memoirs of a Most Respectable Family. Edited by Arthur Pendennis, Esqre. (2 vols.)	1854–5
The Rose and the Ring: or, the History of Prince Giglio and Prince Bulbo. A Fire-Side Pantomime for Great and Small Children. By Mr. M. A. Titmarsh	1855
Ballads	1855
The Virginians. A Tale of the Last Century (2 vols.)	1858–9
Lovel the Widower	1860

*The Four Georges: Sketches of Manners,
   Morals, Court and Town Life*   1860
*The Adventures of Philip on his Way
   Through the World, Shewing who
   Robbed Him, who Helped Him, and
   who Passed Him By* (3 vols.)   1862
Roundabout Papers   1863
Denis Duval   1864

SUGGESTED READING

Vanity Fair and *Henry Esmond.*

Anthony Trollope

1815–1882

Anthony Trollope was born in London, April 24, 1815, the fourth son of an unsuccessful barrister; his mother, Frances Trollope, was one of the most popular of early Victorian novelists, who is remembered mainly today for *Domestic Manners of the Americans*, a malicious, if sometimes uncomfortably accurate, record of her stay in the United States. Anthony attended public school at both Winchester and Harrow, but he failed to win a University scholarship. His father was an improvident man whose bankruptcy finally drove the family to move to Belgium in 1834, where Anthony taught classics for a few weeks in a Brussels school. In the autumn of the same year he returned to London and became a clerk in the general post office. After seven years at his dreary job he was transferred to Ireland as a postal surveyor, which suited him much better, as it raised his income considerably and allowed him to spend more time at fox-hunting and the other outdoor pastimes which he liked so well. In 1834 he married Rose Heseltine, by whom he had two sons.

Shortly before his marriage Trollope began his first novel, *The Macdermots of Ballycloran*, which was published in 1847. Both this story and its successor, *The Kellys and the O'Kellys*, 1848, are concerned with Irish politics, and neither attracted many readers. Trollope's sole attempt at an historical novel, *La Vendée*, 1850, and an unpublished comedy, *The Noble Jilt*, followed before he found his true metier. While wandering around Salisbury Cathedral in 1851, he thought of the germ of a story about cathedral and ecclesiastical society, but it was not until 1855, at the age of 40, that he published *The Warden*, which was the literary turning-point of his life. Around the central figure, a gentle old cleric who is the warden of an endowed hostel for old men, revolves the life of Trollope's mythical county, Barsetshire, and its cathedral town. To the modern reader it is the creation of character and the chronicling of the small beer of a tightly-knit, jealous society which holds most interest, but it was as propaganda against abuse in the handling of ancient endowments that the book was successful with Trollope's contemporaries. Its sequel, *Barchester Towers*, 1857, dropped social criticism for social comedy. It continues the development of the ecclesiastical and social leaders of Barsetshire and introduces one of the great comic characters in English fiction, Mrs. Proudie, the domineering wife of the Bishop. In the next ten years he continued writing his Barset chronicles, the best and most popular group of all his novels. *Doctor Thorne* appeared in 1858, and in 1860-61 *Framley Parsonage* was serialized in *Cornhill Magazine*, then edited by Thackeray; Trollope's name and fortune were made by these stories and by the other Barset novels, *The Small House at Allington*, 1862-4, and *The Last Chronicle of Barset*, 1866-7. They are all concerned with the same set of characters, but after *Barchester Towers* they are not direct sequels to one another.

Meanwhile Trollope had been given steady advancement in the postal service and made frequent journeys in that capacity, including a trip to America in 1861. He was an efficient civil servant and is credited with the invention of the modern English letter box, but he never allowed his postal work to interfere with either his field sports or his writing. He regarded his work as an author as a craft like that of a carpenter, and he applied some of the same rules of work to it, regularly writing 2500 words before breakfast and beginning a new novel the same day he finished the last word on another. Naturally his output was enormous and of varying quality; only a few works can be mentioned here of the sixty-odd which he wrote. Of *Framley Parsonage* he wrote a résumé himself which may serve as a capsule criticism of his whole output: "The story was thoroughly English. There was a little fox-hunting and a little tuft-hunting, some Christian virtue and some Christian cant. There was no heroism and no villainy. There was much Church, but more love-making." His careful observation of middle class manners, his humor and pathos, above all his indestructible interest in the commonplace of English life assure him a lasting place in the literature of his country. Nowhere else in fiction can the reader find such scrupulous recording of the surface trivialities which made up daily living in Victorian England.

During the period of the Barsetshire novels he was also writing such novels of manners as *The Three Clerks*, 1858, for which his memories of his own life as a young man furnished the background; *Orley Farm*, 1861-2, the narrative of a complicated inheritance; and *The Claverings*, 1866-7, the story of Harry Clavering and the two women whom he loves.

In 1867 Trollope retired from the post office and served for a short time as editor of *St. Paul's Magazine*. The following year he went to America to negotiate international postal agreements and copyright laws; on his return to England he stood unsuccessfully for Parliament as a Liberal candidate. He had published his first political novel, *Can You Forgive Her?* in 1864-5, and in 1867-9, the period of his Parliamentary venture, he published *Phineas Finn, the Irish Member*. These two political novels and those which followed, *The Eustace Diamonds*, 1871-3, *Phineas Redux*, 1873-4, *The Prime Minister*, 1875-6, and *The Duke's Children*, 1879-80, form a group second in quality only to the Barsetshire novels. Trollope's interest was always in people rather than institutions; in the Barset stories the center of attention is on clerical society rather than religion, and in the political novels he concentrates more on politicians than politics.

In startling contrast to the equanimity of his other books, *The Way We Live Now*, 1874-5, exposes with merciless anger the state of moral corruption into which Trollope's beloved England had fallen; it is the only one of his novels written in fierce indignation, and some of his critics place it among his greatest works.

During the last decade of his life Trollope travelled extensively, on the Continent, to Australia, New Zealand, Ceylon, South Africa, Iceland, and the United States, and wherever he went he stuck unvaryingly to his writing schedule. Novels, essays, and travel-books flowed out almost faster than they could be read. Perhaps the outstanding book of his later years was none of these but his frank and modest *Autobiography*, written in 1875-6 but published posthumously.

In his old age he had gained both fame and wealth from his writings and had made friends among most of the literary people of London. He loved the club-life of the city, and his closest friend had been that other club-man, Thackeray, whose biography Trollope wrote for the English Men of Letters series. He continued writing until he was stricken by paralysis, which resulted a few week later in his death on December 6, 1882.

BIOGRAPHY AND CRITICISM

Trollope's own account of his life, *An Autobiography* (2 vols., Edinburgh and London, 1883), is the primary biographical source. Hugh Walpole, *Anthony Trollope* (London, 1928) is a brief study in which biography is subordinated to criticism. Perhaps the most generally useful of books on Trollope is by Michael Sadleir, *Trollope: A Commentary* (New York, 1947), which contains a full biography, as well as much information about the Trollope family, sound criticism, and a useful classification of the novels.

PRINCIPAL WORKS

[Since many of Trollope's works were published serially, the date of their publication in book-form is sometimes at variance with that given in the text for their original appearance.]

The Warden	1855
Barchester Towers (3 vols.)	1857
The Three Clerks: A Novel (3 vols.)	1858
Doctor Thorne: A Novel (3 vols.)	1858

Framley Parsonage (3 vols.)   1861
Orley Farm (2 vols.)   1862
The Small House at Allington (2 vols.)   1864
Can You Forgive Her? (2 vols.)   1864
The Belton Estate (3 vols.)   1866
The Last Chronicle of Barset (2 vols.)   1867
The Claverings (2 vols.)   1867
Phineas Finn, the Irish Member (2 vols.)   1869
The Eustace Diamonds (3 vols.)   1873
Phineas Redux (2 vols.)   1874
The Way We Live Now (2 vols.)   1875
The Prime Minister (4 vols.)   1876
Thackeray   1879
The Duke's Children: A Novel (3 vols.)   1880
An Autobiography (2 vols.)   1883

SUGGESTED READING

The Warden and *Barchester Towers*.

Part IV

CHRONOLOGICAL TABLE

	HISTORY	LITERATURE	FOREIGN LITERATURE
1815	Battle of Waterloo Corn Law Passed	SCOTT, *Guy Mannering* WORDSWORTH, *Poems*	CONSTANT, *Adolphe*
1816	Game Law	J. AUSTEN, *Emma* BYRON, *Prisoner of Chillon* *Childe Harold*, III COLERIDGE, *Christabel* *Kubla Khan* PEACOCK, *Headlong Hall* SCOTT, *Antiquary* *Old Mortality* SHELLEY, *Alastor*	BRYANT, *Thanatopsis* GOETHE, *Italiänische Reise*
1817	Death of Princess Charlotte Habeas corpus act suspended	BYRON, *Manfred* COLERIDGE, *Biographia Literaria* KEATS, *Poems* *Blackwood's Magazine* founded Death of J. Austen	

1818	J. AUSTEN, *Persuasion* *Northanger Abbey* BYRON, *Beppo* KEATS, *Endymion* PEACOCK, *Nightmare Abbey* SCOTT, *Rob Roy* M. SHELLEY, *Frankenstein* SHELLEY, *Revolt of Islam*	IRVING, *Sketch Book* SCHOPENHAUER, *Wille und Vorstellung* HUGO, *Odes*
1819	Birth of Queen Victoria Peterloo massacre First Factory Act passed Six Acts passed	BYRON, *Don Juan*, I, II SCOTT, *Ivanhoe* SHELLEY, *Cenci* WORDSWORTH, *Peter Bell*
1820	George IV ascends throne Trial of Queen Caroline	KEATS, *Lamia* LAMB, *Essays of Elia* SHELLEY, *Prometheus Unbound* *London Magazine* founded	LAMARTINE, *Méditations poétiques*
1821		BYRON, *Cain* DE QUINCEY, *Confessions* SCOTT, *Kenilworth* SHELLEY, *Adonais* SOUTHEY, *A Vision of Judgment* *Manchester Guardian* founded Death of Keats	COOPER, *The Spy* GOETHE, *Wilhelm Meisters Wanderjahre*

	HISTORY	LITERATURE	FOREIGN LITERATURE
1822	Death of Castlereagh	BYRON, *The Vision of Judgment* SHELLEY, *Hellas* Death of Shelley	
1823	Monroe Doctrine	CARLYLE, *Life of Schiller* SCOTT, *Quentin Durward*	
1824	Repeal of Combination Laws	BYRON, *Don Juan*, XV, XVI CARLYLE, *Goethe's Wilhelm Meister* (tr.) LANDOR, *Imaginary Conversations* *Westminster Review* founded Death of Byron	
1825	Opening of Stockton-Darlington Railway, world's first Catholic Relief Bill defeated by House of Lords	COLERIDGE, *Aids to Reflection* MACAULAY, *Essay on Milton*	
1826		DISRAELI, *Vivian Grey*	COOPER, *Last of the Mohicans*

1827	Canning P.M. University College, London, founded Arnold headmaster Rugby	KEBLE, *Christian Year* TENNYSON, *Poems by Two Brothers* Death of Blake	POE, *Tamerlane* HEINE, *Buch der Lieder* HUGO, *Cromwell*
1828	Wellington P.M. Repeal Test and Corporation Acts	HAZLITT, *Life of Napoleon* LYTTON, *Pelham* *Athenaeum* and *Spectator* founded	
1829	Catholic Emancipation Act	TENNYSON, *Timbuctoo*	HUGO, *Les Orientales*
1830	William IV ascends throne Grey P.M. Revolution in France, fall of Charles X Manchester and Liverpool railway opened Agricultural Riot suppressed	LYELL, *Principles of Geology* MOORE, *Life of Byron* TENNYSON, *Poems, chiefly Lyrical* *Fraser's Magazine* founded	COMTE, *Cours de Philosophie Positive* GAUTIER, *Poésies* HUGO, *Hernani* STENDHAL, *Le Rouge et le Noir*

	HISTORY	LITERATURE	FOREIGN LITERATURE
1831	Defeat of Reform Bill Bristol Riots British Association for Advancement of Science founded	ELLIOTT, *Corn-Law Rhymes* PEACOCK, *Crotchet Castle* TRELAWNY, *Adventures of a Younger Son*	BALZAC, *Le Peau de Chagrin* HUGO, *Notre Dame de Paris*
1832	Reform Bill passed	DARWIN, *Voyages of Adventure and Beagle* LYTTON, *Eugene Aram* F. TROLLOPE, *Domestic Manners of the Americans* Death of Scott	BRYANT, *Poems* GOETHE, *Faust*, II BALZAC, *Le Curé de Tours*
1833	Keble's sermon "National Apostasy" opens Oxford Movement Factory Act ("Children's Charter") Abolition of slavery in English colonies	E. B. BARRETT, *Prometheus Bound* BROWNING, *Pauline* CARLYLE, *Sartor Resartus* NEWMAN, et al., *Tracts for the Times* TENNYSON, *Poems* Death of A. H. Hallam	BALZAC, *Eugénie Grandet* G. SAND, *Lélia*

1834	Melbourne P.M. Peel P.M. New Poor Law Houses of Parliament burn Organization of Grand National Consolidated Trade Union	LYTTON, *Last Days of Pompeii* Death of Coleridge Death of Lamb	PUSHKIN, *Queen of Spades*
1835	Municipal Reform Act	BROWNING, *Paracelsus* DICKENS, *Sketches by Boz* LYTTON, *Rienzi* WORDSWORTH, *Yarrow Revisited*	STRAUSS, *Das Leben Jesu* BALZAC, *Le Père Goriot* DE TOCQUEVILLE, *La Démocratie en Amérique*
1836	Great trek of the Boers	DICKENS, *Pickwick Papers* LOCKHART, *Life of Scott* NEWMAN et al., *Lyra Apostolica*	LAMARTINE, *Jocelyn* GOGOL, *Inspector-General*
1837	Victoria ascends throne	BROWNING, *Strafford* CARLYLE, *French Revolution* DICKENS, *Oliver Twist* THACKERAY, *Yellowplush Papers* *Bentley's Miscellany* founded	EMERSON, *American Scholar* HAWTHORNE, *Twice-Told Tales* GOGOL, *Dead Souls*
1838	People's Charter published	DICKENS, *Nicholas Nickleby* LYELL, *Elements of Geology* SURTEES, *Jorrocks's Jaunts and Jollities*	HUGO, *Ruy Blas*

	HISTORY	LITERATURE	FOREIGN LITERATURE
1839	Penny Postage Act First Factory Inspectors' Report Opium War	BAILEY, *Festus* CARLYLE, *Chartism* THACKERAY, *Catherine*	POE, *Tales of the Grotesque* STENDHAL, *La Chartreuse de Parme*
1840	Marriage of Victoria Health of Towns Committee Annexation of New Zealand	BARHAM, *Ingoldsby Legends* BROWNING, *Sordello* DICKENS, *Old Curiosity Shop* *Barnaby Rudge*	
1841	Peel P.M.	BROWNING, *Pippa Passes* CARLYLE, *Heroes and Hero-Worship* Newman, *Tract XC* THACKERAY, *Titmarsh* *Great Hoggarty Diamond* *Punch* founded	COOPER, *The Deerslayer* EMERSON, *Essays*, I DUMAS, *Count of Monte Cristo* FEUERBACH, *Essence of Christianity*
1842	Chartist riots Income tax Ashley's Act (Ten Hours Bill)	DICKENS, *American Notes* MACAULAY, *Lays of Ancient Rome* TENNYSON, *Poems* *Illustrated London News* founded	

1843	Free Church of Scotland founded	BROWNING, *Blot in the 'Scutcheon* CARLYLE, *Past and Present* DICKENS, *Christmas Carol* *Martin Chuzzlewit* MACAULAY, *Critical and Historical Essays* J. S. MILL, *System of Logic* RUSKIN, *Modern Painters*, I Death of Southey Wordsworth becomes Poet Laureate
1844	Rochedale Pioneers	E. B. BARRETT, *Poems* CHAMBERS, *Vestiges of Creation* DISRAELI, *Coningsby* PATMORE, *Poems* THACKERAY, *Barry Lyndon* EMERSON, *Essays*, II DUMAS, *Three Musketeers*
1845	Newman joins Church of Rome	BROWNING, *Dramatic Romances* CARLYLE, *Cromwell* DICKENS, *Cricket on the Hearth* DISRAELI, *Sybil* NEWMAN, *Essay on Development* POE, *Raven and Other Poems*

	HISTORY	LITERATURE	FOREIGN LITERATURE
1846	Russell P.M. Potato famine Repeal of Corn Laws	BRONTËS, *Poems by Currer, Ellis, and Acton Bell* DICKENS, *Dombey and Son* G. ELIOT, *Life of Jesus* (tr.)	EMERSON, *Poems* HAWTHORNE, *Mosses from an Old Manse* MELVILLE, *Typee* G. SAND, *La Mare au Diable*
1847	British Museum opened	A. BRONTË, *Agnes Grey* C. BRONTË, *Jane Eyre* E. BRONTË, *Wuthering Heights* LANDOR, *Hellenics* TENNYSON, *Princess* THACKERAY, *Vanity Fair*	LONGFELLOW, *Evangeline*
1848	Continental revolutions Failure of Chartism Public Health Act Communist Manifesto	A. BRONTË, *Tenant of Wildfell Hall* CLOUGH, *Bothie* GASKELL, *Mary Barton* KINGSLEY, *Yeast* MILL, *Principles of Political Economy* NEWMAN, *Loss and Gain* THACKERAY, *Pendennis* Pre-Raphaelite Brotherhood founded Death of E. Brontë	LOWELL, *Biglow Papers* *Fable for Critics* MURGER, *Scènes de la Vie de Bohème*

1849		ARNOLD, *Strayed Reveller*	MELVILLE, *Mardi*
		C. BRONTË, *Shirley*	
		DICKENS, *David Copperfield*	
		MACAULAY, *History of England*, I, II	
		RUSKIN, *Seven Lamps of Architecture*	
		Household Words founded	
1850	Re-establishment English Roman Catholic hierarchy; threat of "Papal Aggression"	BEDDOES, *Death's Jest Book*	EMERSON, *Representative Men*
		E. B. BROWNING, *Poems*	HAWTHORNE, *Scarlet Letter*
		BROWNING, *Christmas Eve and Easter Day*	MELVILLE, *White-Jacket*
	Factory Act	CARLYLE, *Latter-Day Pamphlets*	
	Ministry of Education	KINGSLEY, *Alton Locke*	
		TENNYSON, *In Memoriam*	
		WORDSWORTH, *Prelude*	
		The Germ founded	
		Death of Wordsworth	
		Tennyson becomes Poet Laureate	
1851	Great Exhibition, Hyde Park	BORROW, *Lavengro*	HAWTHORNE, *House of Seven Gables*
		E. B. BROWNING, *Casa Guidi Windows*	
	Window tax repealed	CARLYLE, *Life of Sterling*	LONGFELLOW, *Golden Legend*
	Napoleon III's *coup d'état*	MEREDITH, *Poems*	MELVILLE, *Moby Dick*
		RUSKIN, *Pre-Raphaelitism*	
		Stones of Venice, I	

	HISTORY	LITERATURE	FOREIGN LITERATURE
1852	Derby P.M. Aberdeen P.M. Annexation of Burma Opening of new Houses of Parliament Death of Wellington	ARNOLD, *Empedocles on Etna* DICKENS, *Bleak House* THACKERAY, *Henry Esmond*	HAWTHORNE, *Blithedale Romance* MELVILLE, *Pierre* H. B. STOWE, *Uncle Tom's Cabin* TURGENEV, *Sketches of a Sportsman*
1853		ARNOLD, *Poems* C. BRONTË, *Villette* GASKELL, *Cranford* KINGSLEY, *Hypatia* THACKERAY, *Newcomes* YONGE, *Heir of Redclyffe*	HAWTHORNE, *Tanglewood Tales*
1854	Working Men's College founded Crimean War	DICKENS, *Hard Times*	THOREAU, *Walden*

1855	Palmerston P.M. Florence Nightingale in Crimea Fall of Sebastopol	ARNOLD, *Poems* BROWNING, *Men and Women* DICKENS, *Little Dorrit* E. GASKELL, *North and South* KINGSLEY, *Westward Ho!* MEREDITH, *Shaving of Shagpat* TENNYSON, *Maud, and Other Poems* THACKERAY, *Rose and the Ring* TROLLOPE, *The Warden* *Saturday Review* founded Death of C. Brontë	LONGFELLOW, *Hiawatha* WHITMAN, *Leaves of Grass*
1856	Peace of Paris Limited Liability Act	NEWMAN, *Callista* RUSKIN, *Modern Painters*, III, IV *Oxford and Cambridge Magazine* founded	FLAUBERT, *Madame Bovary*
1857	Sepoy Mutiny Bank Crisis Discovery of gold in Australia	BORROW, *Romany Rye* E. B. BROWNING, *Aurora Leigh* G. ELIOT, *Scenes of Clerical Life* E. GASKELL, *Life of C. Brontë* HUGHES, *Tom Brown's Schooldays* KINGSLEY, *Two Years Ago* THACKERAY, *The Virginians* TROLLOPE, *Barchester Towers*	BAUDELAIRE, *Fleurs du Mal*

	HISTORY	LITERATURE	FOREIGN LITERATURE
1858	Derby P.M. Mutiny crushed, India transferred to Crown Removal of property qualifications for M.P.'s	ARNOLD, *Merope* CARLYLE, *Frederick the Great*, I, II KINGSLEY, *Andromeda* MORRIS, *Defence of Guenevere*	HOLMES, *Autocrat of the Breakfast Table* LONGFELLOW, *Courtship of Miles Standish*
1859	Palmerston P.M. Franco-Austrian War; Italian Risorgimento; Peace of Villa Franca	DARWIN, *Origin of Species* DICKENS, *Tale of Two Cities* G. ELIOT, *Adam Bede* FITZGERALD, *Rubáiyat* MEREDITH, *Richard Feverel* MILL, *On Liberty* TENNYSON, *Idylls of the King* *All the Year Round* founded	HUGO, *La Légende des Siècles*

1860	Garibaldi in Sicily and Naples	COLLINS, *Woman in White*	HAWTHORNE, *Marble Faun*
		DICKENS, *Great Expectations*	
		G. ELIOT, *Mill on the Floss*	
		RUSKIN, *Unto This Last*	
		SWINBURNE, *Queen Mother Rosamond*	
		WILSON et al., *Essays and Reviews*	
		Cornhill Magazine founded	
1861	Death of Prince Albert	G. ELIOT, *Silas Marner*	
	American Civil War begins	MILL, *Utilitarianism*	
		PALGRAVE, *Golden Treasury*	
	Trent Incident	READE, *Cloister and the Hearth*	
	Repeal of paper tax	ROSSETTI, *Early Italian Poets*	
		Death of E. B. Browning	
1862	Lancashire Cotton Famine	G. ELIOT, *Romola*	FLAUBERT, *Salammbô*
		MEREDITH, *Modern Love*	HUGO, *Les Misérables*
	Colenso controversy	C. ROSSETTI, *Goblin Market*	TURGENEV, *Fathers and Sons*
		THACKERAY, *Philip*	
1863		HUXLEY, *Man's Place in Nature*	LONGFELLOW, *Tales of a Wayside Inn*
		KINGSLEY, *Water Babies*	
		READE, *Hard Cash*	RENAN, *Vie de Jésus*
		THACKERAY, *Roundabout Papers*	
		Death of Thackeray	

	HISTORY	LITERATURE	FOREIGN LITERATURE
1864	*Alabama* sunk	BROWNING, *Dramatis Personae* DICKENS, *Our Mutual Friend* NEWMAN, *Apologia* TENNYSON, *Idylls of the Hearth* THACKERAY, *Denis Duval* Death of Landor	
1865	Russell P.M. Death of Palmerston Assassination of Lincoln Fenian Conspiracy	ARNOLD, *Essays in Criticism*, I L. CARROLL, *Alice in Wonderland* RUSKIN, *Sesame and Lilies* SWINBURNE, *Atalanta in Calydon* *Fortnightly Review* founded	WHITMAN, *Drum Taps* TOLSTOI, *War and Peace*
1866	Derby P.M. Suspension of Habeas Corpus Act in Ireland Hyde Park Riots and agitation for electoral reform	E. GASKELL, *Wives and Daughters* G. ELIOT, *Felix Holt* KINGSLEY, *Hereward the Wake* RUSKIN, *Crown of Wild Olive* SWINBURNE, *Poems and Ballads*, I Death of Keble	WHITTIER, *Snow-Bound* VERLAINE, *Poèmes Saturniens* IBSEN, *Brand* DOSTOIEVSKY, *Crime and Punishment*

1867	Disraeli P.M. Second Reform Bill Federation of Canada	ARNOLD, *New Poems* CARLYLE, *Shooting Niagara* MORRIS, *Life and Death of Jason* RUSKIN, *Time and Tide* TROLLOPE, *Last Chronicle of Barset*	IBSEN, *Peer Gynt* MARX, *Das Kapital*, I
1868	Gladstone P.M. Prosecution of Eyre fails	BROWNING, *Ring and the Book* COLLINS, *Moonstone* G. ELIOT, *Spanish Gypsy* MORRIS, *Earthly Paradise*, I NEWMAN, *Verses on Various Occasions*	
1869	Irish Church Act Opening of Suez Canal	ARNOLD, *Culture and Anarchy* MILL, *Subjection of Women* TENNYSON, *Holy Grail* TROLLOPE, *Phineas Finn*	TWAIN, *Innocents Abroad* FLAUBERT, *L'Education Sentimentale*
1870	Irish Land Act Elementary Education Act Franco-Prussian War	ARNOLD, *St. Paul and Protestantism* DICKENS, *Edwin Drood* HUXLEY, *Lay Sermons* MORRIS, *Volsunga Saga* NEWMAN, *Grammar of Assent* ROSSETTI, *Poems* Death of Dickens	

	HISTORY	LITERATURE	FOREIGN LITERATURE
1871	Abolition of Religious Test at Universities Abolition of purchase of Army Commissions	ARNOLD, *Friendship's Garland* DARWIN, *Descent of Man* G. ELIOT, *Middlemarch* RUSKIN, *Fors Clavigera* SWINBURNE, *Songs Before Sunrise*	WHITMAN, *Democratic Vistas*
1872	Secret ballot	BUTLER, *Erewhon* HARDY, *Under the Greenwood Tree* RUSKIN, *Munera Pulveris*	TWAIN, *Roughing It* DAUDET, *Tartarin de Tarascon*
1873	Settlement of Alabama Claims	ARNOLD, *Literature and Dogma* BRIDGES, *Poems* MILL, *Autobiography* PATER, *Studies in Renaissance* Death of Mill	HOWELLS, *Chance Acquaintance* TWAIN, *Gilded Age* RIMBAUD, *Une Saison en Enfer* TOLSTOI, *Anna Karenina*
1874	Disraeli P.M.	HARDY, *Far from the Madding Crowd* MILL, *Three Essays on Religion* SWINBURNE, *Bothwell* THOMSON, *City of Dreadful Night*	FLAUBERT, *La Tentation de Saint-Antoine*

1875	Employees' and Workmen's Act Purchase of Suez Canal Shares	TENNYSON, *Queen Mary* TROLLOPE, *Way We Live Now* Death of Kingsley	EDDY, *Science and Health*
1876	Bulgarian atrocities Royal Titles Bill	G. ELIOT, *Daniel Deronda* MEREDITH, *Beauchamp's Career* MORRIS, *Sigurd the Volsung* TENNYSON, *Harold*	TWAIN, *Tom Sawyer* MALLARMÉ, *L'Après-Midi d'un Faune*
1877	Russo-Turkish War Transvaal annexed	MEREDITH, *Idea of Comedy*	ZOLA, *L'Assommoir* IBSEN, *Pillars of Society*
1878	Congress of Berlin Factory and Workshop Act Zulu War Economic depression	BROWNING, *La Saisiaz* HARDY, *Return of the Native* SWINBURNE, *Poems and Ballads*, II	JAMES, *Daisy Miller*
1879		BROWNING, *Dramatic Idyls*, I MEREDITH, *The Egoist*	CABLE, *Old Creole Days* IBSEN, *Doll's House*

	HISTORY	LITERATURE	FOREIGN LITERATURE
1880	Gladstone P.M.
Compulsory education	BROWNING, *Dramatic Idyls*, II
DISRAELI, *Endymion*
SHORTHOUSE, *John Inglesant*
TENNYSON, *Ballads and Other Poems*
Death of G. Eliot	WALLACE, *Ben-Hur*
DE MAUPASSANT, *Boule de Suif*
ZOLA, *Nana*
DOSTOEVSKY, *Brothers Karamazov*
1881	Defeat at Majuba Hill
Parnell imprisoned
Married Women's Property Act
Irish Land Act
Boycott
Death of Disraeli	CARLYLE, *Reminiscences*
ROSSETTI, *Ballads and Sonnets*
SWINBURNE, *Mary Stuart*
WILDE, *Poems*
Browning Society founded
Death of Carlyle	JAMES, *Portrait of a Lady, Washington Square*
HARRIS, *Uncle Remus*
FRANCE, *Le Crime de Sylvestre Bonnard*
IBSEN, *Ghosts*
1882	Phoenix Park murders
British intervention in Egypt	SHAW, *Cashel Byron's Profession*
SWINBURNE, *Tristram of Lyonesse*
Death of Darwin
Death of Rossetti
Death of Trollope	HOWELLS, *A Modern Instance*
DE MAUPASSANT, *Une Vie*

1883	Fabian Society founded	MEREDITH, *Poems and Lyrics of the Joy of Earth*	TWAIN, *Life on the Mississippi*
		TROLLOPE, *Autobiography*	NIETZSCHE, *Also Sprach Zarathustra*
1884	Third Reform Bill	TENNYSON, *Becket*	TWAIN, *Huckleberry Finn*
			IBSEN, *Wild Duck*
1885	Salisbury P.M.	ARNOLD, *Discourses in America*	HOWELLS, *Rise of Silas Lapham*
	Fall of Khartoum	MEREDITH, *Diana of the Crossways*	DE MAUPASSANT, *Bel Ami*
		PATER, *Marius the Epicurean*	ZOLA, *Germinal*
		RUSKIN, *Praeterita*	
		STEVENSON, *Child's Garden of Verses*	
		TENNYSON, *Tiresias*	
		Commonweal founded	
1886	Gladstone P.M.	HARDY, *Mayor of Casterbridge*	JAMES, *The Bostonians*
	Salisbury P.M.	KIPLING, *Departmental Ditties*	*Princess Casamassima*
	Irish Home Rule Bill	STEVENSON, *Dr. Jekyll and Mr. Hyde*	RIMBAUD, *Les Illuminations*
	defeated in Commons	*Kidnapped*	IBSEN, *Rosmersholm*
		TENNYSON, *Locksley Hall Sixty Years After*	CHEKHOV, *Ivanov*
1887	Queen's Jubilee	DOYLE, *Study in Scarlet*	STRINDBERG, *The Father*
	Trafalgar Square Riots	PATER, *Imaginary Portraits*	SARDOU, *La Tosca*
	First Colonial Congress		

	HISTORY	LITERATURE	FOREIGN LITERATURE
1888	Local Government Act	ARNOLD, *Essays in Criticism*, II KIPLING, *Soldiers Three* MEREDITH, *Reading of Earth* MORRIS, *Dream of John Ball* MRS. WARD, *Robert Elsmere* Death of Arnold	STRINDBERG, *Miss Julie*
1889	Parnell Commission London Dock Strike	BROWNING, *Asolando* MORRIS, *House of the Wolfings* SHAW et al., *Fabian Essays* SWINBURNE, *Poems and Ballads*, III YEATS, *Wanderings of Oisin* Death of Browning Death of G. M. Hopkins	TWAIN, *Connecticut Yankee*
1890	Parnell divorce	FRAZER, *Golden Bough* MORRIS, *News from Nowhere* Kelmscott Press founded Death of Newman	E. DICKINSON, *Poems* IBSEN, *Hedda Gabler* TOLSTOY, *Kreutzer Sonata*

1891	Factory Act Free Education Act Death of Parnell	HARDY, *Tess of the d'Urbervilles* MORRIS, *Poems by the Way* SHAW, *Quintessence of Ibsenism* WILDE, *Dorian Gray*	LAGERLÖF, *Gösta Berling*
1892	Gladstone P.M.	TENNYSON, *Death of Oenone* Death of Tennyson	MAETERLINCK, *Pelléas et Mélisande* ZOLA, *La Débâcle* IBSEN, *Master Builder*

Index

A

Aberdeen, Lord, 54
Achilli, G. G., 230-31
Adams, C. F., 63, 64, 87
Adams, Henry, 64 *n.*, 65 *n.*
Afghanistan, 90, 95
Africa, South, 52, 53, 79, 90, 95, 99, 100
Agnosticism, 80, 201
Alabama, the, 63, 86-7
Albert, Prince Consort, 28, 50, 54, 62, 207, 257, 258
All the Year Round, 182
Alsace-Lorraine, 86
"Apostles," the, 255
Apostolic succession, 40
Arabi Bey, 95
Arnold, Matthew, 42, 67 *n.*, 69, 73, 80 *n.*, 108, 119, 135 *n.*, 137, 149, 150, 153-8, 201, 229, 265
Arnold, Thomas, 41, 147, 153
Australia, 13, 51-2, 198
Austria, 58, 59, 60, 99, 212

B

Balfour, Arthur, 101
Ballot, secret, 32, 75, 126, 128, 131
Bankruptcy Act, 50
Barrett, Elizabeth. *See* Browning, E. B.

INDEX

Beaconsfield, Lord. *See* Disraeli, Benjamin
Belgium, 86, 160, 269
Bentham, Jeremy, 14, 15, 18, 19, 25, 27, 128, 217, 218, 219
Bible, 112, 142-3, 146-9
Biology, 143-4, 198-200
Bishops, 8, 10, 39, 79, 102
Bismarck, 86, 89
Black Sea, 55, 86
Blackwood's Edinburgh Magazine, 256
Boers. *See* Africa, South
Booth, "General" William, 81
Boroughs, 9-10, 21, 125-6, 127
Boycott, Captain, 92
Bridges, Robert, 106
Bright, John, 30 *n.*, 54, 64, 67, 98, 118, 139
Bristol, 9, 21
Broad church, 205
Brontë, Anne, 160-63
Brontë, Charlotte, 44, 49 *n.*, 132 *n.*, 159-63
Brontë, Emily, 44, 159-63
Brookfield, William, 261, 264
Brown, Ford Madox, 236, 243
Browning, Elizabeth Barrett, 26 *n.*, 43, 59 *n.*, 69, 117, 166-9, 265
Browning, Robert, 24, 43, 64, 69, 75, 89, 98 *n.*, 104, 105, 147 *n.*, 164-70, 223
Buchanan, Robert, 238
Bulgaria, 88
Burma, 51
Burns, John, 101, 103 *n.*
Butler, Samuel, 106, 145, 146 *n.*
Byron, Lord, 4, 11 *n.*, 18 *n.*, 29 *n.*

C

Cambridge, 9, 18, 19, 24, 75, 144, 204, 207, 255, 261
Canada, 51, 62, 67
Canning, George, 16, 18, 19
Carlyle, Jane Welsh, 172-5
Carlyle, Thomas, 4, 11 *n.*, 23, 29, 31 *n.*, 32, 37 *n.*, 43, 66, 68, 72, 75, 89, 104, 107, 118, 120, 136, 137 *n.*, 138, 164, 171-7, 206, 213
Castlereagh, Lord, 15, 16, 18
Catholic Emancipation, 6, 19, 39
Cavendish, Lord Frederick, 93

Chamberlain, Joseph, 74, 98
Chapman, John, 187
Charlotte, Princess, 6, 7
Chartered companies, 100
Chartism, 28, 31-4, 43, 46, 75, 131, 132, 139, 205, 206
Child labor, 117
China, 53
Christian Socialism, 205-06
Church rates, 10
Church, state, 10, 39, 112
Civil Service, Home, 76
Clough, A. H., 153
Cobbett, William, 16, 139
Colenso, J. W., 78-9
Coleridge, S. T., 218
Collins, Wilkie, 72
Combination Laws, 12, 36
Conservatives, 25, 29, 46, 66, 67, 76, 94, 97, 99, 134
Co-operative movement, 36
Cornhill Magazine, 243, 265-6
Corn Law, 11, 16, 30, 31, 38, 130
Counties, 9, 125
Crimean War, 51, 53-6, 58, 59, 131
Crimes Act, 101
Cross, Mary Ann. *See* Eliot, George
Crystal Palace, 51, 120, 142
Cumberland, Duke of (King of Hanover), 7

D

Darwin, Charles, 72, 75, 77, 104, 108, 143-6, 149, 199, 200, 206
Darwin, Erasmus, 143
Davis, Jefferson, 60, 61 *n.*, 62
Democracy, 122-39
Derby, Lord, 58, 67-8
Dickens, Charles, 26, 29, 38, 43, 50 *n.*, 70, 74, 104, 117 *n.*, 119, 129 *n.*, 141, 178-85, 262, 265
Disraeli, Benjamin, Earl of Beaconsfield, 23, 31, 44, 58, 67-8, 74, 76, 77 *n.*, 84, 86, 87-8, 89, 90, 91, 104, 106, 120, 131

E

Edinburgh Review, 9 *n.*, 23, 173
Education, 47, 75, 85, 94, 101, 134-6, 154, 199-200, 201-02

Education Bill, 135
Egypt, 65, 76, 88, 95-7, 100
Eliot, George, 71, 104, 106, 147 *n.*, 186-91
Elliot, Ebenezer, 29
Employers' and Workmen Act, 88
Engels, Friederick, 29 *n.*, 116
Essays and Reviews, 78, 79
Evangelicals, 14 *n.*, 15, 35, 81
Evans, Mary Ann. *See* Eliot, George
Evening Chronicle, 179
Evolution, 77, 143, 145-6
Eyre, Governor, 65-6

F

Fabian Society, 83
Factory Acts, 16, 26, 47, 101
Fenian Brotherhood, 84
Fitzgerald, Edward, 70, 261
Forster, W. E., 85
France, 3-4, 10, 20, 22, 33, 38, 44, 45, 53, 59, 60, 61, 76, 85, 86, 88, 95, 99, 112, 121, 129, 153-4, 219, 220
Fraser's Magazine, 173, 206, 243, 262
Froude, J. A., 243
Froude, R. H., 229

G

Game Laws, 11, 94
Gaskell, Mrs. Elizabeth, 71, 118, 120
Geology, 142-3
George, Henry, 82
George III, 4, 5, 10, 111, 113, 114, 128
George IV. Prince Regent, 5-6; King, 17, 19, 20
Germ, The, 236
Germany, 7, 23, 44, 77-8, 85-6, 99, 147, 156, 187, 210, 262
Gladstone, W. E., 22, 47, 50, 59, 61, 67-8, 74, 76, 77, 80, 83, 84, 86-7, 88, 90, 91-5, 97-9, 101-4, 131-3
Goethe, 218, 262
Gordon, General Charles, 92, 96-7
Gordon Riots, 129
Greville, Charles, 5 *n.*, 7 *n.*, 25 *n.*
Grey, Earl, 21, 22, 27, 39

H

Hallam, A. H., 255, 256, 257
Hardie, James Keir, 74, 83, 103 *n*.
Hardy, Thomas, 107, 192-7
Helgoland, 99
Home rule, 91, 94, 97-9, 102-03
Household Words, 181, 182, 211
Hughes, Thomas, 47, 66, 205
Hunt, W. Holman, 236
Huxley, Thomas, 66, 73, 80, 98, 108, 141, 143, 149, 198-203, 206

I

Imperialism, 76, 90, 99-100
Income tax, 16, 30
India, 19, 51, 53, 56-8, 65, 131
Industrial revolution, 111-21, 142
Ireland, 19, 30, 39, 43, 77, 83-4, 91, 92-4, 98-9, 101-03
Irving, Edward, 171-2
Italy, 44, 45, 54, 58-60, 71, 165, 166-7, 189, 212, 213, 229, 249, 250

J

Jeffrey, Lord, 9 *n.*, 173
Jingoism, 89
Jones, Edward Burne-, 222, 223, 237, 243
Jowett, Benjamin, 78, 80, 153
Joyce, James, 102 *n*.

K

Keats, John, 164
Keble, John, 39-40, 42, 229
Kent, Duke of, 7
Kingsley, Charles, 42, 47, 66, 71, 82 *n.*, 104, 117 *n.*, 120, 149-50, 199, 204-09, 211, 231-2
Kipling, Rudyard, 28, 42 *n.*, 58, 77, 96 *n.*, 97 *n.*, 107
Kitchener, Lord, 97

L

Labor, 11, 12, 13, 127-8, 132
Labor party, 34, 87-8, 115, 134

Laissez-faire, 117, 118, 145
Lamarck, J. B., 145, 146 *n*.
Land Acts, 84, 93
Land League, 93-4
Landor, W. S., 249
Lewes, G. H., 187-90
Liberal party, 21, 67-8, 74, 76-7, 87-8, 91, 97-9, 104, 128, 134
Limited Liability Act, 48
Lincoln, Abraham, 60, 61, 62, 65, 124
Local Government Act, 101
London Magazine, 172
London Review, 219
Louis Philippe, 20, 44
Lyell, Charles, 143

M

Macaulay, Thomas Babington, 4, 18, 20, 21, 23, 28, 33, 57 *n*., 72, 76, 111, 121, 126, 129, 147
MacDonald, Ramsay, 101
Macready, W. C., 165
Mahdi, the, 96
Majuba, 95
Manchester, 9, 16, 29 *n*., 37, 65, 84 *n*., 116, 127
Manning, Cardinal, 101
Married Women's Property Act, 94
Marx, Karl, 29 *n*., 33, 82 *n*., 116 *n*.
Maurice, F. D., 199, 205
Melbourne, Lord, 27, 28-9
Meredith, George, 45, 54 *n*., 69, 71, 107, 193, 195, 210-16, 249
Mill, James, 217, 218, 219
Mill, John Stuart, 15, 58, 60, 62 *n*., 63, 64, 66, 67 *n*., 68, 72, 75, 94, 108, 137, 174, 217-21
Millais, Sir John E., 236, 242
Monarchy, 4-7, 124, 129
Monroe Doctrine, 18
Morley, John, 250
Morris, William, 69, 82, 89, 101 *n*., 105, 136, 138, 139 *n*., 222-7, 237, 249

N

Napoleon, Louis, 33 *n*., 53, 55, 59, 60
Newman, John Henry, 40-2, 73, 104, 108, 208, 228-34

INDEX 305

New Zealand, 52
Niebuhr, B. G., 147
Nightingale, Florence, 55

O

Oligarchy, 126
Once a Week, 212
Orange Free State. *See* Africa, South
O'Shea, Captain, 102
Owen, Robert, 34-6, 49, 118
Oxford, 9, 19, 20, 75, 153, 155, 222-3, 228-30, 237, 242, 244, 248-9, 258
Oxford and Cambridge Magazine, 223, 237
Oxford movement, 38-41, 81, 229-30

P

Palmerston, Lord, 46, 55, 58, 59, 61, 66, 74
Paris, Treaty of, 86
Parliament: House of Commons, 8-10, 21, 25, 27, 67, 87-8, 91, 94, 97, 99, 103, 124-31, 133-4; House of Lords, 8, 10, 19, 21, 27, 67, 84, 88, 92, 94, 99, 103, 124, 126, 130-1, 133, 134
Parnell, Charles Stewart, 74, 91, 92-3, 97-9, 101-03
Patmore, Coventry, 42, 68, 106
Peacock, Thomas Love, 210-11
Peel, Sir Robert, 16, 19, 20, 25, 27, 29, 30-1, 34, 39, 74, 119, 126, 257
"Peelers," 20, 33, 43
Peterloo, 17, 20
Pitt, William, 4, 8, 18
Poor Law, 26-7, 179
Pre-Raphaelitism, 120, 236-7, 242, 249
Public Health Act, 27, 88
Punch, 61, 65, 182, 263
Pusey, Edward Bouverie, 229

Q

Quarterly Review, 256

R

Railways, 37-8, 114, 121
Reade, Charles, 71

Red Cross, 55
Reform Bills: *1832*, 3, 4, 5, 10, 15, 21-3, 31, 34, 42, 66-7, 112, 114, 124 *n.*, 128, 130, 133; *1867*, 22, 50, 68, 75, 91, 94, 120, 126, 131, 135, 174; *1884*, 75, 82, 94, 132-3; *1918*, 133; *1928*, 133
Rhodes, Cecil, 100
Risorgimento. *See* Italy
Roberts, Lord, 90, 95
Rosebery, Lord, 101, 103
Rossetti, Christina, 69, 81, 106, 235, 239
Rossetti, Dante Gabriel, 69, 104, 105-6, 223, 225, 235-40, 243, 249
Royal Titles Bill, 88
Ruskin, John, 43, 66, 72, 89, 104, 107, 120, 137, 223, 225, 236-7, 241-7, 249, 266
Russell, Lord John, 59, 61, 63-4, 66, 74, 130
Russia, 53-6, 61, 86, 89, 90, 122

S

Salisbury, Lord, 68, 74, 76, 77, 94, 99
Saturday Review, 250
Science, 140-50
Scott, Sir Walter, 4, 23, 48, 75, 137
Sepoy mutiny, 53, 56-7, 131
Shaw, G. B., 83, 96 *n.*, 107
Shelley, Percy Bysshe, 4, 5, 16 *n.*, 17, 18 *n.*, 164, 249
Shorthouse, J. H., 42, 107
Six Acts, the, 17
Slavery, 14, 26, 96, 121
Socialism, 82-3, 138, 225
Southey, Robert, 4
Speedhamland Act, 13
Spencer, Herbert, 187
Stanley, A. P., 147
Sterling, John, 174
Stevenson, Robert Louis, 107
Strauss, D. F., 187
Sudan. *See* Egypt
Swinburne, Algernon Charles, 70, 98, 105, 237, 248-53

T

Tennyson, Alfred, 4, 11 *n.*, 13 *n.*, 24, 43, 45, 54, 57 *n.*, 59 *n.*, 68, 75, 98, 100 *n.*, 103, 104, 105, 144 *n.*, 195, 254-60, 261, 265

Test and Corporation Acts, 19
Thackeray, W. M., 5 n., 44, 62 n., 70, 75, 119 n., 162, 243, 261-8, 273
Thomson, James, 106
Times, The, 55, 101-2, 262
Toynbee, Arnold, 113-14
"Tracts for the Times," 229-30
Transvaal. *See* Africa, South
Trade Unions, 12, 37, 49, 50, 83
Trafalgar Square Riot, 100
Trevelyan, G. B., 98
Trevelyan, G. M., 9, 13 n., 23 n., 133
Trollope, Anthony, 71, 106, 266, 269-74
Trollope, Mrs. Frances, 269
Turkey, 45, 53-4, 55, 88-9
Turner, J. M. W., 242

U

Ulster, 84, 92, 98-9, 103
Unionists, 77, 99, 100
United States, 18, 60, 61, 62-5, 123, 156, 180, 183, 201, 264, 269, 271, 272
Ussher, Archbishop, 143
Utilitarianism, 15, 218, 220

V

Veto, royal, 5
Victor Emanuel, 59, 60
Victoria, Queen, 7, 16, 27-8, 33, 51, 56, 58, 62, 76-7, 86 n., 88, 90, 92, 97, 100, 207, 257, 258

W

Wallace, A. H., 145
Ward, Mrs. Humphry, 42
Waterloo, 3, 16, 17, 43, 54
Wellington, Duke of, 5, 7, 16, 18, 19, 20, 21, 22, 27, 33, 74, 124, 127
Westminster, 9, 22
Westminster Abbey, 18, 100, 146, 168, 175, 184, 195, 258
Westminster Review, 19, 187, 219
William IV. Duke of Clarence, 6-7; King, 7, 20, 21, 22, 27, 126

Wordsworth, William, 4, 117 n., 218, 257
Working Men's College, 47, 199, 243

Y

Yeats, William Butler, 106
Yonge, Charlotte, 42
York, Duke of, 6
Young, G. M., 148

Z

Zulus. *See* Africa, South